**Alan Cohen** is Lecturer in Education at Durham University. He taught in primary and secondary schools in Britain and the USA and in Colleges of Education before taking up his appointment in the School of Education at Durham. His publications include: *Readings in the History of Educational Thought* (with N. Garner), *A Student's Guide to Teaching Practice* (with N. Garner), *Primary Education: a Sourcebook for Teachers* (with L. Cohen), *Special Educational Needs in the Ordinary School: a Sourcebook for Teachers* (with L. Cohen), *Early Education: The School Years: a Sourcebook for Teachers* (with L. Cohen).

**Louis Cohen** is Professor of Education at Loughborough University of Technology. He, too, taught in primary and secondary schools in Britain and the USA and in Colleges of Education before taking up appointments at Bradford University and at Loughborough University of Technology. His publications include: *Educational Research Methods in Classrooms and Schools, Experiments in the Social Sciences* (with G. Brown and D. Cherrington), *Statistics for Education and Physical Education* (with M. Holliday), *Statistics for Social Scientists* (with M. Holliday), *Perspectives on Classrooms and Schools* (with L. Manion), *A Guide to Teaching Practice* (with L. Manion), *Multicultural Classrooms* (with L. Manion), *Linking Home and School* (with M. Craft and J. Raynor), *Educational Research and Development in Britain, 1970–1980* (with J.B. Thomas and L. Manion), *Multicultural Education: a Sourcebook for Teachers* (with A. Cohen), and *Disruptive Behaviour: a Sourcebook for Teachers* (with A. Cohen).

# EARLY EDUCATION: THE PRE-SCHOOL YEARS

## A Sourcebook for Teachers

Edited by
**ALAN COHEN**
*University of Durham*
and
**LOUIS COHEN**
*Loughborough University of Technology*

Paul Chapman
Publishing Ltd

All rights reserved

First published 1988

Paul Chapman Publishing Ltd.
144 Liverpool Road
London N1 1LA

British Library Cataloguing in Publication Data

Early education : the preschool years : a sourcebook
  for teachers.
  1. Education, Preschool—Great Britain
  I. Cohen, Alan, *1928-*    II. Cohen, Louis
  372'.21'0941    LB1140.2

ISBN 1 85396 007 1

Typeset by Inforum Ltd, Portsmouth
Printed and bound by Athenaeum Press Ltd,
Newcastle upon Tyne.

A B C D E F G        5 4 3 2 1 0

# CONTENTS

## Section Three
## TEACHERS AND CHILDREN

## Section Four
## TEACHERS, PARENTS AND CHILDREN

# INTRODUCTION

*Early Education — The Pre-school Years: A Sourcebook for Teachers* aims to introduce student teachers and teachers to what the editors consider to be some of the most important problems and issues facing those concerned with the education of pre-school children today. The very idea of 'educating' pre-school children has a long, controversial history, rooted in and influenced by long-held traditions of family and child-rearing patterns and by the widely held belief that childcare is primarily the responsibility of women (Duxbury, 1986). It was an accepted view in the nineteenth and early twentieth centuries that women were by nature responsible for the care of their children. The enormous demand for labour which accompanied the Industrial Revolution accelerated the need to initiate means of caring for young children outside the home, and, as a consequence, schools for 'infants' first made their appearance in England in the early nineteenth century. Some years later, the introduction of compulsory schooling for children over the age of five was accompanied by a changing attitude towards the benefits that education could confer. But nursery facilities were still regarded as necessary only for socially disadvantaged children whose mothers, for economic reasons, were forced to seek employment outside the home. Even as late as the 1930s, public authorities' pronouncements and perspectives on nursery provision were couched in nineteenth-century terms. The subsequent advances and setbacks in the history and development of pre-school education demonstrate (probably more than in any other 'sector' of education) that policies, practices and decisions are inextricably influenced by wider social, economic and historical perspectives. For example, it is certainly the case that economic conditions and the psychological climate of the early 1960s were not conducive to the expansion of pre-school education, not just because of the shortage of qualified staff and resources, but also because of research studies which purported to show the effects of early maternal deprivation and its debilitating long-term influence on the development of the young child (Clark and Cheyne, 1979).

In the early 1970s educational policy in Great Britain focused on the early childhood years. Evidence presented in the Plowden Report (CACE, 1967) that 'low economic status is associated, even by the age of seven, with low educational attainment and high maladjustment' (p. 534) led to recommendations for the expansion of pre-school education, for positive discrimination in the form of intervention programmes for children in deprived areas (educational priority areas), and for improving home–school links by encouraging parental participation and involvement in schools. Such programmes had a *compensatory*[1] emphasis and predominantly *language*-oriented goals (Clark and Cheyne, 1979). Research undertaken in the United States and in the United Kingdom concentrated its attention on the role of language and the importance of improving the cognitive functioning of children's learning experiences in the early years, since their 'disadvantage' was largely attributed to a lack of sufficient stimulation in their home background. Thus, the *Head Start* programmes in America had considerable influence on the development of corresponding projects within the educational priority areas in the UK. Experimental programmes introduced in Great Britain included structured language programmes, community education projects and initiatives to involve parents in their children's education as well as pre-school home-visiting schemes.

The 1972 Government White Paper: *Education: A Framework for Expansion* emphasized that 'the value of nursery education in promoting the social development of young children has long been acknowledged. In addition, we now know that, given sympathetic and skilled supervision, children may also make great educational progress before the age of five. They are capable of developing further in the use of language, in thought and in practical skills than was previously supposed. Progress of this kind gives any child a sound base for his subsequent education.'[2] The White Paper's proposal to provide free nursery education for all three- and four-year-olds was never fully realized because of further economic crises and consequent cuts in government expenditure,[3] as well as, of course, the non-mandatory nature of the proposed provision. Increasingly, during the 1970s, politicians had become disillusioned with the proposition that economic growth could be stimulated by educational investment. Furthermore, many educationists were coming to realize the limitations of their influence on individual and social development and to appreciate that their belief that the *extension of educational provision* would produce socially equalizing effects and fulfil democratic ideals had not happened on anything like the scale they had originally envisaged.[4] Further disillusionment grew with the initial evaluations of pre-school programmes which were based on the premises that socially disadvantaged children are necessarily restricted in their linguistic competence and that 'remediation' ensues as a result of early intervention in the form of structured language learning programmes. There was widespread disenchantment with the idea that early injections of money to fund intervention schemes could make up for the debilitating conditions of socially disadvantaged children. The initial evaluations of *Head Start* programmes tended to demonstrate few lasting effects, and in any case subsequent research pointed to a rejection of the theory of language deficit as the most important explanation of educational failure. Recent research, however, has demonstrated more positive findings and a much more optimistic prognosis concerning the effects of early intervention schemes.[5]

The disparate nature of provision for children under five years old highlights the polarity of opinions as to whether the provision on offer is concerned with *care* or with *education*. Pre-school provision ranges from nursery classes and schools, day nurseries and nursery centres, voluntary playgroups, crèches, family centres and childminders, reception classes, vertically grouped classes in infant, primary and first schools, to parent and toddler clubs. Northam, in Reading 2, shows how the use of the all-embracing term 'pre-school' to refer to the varieties of provision made for children under the age of five implies a similarity of purpose and practice which does not correspond to reality. She argues that the general use of the term has helped to sustain a myth that it is possible to think of all the differing organized settings as essentially similar, as unified in purpose, style and effect.

There is continued controversy in the pre-school debate over fundamental questions about how young children should be educated and particularly about the content of their education. For example, Cleave et al. (1982) investigated differences and continuity between pre-school units and reception classes. Their study contrasts the very wide choice element which is available to children within most pre-school units and the emphasis and focus on 'play' as the context for learning, with that of the reception class ethos of more teacher-directed learning even when children were in groups – where 'work' was the expression for the 'educationally' valued activities, and 'play' consisted of what was permitted when work was finished on entry to the reception class. Clark (1983) comments on the importance of considering 'the balance of activities which are termed "work" and "play" and to consider whether play as a learning strategy has a wider role in the reception class and beyond, likewise whether younger children are more capable of sustained "work" and cognitively challenging activities than is sometimes appreciated – provided they see a purpose in the effort' (p. 116). Hughes, in Reading 10, illustrates this very point, demonstrating that there is evidence to suggest that most pre-school children do possess considerabl~ numerical competence and may well possess from a cognitive point of vie` the prerequisite skills for learning arithmetic. Hughes suggests that the skill~ the young children may lack appear to be primarily linguistic in nature. Th implications of his findings suggest the need to shift the emphasis withi early mathematics education away from the use of concrete activiti~ designed to develop numerical concepts and towards their use in a variety c communication situations (Clark, 1983, p. 118).

It is a truism that policies, provision and practices in any sector o 'education' are influenced not only by the social/historical context in whicl they have developed, but also by the changes and developments in contem-porary society. It may be that, like 'special education', a pervasive benevo-lent humanitarianism is implicit in the rhetoric of pre-school educational provision so that it becomes very difficult to subject its aims, forms and content to critical scrutiny. In this sense, humanitarian and philosophical approaches tend to beg such questions as who has the power and the expertise to decide what form 'good' pre-school education shall take, or who controls it, what are its ultimate aims, and who can give or withhold resources for its implementation and development. For example, Lloyd (1983) affirms that a growing body of evidence accumulated over the past 20 or so years substantiates the claim that the early years of a child's life are crucial to future development. He poses the question: 'If, then, this period of a child's life is as important, if not more important than later stages, then why in the literature has the logical conclusion that nursery education should also be compulsory not been drawn? . . . If it is beyond reasonable doubt that early education has great advantages for achievement in later school life, then there is a strong *prima facie* case for making it compulsory especially if compulsory education has been accepted as an arrangement at a later and less critical stage' (p. 125).

Teachers themselves operate in a context which is markedly influenced by social and historical values and beliefs – hence the need for them to acquire a deep understanding of the social, historical, political and economic forces which shape their views about, for example, pre-school education, as well as the pedagogical skills and techniques with which to teach their pupils. Changes and developments in contemporary society influence policy, provi-sion and practice in pre-school education. One important development in recent years has been that pre-school education has suffered as policy makers ceased to be committed to providing equality of access to education-al opportunity. As a result, commitment in Great Britain has shifted to support the voluntary sector for an expansion of pre-school provision. In 1978 government policy recognized the inadequacy of resources which were available for the under-five age-group and urged local authorities to make maximum use of existing resources in the education, social services and health fields provided by statutory authorities and also by the community self through volunteers or voluntary bodies (Sestini, 1985).

The principle of involving parents and the community in children's early education is nowadays widely accepted. As one writer puts it, 'Parents in act have been discovered as critical to the education and development of their children' (Grotberg, 1979). In examining the relationship between early education and the community Hughes (1986) evaluates the substantial body of recent research on the influence of the home on young children's learning. He describes one common set of assumptions underlying many of the approaches to community and parental involvement, calling it the 'deficit' model, since it assumes that particular groups of parents, for example working-class or ethnic minorities, are defective in their provision of an educational environment for their children. Thus the purpose of involving such parents would be to encourage them to alter their child-rearing practices by modelling them on those of teachers. Hughes shows that research provides little evidence to support this 'deficit' model; indeed, he asserts, 'the homes of most (if not all) young children provide a rich learning environment, and that the conversations which take place between young children and their mothers are in many respects richer than those involving young children and their teachers' (p. 32). He argues that young children grow up in a rich community based on their family and that their early learning is firmly embedded within this community. Because the kind of learning demanded of children at school makes few connections with this earlier, community-based experience, the task of the school must be to help the children to make connections between these two kinds of learning.

Another development in contemporary society which has influenced the pre-school scene concerns young children with various learning difficulties. Increasingly, since the 1981 Education Act, more and more children with special educational needs are being integrated into all kinds of pre-school institutions. Over the past 20 years or so there has been a developing interest in the early identification of difficulties suffered by children. Lindsay (1984) writes that the rationale is simple: the earlier such problems can be identified or diagnosed the sooner appropriate action can be taken. The action can be curative or ameliorative. The range of problems and the numbers of young children involved have led to the development of simple and quick methods of identification – screening. Screening programmes are in use at various stages from before conception to about the seven-plus age-level and are concerned with the physical, psychological, linguistic and social development of children.

Lastly, in our introduction, we turn to another important development in contemporary society. We are now an ethnically mixed and culturally varied nation. The debate on multicultural education has shifted considerably during recent years and is now beginning to reflect greater concern for the role of education in countering the pernicious effects of racism both within schools and in society at large. And yet, as the Swann Report (1985) observes, 'This concern with racism is not yet however regarded by the majority of teachers as a valid part of multicultural education as they perceive it . . .'. Day-care provision within the social services departments plays an increasingly important role in supporting families in their parenting tasks, in providing young children with an enriching and stimulating pre-school experience, and in contributing as part of a wider social strategy to preventive work with vulnerable families. Day-care provision has expanded most significantly in urban areas where most ethnic minority communities are concentrated, communities who suffer disproportionately from unemployment, under-employment, low wages, the effects of poor housing and, often, the insidious and long-term effects of racism. A body of research strongly suggests that teachers are inclined to form expectations of children on the basis of ethnic and social stereotypes, and that these expectations are likely to influence their classroom behaviour and, as a result, affect children's attitudes and performance in school. Other research demonstrates that although it is commonplace to hear teachers of young children assert that the very young child cannot be sexist, racist or otherwise discriminatory, young children of three and four do, in fact, notice colour and ascribe certain values and status to it (Milner, 1975, 1983). It would seem to follow that the establishment of effective anti-racist policies and practices in the education of children must begin when they are very young.

## NOTES

1. The 'compensatory' tradition in pre-school educational provision has a very long history. From the mid-nineteenth century onwards, kindergartens or nurseries for middle-class children continued to expand. Their underlying aim was concerned with 'educating' children, which contrasts markedly to the existing infant schools' preoccupation with the physical and moral protection of young children. Browne (1986) comments that 'in pre-school provision, the dichotomy of purpose along class lines continued into the twentieth century. The provision for middle-class children concentrated on "education", while that for working-class children emphasized "rescue" from inadequate homes and environments' (pp. 12–13). Finch (1984), in Reading 4, examines the question of how far voluntary playgroups can be seen as providing a form of pre-school education comparable with,

or even superior to, nursery schools, given that the voluntary playgroup movement has been the major growth area in the pre-school scene since the mid-1960s and has expanded beyond the middle-class areas in which it originated. Specifically, she asks: 'If pre-school provision for working-class children is seen as a form of compensatory education, there is a rather obvious tension between that rationale and the principle of self-help . . . to express this crudely, if you want pre-school experience to counteract a child's home, you can hardly let mothers do it themselves; conversely, if you do foster self-help among the working classes, you may get a form of pre-school provision which reinforces rather than counteracts the "undesirable" home setting' (p. 55).

2. *Education: A Framework for Expansion* (1972 White Paper), Cmnd 5174. London, HMSO, p. 17.

3. By 1976 a package of public expenditure cuts totalling £6000 million was introduced. Capital expenditure for nursery education peaked at £46 million in 1975–76 and fell to less than £15 million in succeeding years. What *did* contract during this period was *planned* expenditure for the expansion of the education service (Richards, 1982).

    The failure of the anticipated expansion in nursery education since 1972 is shown by the fact that the percentage of three- to four-year-olds in nursery classes rose from 10 to only 21 per cent between 1975 and 1981 (DES, 1982). Of the 3 million under-fives in Great Britain, 22 per cent receive nursery education, a further 18 per cent are admitted to primary school at four years or more, and only 1 per cent attend council day nurseries. These figures are in sharp contrast, for example, to France, where the government provides full-time care for 33 per cent of two-year-olds and 88 per cent of three-year-olds. Thus, Britain has one of Western Europe's poorest records of childcare provision in the maintained sector, yet the best voluntary and self-help record (Duxbury, 1986, pp. 34–5.) The outlook for the future of pre-school provision in this country looks equally bleak. Sue Duxbury writes that 'there are no plans to increase day-nursery provision; rather, its range of customers is contracting, unlike in many countries where every child is regarded as an equal priority. Despite the plans to develop nursery education after Plowden, the 1980 Education Act absolved local education authorities of the obligation to provide it, leaving it a discretionary matter. Proposals to extend nursery school hours arouse debates as to whether the children of working parents would be segregated or whether staffing problems could be overcome. Only three British education authorities currently operate such a service, compared to France's coverage for 85 per cent of 3- to 5-year-olds and 23 per cent of 2-year-olds' (Duxbury, 1986, p. 47). Browne and France (1986) comment, 'It is paradoxical that developmental psychologists, psychoanalysts and doctors have all stressed the unique importance of an individual's first five years, and yet British governments have consistently refused to recognize this through the provision of adequate finance and support to carers of young children' (p. 31).

4. Taylor (1980) comments that 'unless some major and unforseen upset in the social and political structure takes place, change in educational provision over the next decade is likely to be evolutionary rather than revolutionary. It follows that efforts to reduce educational inequalities, to enhance opportunity and secure greater equality of outcome are likely to be piecemeal and ameliorative rather than thorough-going and radical' (p. 10).

5. See Jowett and Sylva (1986). The research demonstrates how the behaviour of

working-class children in the reception class can be influenced by their pre-school experiences. Two groups of working-class children, half of whom had attended a nursery class provided by the local education authority and half who had attended playgroups, were compared using systematic observations as well as the Boehm Test of Basic Concepts and the Adjustment to School Scale. Children were observed in their first term in reception class and again six months later, so that a total of 120 hours of the behaviour of 90 children was documented. Data were collected about children's activities and the cognitive challenge they gained from them, their social participation, conversations, and their reactions to difficulties. The findings show the greater gains made by the nursery children. These children were more 'ready' for school than a matched group who had attended a play-group. They concentrated better when alone or parallel to others, their play was richer, they were more independent, and they approached teachers as resources for learning rather than for aid. The authors conclude that 'it seems that playgroup routines which are often characterized by limited space/resources and the need to clean up after each session result in a pre-school programme with less emphasis on children's independence and fewer opportunities for children to solve their own problems or tackle "educational" toys' (p. 30).

See also Woodhead (1985). This very comprehensive review of the effects of pre-school education reports that pre-school intervention projects are now beginning to claim dramatic long-term follow-up findings which appear to support the contention that pre-school can serve as an 'inoculation against failure'. Woodhead argues that neither the revival of this model nor its extension by the idea of a 'sleeper effect' is justified. He claims that a 'transactional' model best accounts for the data, whereby short-lived improvements in competence coupled with increased motivation, parental aspirations and school expectations, were sufficient to trigger a mutually reinforcing positive cycle of achievement (p. 133). Woodhead asserts that the effectiveness of pre-school may also be conditional on certain features of the educational and family context in which intervention took place, in particular those specific procedures which the school adopts for dealing with children who present difficulties, which could serve to amplify or attenuate the initial effects of pre-school.

# PERSPECTIVES ON
# PRE-SCHOOL EDUCATION

# INTRODUCTION

This part of the sourcebook consists of four readings, the first of which traces the trend in recent years towards the polarization of the purposes and practices of nursery schools – a trend which the author suggests 'not only militates against unbiased thinking about early childhood education but is also potentially dangerous in terms of political repercussions in pre-school provision' (p. 12). Tamburrini asserts that the purposes and practices of nursery schools have been polarized as providing either education or a shared child-rearing support system. She offers compelling evidence about the ways in which young children's intellectual functioning and development seem to be most facilitated, making nonsense, she writes 'of the notion that a formal curriculum is concerned with education whereas an informal one is not' (p. 17). Reading 2 examines the effects of categorizing all forms of provision for young children under the single heading 'pre-school'. The author describes how the term is encountered in different ways, and thus associated with different meanings, from one context to another. Northam asserts that the general use of the term 'pre-school' 'has therefore helped to sustain a myth that it is possible to think of all the differing organized settings in which young children meet with adults and each other as essentially similar, as unified in purpose, style and effect' (p. 28). The author offers a detailed examination of the varieties of 'pre-school' provision and discusses their differences in ethos and organization, concluding that the 'pre-school', while mythically powerful, is empirically non-existent. The suggested further readings add support to the contention that the great variety in pre-school provision has important effects on styles of practice and on the ways in which teachers regard the children in their care.

Durrant and Kidner, in Reading 3, present a detailed analysis of one of the most important issues in present-day society – racism. They explore its powerful and debilitating effects, commenting that 'we cannot realistically stress the importance of the pre-school years on a child's physical, intellectual and emotional development whilst ignoring the importance of those years on the development of racial attitudes in both black and white children'. The authors examine the common misconception that small children do not have a racial or cultural awareness, and that because the vast majority of small black children have now been born in Britain they do not have any particular needs in this area. Durrant and Kidner offer a number of practical suggestions for teachers to consider when adopting and initiating anti-racist strategies in schools, examining the use of a variety of teaching materials and activities which impinge on the lives of children. The suggestions for further reading highlight the important point of just how much young children notice differences between people and how perceptive they are about the way in which people are depicted.

In Reading 4 Finch poses the question: 'How far can voluntary playgroups be seen as providing a form of pre-school education comparable with, even superior to, nursery schools?' This is an important question given that the voluntary playgroup movement has been the major growth area in the pre-school scene since the mid-1960s. The author offers an evaluation of the voluntary playgroup as pre-school experience, drawing on data from a study of playgroups in predominantly working-class areas, run on a voluntary basis by local women. The crux of Finch's argument is that 'If pre-school provision for working-class children is seen as a form of compensatory education, there is a rather obvious tension between that rationale and the principle of self-help. The tension is particularly acute if one envisages self-help provision by those sectors of the working classes who would be considered most "disadvantaged". To express this crudely, if you want pre-school experience to counteract a child's home, you can hardly let the mothers do it themselves; conversely, if you do foster self-help among the working classes, you may get a form of pre-school provision which reinforces rather than counteracts the "undesirable" home setting' (p. 55).

# Reading 1
# NEW DIRECTIONS
# IN NURSERY EDUCATION
## *J. Tamburrini*

## POLARIZATION

One of the most detrimental influences on educational thought and practice is the tendency to polarize practices. Polarities are useful when they draw attention to valid distinctions that may have been neglected, but their danger is that practices and their underlying assumptions and values are usually oversimplified, sometimes to the point of caricature. The result is that myths are perpetuated and both theorists and practitioners are driven into defensive entrenched positions when what is required instead is unprejudiced reconsideration of old practices and consideration of new ones.

In recent years a polarization of the purposes and practices of nursery schools has emerged which not only militates against unbiased thinking about early childhood education but is also potentially dangerous in terms of political repercussions in pre-school provision. The purposes and practices of nursery schools have been polarized as providing either education or a shared child-rearing support system. Marion Blank (1974), for example, has drawn a distinction between two types of pre-school: 'shared rearing pre-schools' and 'academic pre-schools'. The former, she suggests, stems from the desire of women to have support services in the rearing of their children while the latter originate with the concern to prevent future academic failure. Thus the two institutions differ in terms of purpose. The major purpose of the shared child-rearing pre-school, she asserts:

> is not to change, educate, alter or modify the child along particular lines, although this may occur. Rather it is to provide, during the hours of the day when the children are in school, a secure benign environment that is compatible with the interests and predispositions of the young child.

By contrast, in the 'academic pre-school':

> . . . the central goal is not day care, but education . . . it is a basic alteration in the child's level of functioning so that not only all present academic learning, but all future academic learning will be enhanced.

The implication of Blank's analysis is that the traditional British nursery

Tamburrini, J. (1982) 'New directions in nursery education', in Richards, C. (ed.) *New Directions in Primary Education*. Lewes, Falmer Press, pp. 97–110.

school engages not in education but in child rearing. Education goes on in schools whose more formal structured programmes are typified by those based on the Bereiter and Engelmann programme or the Peabody Language Development Kit.

In a reply to Marion Blank, Tizard (1974) rejects this polarization, but she does so, not to produce a more elaborate, non-polarized conceptualization of nursery school practice but, instead, in order to reject the distinction altogether. Paradoxically, by doing so she arrives at a similar position to Blank's in her view of the traditional British nursery school when she claims that:

> the curriculum of the nursery school can hardly be distinguished from that of the home.

The main distinction between parents and teachers as educators, she claims:

> is ideological – that is both parents and teachers provide the same kind of learning experiences for the child, but the teacher formulates her objectives and has theories about her methods.

Tizard's purpose is a worthy one. She expresses anxiety about the implications for practice of Blank's distinction, particularly in terms of the tendency for 'most adult–child contacts (outside the nursery school to be) down-graded to "child rearing" ', rather than for child rearing to be seen as a pervasive process in which 'all adult–child contacts are potentially important and fruitful'. Nevertheless, to blur the distinction between what does or should go on in a nursery school and what goes on in the home, the day nursery or in childminding deprives the nursery school teacher of a professional role, even though Tizard expresses a desire to avoid doing so.

Tizard's argument rests on two major points. First, she argues that both upbringing and education go on in the home, and second, that much of what a child learns at home and at school is incidental or unintended rather than the intended outcome of an attempt to educate. These arguments would seem strange if they were applied to children of compulsory school age, but parents do to a greater or lesser degree attempt to educate older children and all schools have a 'hidden curriculum' which produces incidental or unintended learning. It would seem that Tizard, like Blank, bases her argument on the fact that the traditional nursery school curriculum is more informally structured than that of the compulsory schooling sector.

Tizard and Blank are by no means the only theorists to argue that traditional nursery schools are not primarily educational institutions. Van der Eyken (1977), for example, has also argued that the nursery school ethos does not 'place the emphasis where it belongs – on educational needs'.

Van der Eyken's evidence for this claim is drawn largely from the findings of the survey conducted by Taylor et al. (1972) for the Schools Council. The survey was carried out among 578 teachers. Part of the questionnaire completed by the teachers was concerned with the main purposes of education. There were five aims focused on intellectual development, social and emotional development, physical development and the creation of an effective transition from home to school. Each of these aims was derived from discussion with teachers. Another section of the questionnaire was concerned with objectives, that is with more specific goals related to these aims. Thirty objectives were derived representing a range of capabilities, skills, attitudes, values and dispositions, and were related to the four developmental areas – social/emotional, intellectual, physical and aesthetic – included among the aims. The teachers were required to place each of the five aims in rank order from one to five in terms of the priority they would give it relative to the other aims. The section dealing with objectives required the teachers to rate each one on a five-point scale.

Van der Eyken's report of the findings of the survey claims that 'the teachers gave a considerably greater weighting to the social and emotional development of children, and considered that intellectual development was, if a choice had to be made, the least important'. Concerning the objectives Van der Eyken reports that 'once again, intellectual or cognitive development took a low priority'.

Before examining Van der Eyken's reporting of the findings, some reservations concerning the survey itself need to be kept in mind. First, with regard to aims, a choice of priorities had to be made: if a teacher was reluctant to place the aims in rank order believing each of them to be equally important, she had either to rank them in spite of her reluctance or to fail to return the questionnaire. Second, this section required only a ranking of the aims not a statement of the reason for the ranking given. Let us suppose a teacher conceives intellectual development to be of supreme importance, but believes that attempts to bring it about will be fruitless unless favourable social and emotional factors predispose a child to be receptive to the teacher's efforts. She might then give social and emotional development a higher ranking than intellectual development for that reason. As Van der Eyken himself says, 'so much depends on how the respondents interpret the questions'.

The same criticism cannot be made of the section of the questionnaire dealing with objectives, since teachers were not required to put them in rank order but instead had to rate each one on a five-point scale. It was found that objectives concerned with the child's psychological awareness of self and others was most likely to be emphasized. Next came areas concerned with school expectations, physical development and general social awareness, with creative, aesthetic objectives only a little way behind. Finally came intellectual or cognitive objectives. However, in interpreting these results it is important to note that, as Taylor and his associates emphasize, some objectives serve more than one area of educational intentions. For example, 'to help the child understand and recognize the feelings, needs and attitudes of others' has an intellectual component as well as one relating to self–other objectives.

Even if these reservations were not valid, Van der Eyken has overstated the case. It is in the section dealing with objectives that the cognitive domain emerged with the lowest score, and this was in contradiction to the ranking given to intellectual development in the section on aims, where it emerged not last but second in rank order. In addition, as Taylor and his associates with more caution than Van der Eyken point out, 'no great gulf separates any of the objectives from any other. All are considered important, though it is reasonable to infer that some will be given priority, depending on the child and the circumstances.'

Taylor et al. conclude that these unresolved complexities and contradictions, indicated in their research, are 'likely to have arisen from the difficulties of translating broad statements of educational intent into specific aspects of practical action'. What does seem certain from the Schools Council survey is that most nursery school teachers have a strong resistance to 'formal' curricula, to structured programmes exemplified by the Peabody Language Development Kit or the Bereiter and Engelmann programme. Instead they favour a curriculum based largely on children exercising choice of activity from a wide range of materials, few of which are tightly pre-structured. Within this context, according to Taylor and his associates, 'cognitive objectives are seen as only a little less important than social and emotional ones'.

A more powerful source of evidence that nursery school teachers may give relatively low priority to cognitive development comes from studies of practice. Thomas (1973) observed a small sample of children for a complete day, recording every response uttered by and to them and noting their activities and the time spent on each. She found that the teachers accepted minimal verbalization from children and that their own verbal exchanges with a child rarely extended either his language or his thinking. In addition the experiences and pattern of activities tended to be repetitive. In sum, little attention seemed to be paid to intellectual objectives in general and to developing language in particular.

Another study of nursery school teachers' practice, particularly their use of language, was carried out by Tizard et al. (1976). Twelve pre-school centres were studied. Four were day nurseries rather than schools and, since the staff were not teachers, need not concern us here. Of the remaining eight institutions four were 'traditional' nursery schools and four 'had departed from tradition to the extent of including a special language programme in the school day'. The results showed significant differences between these two types of nursery school. In the schools with a language programme staff spent more time interacting with the children and these interactions had more 'cognitive content' than those of staff in the 'traditional' schools. There appears to have been some match between the beliefs of the staff concerning the functions of the institution and their behaviour:

> in those centres where the staff saw their main function as looking after children whilst their mothers worked or providing them with an opportunity to play with other children, the staff interacted less with the children and in a more supervisory capacity than did staff in centres with avowedly educational aims.

A more recent study by Tizard (1979) examined video-tapes of the same children in their nursery schools and at home, and concluded that there was more connected discourse in the latter.

One should, however, be wary about drawing a firm conclusion from these studies that nursery school teachers have a relative lack of concern for intellectual development and for extending children's language. None of the studies finds that teachers' exchanges with children do not have cognitive content, but rather that the proportion of such exchanges is relatively small. Sylva et al. (1980), in their study that was part of the Oxford Pre-school Project, certainly found instances of exchanges involving 'tutorial' dialogue. Unfortunately these instances were infrequent. What we do not know is whether this state of affairs reflects a relative lack of concern with the cognitive domain or whether it is the result of managerial demands in the ecology of the typical nursery school. Bruner (1980) in his overview of the Oxford Pre-school Project, suggests this may be the case:

> Teachers talking non-managerially with children can and do produce long and rich dialogues. But management duties must preclude such dialogue. And for chillingly good reasons when one computes the statistics of the situation. Take the typical preschool group . . . It will contain, say, twenty-five children and three adult staff. The study by Sylva, Roy and Painter computes that, on average, a child will talk conversationally three minutes in an hour with an adult. Assume that for each child each hour this constitutes three three-turn conversations with an adult . . . This makes about twenty-five connected conversations for each adult each hour . . . Is it realistic to expect much more conversational activity from a

teacher in preschool settings as organized?

Some support for the suggestion that the problem may be a managerial one comes from the Oxford Pre-school Project evidence. It finds that staff–child ratio is a potent factor determining the quality of staff–child interaction. The centres studied were divided into those with good staff–child ratios (1 : 8, 1 : 9 and 1 : 10) and those with excellent ones (1 : 7, 1 : 6 and 1 : 5). It was found that:

> children in centres with excellent ratios are more prone to conversation. Interestingly, they speak less to one another but twice as much with staff members. The magnitude of the difference is surprising, as there were not twice as many adults around to serve as conversational partners.

## FOSTERING INTELLECTUAL DEVELOPMENT

Whether the comparative infrequency with which teachers in traditional nursery schools seem to engage in dialogues where the intention is to stimulate and extend children intellectually is the result of cognitive objectives not being given priority or to managerial demands, it is nonetheless important that this state of affairs changes. If it does not, Tizard's claim, that nursery schools do little more than other agencies in educating young children, and attempts by politicians and administrators to close down nursery schools or to replace teachers with staff who have had no teacher training will be difficult to combat. It would be an equally sad state of affairs if Tizard's claim were to affect change in the direction of nursery school teachers being driven to adopt a curriculum consisting primarily of formal, highly structured programmes of the kind they have previously rejected. The remainder of this chapter will be concerned with evidence about the ways that young children's intellectual functioning and development seem to be most facilitated. It will be argued that the evidence suggests that the conventional wisdom of nursery school teachers, that the curriculum should be one in which children's intentions are given a central place, is well grounded, but that within such a context a teacher needs to interact with children in ways that require knowledge and skills of a professional kind, making nonsense of the notion that a formal curriculum is concerned with education whereas an informal one is not.

The work of Piaget has dominated the psychology of intellectual development for several decades. There is not the space here to go into details concerning his work. The important thing to note is that his description of the thinking of pre-school children is mainly in terms of their incompetence; of how, that is, they cannot yet reason. The major characteristic of young children's thinking, according to Piaget, is that they are unable to 'decentre', that is they focus on a limited aspect of an object or situation, resulting in false conclusions or 'illogical' thinking. Just a few examples must suffice to illustrate this. The young child cannot put himself at the point of view of another person when it is different from his own: he 'centres' on his own point of view. If the shape of some malleable substance is changed (if a ball of clay, for example, is rolled into a sausage shape), a young child believes the quantity has either increased or decreased. He does so because he centres either on the increase in length and ignores the decrease in width or vice versa. Young children generally centre on similarities between objects and ignore dissimilarities. Piaget's example is of a child who, on a walk, saw first one slug and then another slug and concluded they were the same slug. Conversely and paradoxically, a child may sometimes centre on dissimilarities and ignore similarities. This leads him to conclude, for example, that there are several suns because he has seen the sun in different places. This account of young children's thinking is in terms of incompetence; of what they cannot yet understand; of how they cannot yet think. It creates a problem for those concerned with the education of young children, when their traditional wisdom has been that it is important to start with what a child can do and understand; with his competencies rather than his incompetencies.

There is now, however, a considerable amount of evidence that, given certain conditions, young children's intellectual capabilities are greater than Piaget's tests might lead us to believe. Tamburrini (1981) has argued that it should not be inferred from this evidence that Piaget's tests are invalid, but rather that Piaget's tests assess some overall generalized competence that will be shown by a child in all relevant contexts, whereas there are some specific contexts where a child will think at a higher level than he does in a standard Piagetian test. What the characteristics of these contexts are must therefore now be examined.

First, it would appear that, if we want a young child to function intellectually at his most capable, we must ensure that the way we ask him to express his understanding is appropriate to his level of understanding and development. A comparison between children's responses on Piaget's standard tests for egocentricity and those in a test devised by Borke (1978), which modifies the standard test only slightly, illustrates this principle. 'Egocentricity' is the term Piaget uses for the inability of the young child to put himself at the point of view of another person when it is different from his own. In Piaget's test the child is shown a three-dimensional model of three mountains each of which has a feature clearly distinguishing it from the other two. The child is required to select from photographs of the mountains from different points of view the one representing the perspective of a doll which is placed *vis-à-vis* the mountains in a position different from that of the child. On this standard test few children under the age of seven are able to select the correct photograph. Most young children select the photograph representing their own point of view. Borke modified the test in a simple way. Instead of selecting from photographs the child had to demonstrate the point of view of the doll by turning a turntable. Many children of four and some of three years of age were able to do this correctly.

A second condition favourable to children thinking at their most capable is the familiarity of the materials involved. In a further modification of Piaget's 'mountains' test for egocentricity Borke substituted for the three mountains a three-dimensional model consisting of miniature people and animals in familiar domestic settings. As in the previous experiment the turntable was used instead of a selection of photographs. Under these conditions even more young children were able to give a correct response than in the other experiment by Borke discussed above.

A third important condition affecting the level of young children's thinking is one particularly stressed by Donaldson (1978) involving the extent to which they understand the intentions of the participants in a situation. She reports an experiment carried out by McGarrigle which again involved a minor modification to a standard Piagetian test. One of Piaget's tests for conservation of number involves showing the child two rows of five objects, say counters, aligned so that each counter in the second row is placed underneath the corresponding counter in the first row. The experimenter then spreads out the second row and the child, who has agreed that there was the same amount of counters in each row when they were aligned, is now asked whether there is still the same amount. In McGarrigle's version of the task the rearrangement was ostensibly the result of accident rather than of the intentional act of an adult. This was achieved by introducing a teddy bear, called 'naughty Teddy', who rearranged the elements. In this modified version more young children gave the correct response than normally happens in the standard test. Donaldson comments that in the standard test the young child tries to make sense of the experimenter's intention in terms of his experience of adults' intentions in his everyday transactions with them. If an adult arranges some objects, asks if they are the same amount, rearranges them, and then again asks if there is the same amount, a young child is likely to assume that the answer must be that the amount has changed, because in his experience adults do not carry out an action on things if their state is to remain the same as it was before.

A fourth condition affecting young children's understanding is, perhaps obviously, the complexity of relationships involved in a situation. For example, Light (1979), investigating egocentricity or role-taking abilities in a group of four-year-old children, used a number of tasks varying in complexity but each one requiring the child to identify another's point of view that was different from his own. One of Light's tasks used a three-sided pyramid with a different toy illustrated on each of its faces. The child was required to say which toy the experimenter who sat opposite him could see. In a more elaborate version of the task a doll was used and placed in each of five positions from two of which it would 'see' only one toy and from the other three of which it would 'see' two toys. The child was required to identify the toy or toys the doll would 'see' from the various positions. Out of a group of 60 children only 5 gave the correct response on all trials in the second task, whereas 23 did so in the first task.

These findings lend support to the conventional wisdom of the traditional nursery school that children need to explore and play with materials in their own way and in their own time. Further support for this practice comes from a comparative study carried out by Sylva et al. as part of the Oxford Pre-school Project. A comparison was undertaken between pre-school centres in Oxfordshire and in Miami, Florida. In the Oxfordshire schools a large range of equipment was available from which, for the most part, a child selected what he wanted when he wanted it. By contrast, in most of the Miami centres a limited range of materials, such as three Rs materials, was laid out at any one time, and choice was firmly controlled by the teacher for large parts of the day, even in some cases in so-called free play periods. Sylva and her associates found that the Miami children were not stretching themselves intellectually as much as the Oxfordshire children, and this was in spite of the greater emphasis in the Miami centres on school-like activities and in spite of the much greater frequency in them of prescribed work as compared with the Oxfordshire centres.

While the evidence suggests the need for children to have ample opportunity to explore and play with materials in their own way and in their own time, it would be wrong to conclude that all the adult needs to do is to provide appropriate materials and then to adopt only a supervisory role. Evidence is beginning to accrue of differences in children's social experience that are associated with differences in their intellectual functioning. This evidence supports the view that nursery school teachers should adopt an active rather than passive role with respect to the cognitive domain.

In the investigation by Light mentioned above, there were individual differences among the 60 four-year-old children in relation to their ability to role-take. He used a number of role-taking tasks among which there was sufficient intercorrelation for him to obtain a composite score for each child. These scores were then related to other factors including aspects of maternal style. One of these aspects was the mothers' teaching strategies with respect to a simple task. The mothers were first shown how to arrange some coloured blocks in a prescribed pattern. They then had to teach the task to their children, and the way in which they did so was observed by the experimenter. Two different maternal styles emerged, one in which the mother corrected an error immediately a child made it, and the other in which correction was delayed until a child was himself aware of a problem because the difficulties arising from an error were clear to him. In other words the second style synchronized more with the child's perceptions than the first one did. A significant association was found between competent role-taking and the maternal style involving deferred correction.

Another aspect of maternal style explored by Light concerned social control and was based on the distinction made by Bernstein in terms of a personal/positional dimension. Bernstein (1971) has suggested that in a 'person-oriented' family a child's awareness of self and others develops and differentiates as the motives and intentions of the family members as individuals are realized in their speech to one another. By contrast, in the 'positional' family reference is to status or position and a child learns a less differentiated role. Light was able to analyze transcripts of his sample of mothers in an open-ended interview that included questions about social control. He found a great variation in the frequency with which personal rationales in relation to social control of the child were given. These comments, Light says, 'get below the surface of the child's behaviour and consider things from the point of view of the child's feelings, intentions and character'. Light found a positive correlation between a frequent use of person-oriented rationales by the mother and good role-taking abilities on the part of the child, which was particularly notable when compared with the absence of a significant relationship between the use of such rationales and the child's IQ.

In Light's study these differences were not associated with social class differences, partly, perhaps, because his sample drawn from Cambridge and its environs was not strongly differentiated in terms of conventional social class distinctions. However, social class differences have been found in other studies of maternal teaching styles and of parents' language in different social class groups.

The traditional nursery school gives a central place to children's play. Other pre-school services also emphasize play: the term 'pre-school play group' speaks for itself. In the study carried out by Sylva et al., however, there seemed to be a reluctance among staff to see children's play as varying in quality and in value. This may well spring from the fairly widespread assumption that play is such a natural and universal phenomenon that it will occur in spite of what adults do. It is probably reasoned that any intervention will destroy the spontaneity of play and that, since it is a 'natural phenomenon', all play is of equal value.

There is now, however, considerable cross-cultural evidence (see Feitelson, 1977) to suggest that make-believe play varies in extent and quality depending on the attitudes towards play of the adults in a community. El'Konin (1966) has concluded that make-believe play does not develop spontaneously but, instead, arises in interaction with adults who suggest it.

The findings of cross-cultural studies of children's play have led to a number of tutoring studies whose primary purpose was to improve the imaginative quality of children's play through adult modelling. Freyburg (1973), for example, carried out a study with a group of 80 five-year-old children from low socioeconomic class families. The children were evenly divided into a control and experimental group, and the children in the experimental group were given eight 20-minute training sessions in small groups of four children at a time. They were taken to a room equipped with a large table on which were spread pipe-cleaners, a variety of fabrics, clay, Playdoh, bricks, Tinkertoy sets and a wide variety of wooden shapes. During each of the eight sessions the investigator introduced a theme based on the children's interests and began to enact small plots in which pipe-cleaner figures were made to talk and to engage in make-believe roles. The children were encouraged to adopt a role using play equipment of their own choosing. Compared with the control group the experimental group improved significantly in the imaginativeness of their play and in the degree of concentration shown in it. Moreover when the children's play was re-examined two months later these changes had persisted.

Some other tutoring studies have, in addition, examined other outcomes of adult modelling for imaginative play. Several have found that experimental groups who have been tutored not only improve in the quality of imaginativeness in their play but, subsequently, also achieve higher scores on a creativity test than children in the control group. Golomb and Cornelius (1977) even found that children tutored for play performed better in Piagetian tests than did children in the control group.

Smith and Sydall (1978) have suggested that it is not the specific tutoring for play so much as adult interaction which is effective in producing these outcomes. This is to some extent borne out by the findings of the study carried out by Sylva et al. Two aspects of children's play were examined; its cognitive complexity and the degree of concentration shown by the children. Cognitive complexity was examined in terms of the sequential organization and elaboration in a bout of play and concentration was assessed in terms of duration of a bout of play – a 'bout' being a sequence of activity having a coherent thread. It was found that there was an upward shift in the complexity of play associated with adult interaction of any kind, but particularly when the interaction involved the adult in a tutorial capacity; that is 'when she deftly expands the child's scope of action or conception, often using the concrete task as a take-off point for discussion in a more abstract or imaginary vein'.

In sum, research into differences in maternal style and their outcomes and into the effect of adult interaction on the quality of children's make-believe play and some cognitive outcomes suggest that nursery school teachers need to do more than provide a rich range of materials with which children generate and direct their activities. They need also to adopt a role which includes interacting with children in a way that synchronizes with their intentions and purposes.

It would seem then that the task for the teachers is threefold: first, she needs to diagnose a child's intentions; second, to comment on or elaborate them in some way that has cognitive potential; and third, to ensure that the child understands her, the teacher's, intentions. Each of these three components in an interaction require considerable knowledge and skill on the part of a teacher.

When a teacher is concerned with children between the ages of three and five years, diagnostic skill is not something she should expect to 'come naturally' as it seems to in the studies of the mother–infant dyad such as Schaffer's (1971). Diagnosis on the basis of the child's language is a highly professional matter. Tough's project for the Schools Council on Communication Skills has categorized the various functions, some more cognitively loaded than others, that a child's language use may serve. Even when a teacher has studied these functions, diagnosis is no simple matter. As Stannard (1980) emphasizes in his comments on the work of Tough, it is not always easy to determine a child's intention from the language he uses, as often what a child says will serve more than one purpose: a statement about some object or event may at its face value serve to communicate information about that object or event, but it may also be concerned with maintaining the personal identity of the speaker.

In addition, the diagnosis of language is often only a first step in assessing a child's level of intellectual functioning. For example, a statement by a child that serves a clear purpose of maintaining personal identity may not inform a teacher whether that child is capable of role-taking, of taking another person's point of view. To elicit such information, further dialogue is necessary and successful dialogue, in this instance, requires knowledge of the development of role-taking abilities.

There are many occasions, however, when it is not from what a child says but from what he does that a teacher needs to assess his level of development. Correct assessment requires more than 'common-sense' or everyday experience of children. It requires professional knowledge. The development of children's drawings illustrate this. Younger pre-school children draw what they claim to be representations of the human figure that are usually unrecognizable as such, with elements totally separate – facial features, for example, appearing outside the head. Slightly older children draw features enclosed within the head of a figure that is tadpole-like, having no torso. At this stage arms are often omitted but legs seldom are. The 'common-sense' layman's assumption accounts for these differences in terms of the child's manual coordination abilities. As Goodnow (1977) has shown, this is a false explanation. Correct assessment requires a knowledge of children's drawing strategies that should be part of a teacher's professional training. Similarly the ability to diagnose correctly a child's development with respect to classificatory concepts, from how he arranges miniature animals and objects in the sand tray or with respect to mathematical concepts from his play in the 'home corner', requires professional knowledge.

Diagnosis of a child's intentions or level of development is, of course, of nothing more than academic interest unless it is followed by an attempt to extend that child's understanding or to elaborate his intentions into educationally fruitful activity. It has been argued here that the nursery school curriculum should be one in which a teacher's interactions with her pupils synchronize with their intentions and levels of understanding. Thus, skilful extension requires skilful diagnosis. But professional knowledge of what constitutes a worthwhile curriculum in educational terms at this stage is also necessary. If, as Bruner has suggested, the managerial demands in a nursery school are considerable, a teacher, when not dealing managerially with children, has to decide where it would be most educationally profitable to engage in tutorial dialogue. Even though a teacher has provided materials that she considers have the greatest potential for provoking educationally fruitful activities, children will generate problems and activities that will differ in their educational potential. A child who has discovered that he can use constructional materials to build an edifice that remains stable if it is symmetrical has encountered a problem of considerable mathematical importance. If a teacher first makes explicit for him his formulation of the problem and his solution, then directs him to an activity with the balance scales and an assortment of objects and, yet later, confronts him with how to account for an asymmetrical structure that balances, he may well begin to understand that it is equal distribution of weight rather than symmetry that determines balance. The decision to interact with this child rather than with a group of children who, at the same time, are using the same equipment to symbolize objects at a make-believe tea party would be justifiable on educational grounds. On another occasion a group of children holding a make-believe tea party that seems to lack elaboration or imaginativeness may well be the ones who should be selected for attention in terms of a tutorial dialogue to improve the imaginative quality of their play.

In sum, the education of pre-school children requires professional knowledge of both child development and of the kinds of skills and concepts that may be acquired by children in that age range and that are educationally powerful. The fact that the context in which this takes place is not that of a formal curriculum, but an informal one in which a large proportion of their activities are generated by the children does not mean that teachers are merely engaged in a shared child-rearing exercise. On the contrary, a high level of professional expertise is required to educate young children within an informal curriculum where there is a synchrony between children's intentions and the educational dialogues a teacher initiates.

## TOPICS FOR DISCUSSION

1. Critically evaluate the evidence which, Tamburrini suggests, supports the claim that 'the conventional wisdom of nursery school teachers that the curriculum should be one in which children's intentions are given a central place' is well grounded.
2. Tamburrini cites four conditions which affect young children's thinking and understanding, offering research evidence to support her contention that there are some specific contexts where a child can think at a 'higher level'. How far do these findings lend support to the 'conventional wisdom of the traditional nursery school'?
3. 'Differences in children's social experience are associated with differences in their intellectual functioning.' Discuss three or four research findings which support this statement.

## SUGGESTIONS FOR FURTHER READING

1. Tizard, B. and Hughes, M. (1984) 'The gap between home and nursery school', in *Young Children Learning: Talking and Thinking at Home and at School*. London, Fontana, chap. 10, pp. 235–48.

The nursery schools and classes studied by Tizard and Hughes were found to create 'a child-centred play environment in which children had relatively few encounters with adults. When they did encounter the school staff, they found the staff's expectations of them were very different from their mothers' (p. 235). The authors examine the range of differences which face the young child on entering nursery school and carefully detail the ways in which children respond and behave to the two very different environments of home and mother and school and teacher. Of particular interest is their discussion of typical effects on working-class children, and the strategies employed by *all* the participants – parents, teachers and children – to bridge the gap between home and school – interestingly, a task that seemed harder for the teachers than for the mothers. How the children tried to bridge the gap is demonstrated in a variety of ways. For example, the authors note that it is obviously necessary that young children should learn how to give teachers appropriate information in a clear and intelligible form. When staff don't ask the right questions, however, quite bizarre results can happen:

> The following conversation failed to establish communication because Lynne did not explain that Polly was her grandmother's dog who had just spent a night with her, and the nursery assistant did not ask who Polly was, or where her home was.
> Child: Polly's back. Polly comed up yesterday, but she's gone home. Polly.
> Staff: Polly?
> Child: Yeah, my Polly.
> Staff: Oh!
> Child: We had some biccies up there. When we taked her home. She bringed us some sweeties.
> Staff: Oh, that was nice.
> Child: A packet.
> Staff: A packet? What kind? (Child did not reply, and staff talks to other children.) (p. 238)

Some of the problems which ensue when staff attempt to bridge the home–school gap by asking children questions about their home life are the result of the teachers having no means of evaluating the children's replies. Similarly, it was found that because mothers were familiar with the school routine, conversations at home about school presented fewer problems than conversations about home at school. Tizard and Hughes conclude this very useful chapter with an examination of the implications of the home–school gap.

2. Donaldson, M. (1978) 'Disembedded thought and social values', in *Children's Minds*. London, Fontana, chap. 7, pp. 76–85.

Donaldson reminds us that it is in situations of fairly immediate goals and intentions and familiar patterns of events that we feel most at home. Thus, 'even pre-school children can frequently reason well about the events in the stories they hear' (p. 76). It is when thinking moves beyond the bounds of familiar patterns of meaningful events, to 'formal' or 'abstract' situations or, as Donaldson calls it, 'disembedded' thinking, that there are dramatic differences in children's abilities to cope. Donaldson illustrates this move beyond the bounds of human sense to the *form* or logical structure of the reasoning (with its attendant difficulties) with the following example:

> Nial (aged 4 years):  But how can it be (that they are getting married)? You have
>                                        to have a man too.
> (The book contains an illustration of a wedding in which the man looks rather like a woman. The child thinks it is a picture of two women.)
> (*Premises*: (1) You need a man for a wedding; (2) There is no man in the picture. *Conclusion*: It can't be a wedding.) (p. 55)

The 'form' or 'structure' of this argument involves breaking the reasoning into separate statements or propositions. Two propositions, together with the negations of the two, are involved: *there is a wedding* and *there is a man*. The 'pure' form of reasoning, given that

> *there is a wedding* = the symbol *p*, and
> *there is a man* = the symbol *q*, becomes
>> If *p*, then *q*.
>> *Not q*.
>> Therefore *not p*.

Put like this, Donaldson comments, the reasoning, for many people, becomes mind-boggling, for we do not easily engage in manipulating meaningless symbols. But note that Nial, aged only four, can very easily *reason* about men and weddings (p. 77). The author wryly remarks that in our society, the better you are at coping with problems without having to be sustained by human sense, 'the more likely you are to succeed in our educational system, the more you will be approved of and loaded with prizes'. Donaldson's argument is that you cannot master *any* formal system unless you have learned to take at least some steps beyond the confines of human sense, and that the problems involved in helping very young children to begin to do this at the very beginning of their schooling – or even earlier – have been neither properly recognized nor adequately tackled. The paramount task, then, for teachers of the young, is to teach the disembedded modes of thinking more successfully (p. 82). The lucid discussion of just what teachers *ought* to be doing is of particular importance and relevance to topics for discussion (no. 2) in Reading 1 (p. 25).

3. Tizard, B. and Hughes, M. (1984) 'An afternoon with Donna and her mother', chap. 7, pp. 161–79, and 'The working-class girls, including Donna, at school', chap. 9, pp. 214–34, in *Young Children Learning: Talking and Thinking at Home and at School*. London, Fontana.

Donna was chosen as an object of study because, the authors assert, she was an extreme example who confirmed the popular, stereotyped picture of a working-class upbringing. However, in spite of the fact that Donna was a demanding child, that much of the time at home was occupied by wrangles and disputes and, in addition, her mother spent little time with her engaged in the kind of educational play so valued by nursery school teachers, Tizard and Hughes maintain that the overall picture did not confirm any stereotypical view of the inadequacies of working-class language. Indeed, the authors claim, Donna's home provided a rich learning environment. Tizard and Hughes present a fascinating vignette of Donna's typical interactions with her mother, demonstrating how the parent was invariably prepared patiently to follow along with the child's thinking, was concerned to understand what her daughter was trying to say, and offered many explanations which were detailed and specific, giving Donna a clear picture of the constraints and realities of her life. Other episodes demonstrate the mother's concern with helping Donna to acquire what was considered to be essential learning, namely knowing her letters and numbers. Moreover, Donna's mother was one of a minority of working-class mothers who did not hold the viewpoint that play was important, for she was critical of the nursery school for providing only play, supplementing the school's activities by teaching her child the alphabet and to spell and copy her name. In one afternoon session the authors recorded 69 conversations between mother and daughter, 77 questions which included 28 'Why' questions, and noted that Donna and her mother contributed nearly equally to *initiating* and *sustaining* the conversations. This was, however, as the authors affirm, a very disputatious working-class family and many of the interactions were to do with discipline so that the range of information given to the child was often relatively limited, given to explanations which were often brief and somewhat implicit. The mother seemed to see her own educational responsibilities much more in terms of encouraging formal school skills than in developing and extending general knowledge or vocabulary.

Chapter 9, 'The working-class girls, including Donna, at school', provides evidence which clearly supports the contention that working-class children are adversely affected by the school setting. Tizard and Hughes teased out the evidence by comparing the way in which middle-class and working-class children behaved at home and at school, showing that working-class children were *much more affected* by the demands made on them by the school. For example, whereas at home conversations between mother and child were more evenly balanced, at school it was the staff who did most of the talking. Working-class children contributed only 15 per cent of sustaining remarks in conversation with the staff, and the discrepancy between the proportion of adult talk to child talk at home and at school was significantly greater in the case of working-class children. Such youngsters, in a wide range of situations and behaviours, appeared more subdued and immature at school than at home, and since the teachers adjusted their demands to the perceived immaturity of the children, they in no way *compensated* for any inadequacies in their homes. The authors contend that 'what we *do* know is that the working-class children were already appearing at a disadvantage in nursery school'.

## Reading 2

# THE MYTH OF THE PRE-SCHOOL

## *J. Northam*

### INTRODUCTION

The use of the all-embracing term 'pre-school' to refer to the varieties of provision which are made for children under the age of five implies a similarity of purpose and practice which does not correspond to the situation. The concept of the pre-school has, however, influenced research in the field of early childhood and can be detected in policy regarding provision. The general use of the term has therefore helped to sustain a myth that it is possible to think of all the differing organized settings in which young children meet with adults and each other as essentially similar, as unified in purpose, style and effect. Though there is no such form of provision in Britain as 'the pre-school', the supposed validity of the concept has deflected attention from marked differences between settings. Underlying the con-

Northam, J. (1983) 'The myth of the preschool'. *Education 3–13*, **11**, 2, 37–40.

cept there is a stereotype of 'the child' which does not reflect either the variety in children's needs or the active way in which children may participate in their social world.

This article is concerned with the effects of categorizing all forms of provision for young children under one heading, that of 'pre-school'. The term is encountered in different ways, and associated with different meanings, from one context to another.

## VARIETIES OF 'PRE-SCHOOLING'

[. . .]

At least nine major forms of early childhood provision can be distinguished. There are nursery schools and classes; low-cost nursery educational provision; combined family and nursery centres; local authority day nurseries; workplace day nurseries; private day nurseries; private schools which admit under fives; childminders; and playgroups. Each of these forms includes wide variations, but they have been classified according to major differences in organization, financing, staffing, purpose and patterns of attendance. That these differences have an important effect on styles of practice and on the ways in which practitioners regard the children in their care can be seen by comparing the reports of the Oxford Pre-school Research Project, especially those by Garland and White (1980) and Bryant et al. (1980).

## PLAYGROUPS

It is perhaps among playgroups that the greatest variation can be found. It is arguable that there is such diversity that to place all these groups in one category could be misleading. There are at least 16 different ways of organizing playgroups. Examples of organizing bodies in England and Wales include playgroups run by one person who is in sole charge of financing and administration and who does not refer any decisions to parents; playgroups run by a parents' committee in which all parents are invited to committee meetings and are consulted on every decision, major and minor; and playgroups run by a Church or community association committee, who make all decisions without reference to parents, including the selection and employment of the supervisor and the definition of the recruitment area of the playgroup. In staffing and adult help at sessions playgroups vary. At some a team of six or more staff, all designated 'supervisor', divide the number of sessions between them so that no one person attends more than two-thirds of the sessions at most; parents may also be included in the child/adult ratio, taking it in turns to attend sessions on a helper rota. At others, the same team of three staff, hierarchically organized, attend every session and do not involve parents as helpers. Children's attendance is typically sessional; two or three sessions per week is a usual pattern. In groups which have a highly variable and part-time pattern of attendance on the part of both children and adults, the children may well encounter a rather different group from session to session. At some play-groups it seems perfectly possible for a session to be a unique event in that the particular combination of people present may never be repeated exactly. To assume, therefore, that children's experience at playgroups is broadly similar would seem to be unjustified, unless one also assumes that children do not notice whether the same people are present from session to session, or if they do, it is of little consequence to them. Therefore, to subsume all these different types of organization under one heading for the purpose of studying, for example, the transition from home to organized group provision implies some curious assumptions about the ways in which young children behave.

## DIFFERENCES IN ETHOS AND ORGANIZATION

In a number of recent studies, nursery schools and classes as well as varieties of playgroup are placed under the heading of 'pre-school'. It is doubtful whether an establishment may usefully be termed both 'school' and 'pre-school' at one and the same time. As King (1978) has pointed out, 'play' in schools has a special meaning, associated with the ways in which teachers regard children and the purposes of education. The definition of play therefore is related to the school curriculum, the assessment and typification of children as individuals and theories about development during childhood. Unlike most playgroup supervisors, teachers are *in loco parentis*, which affects their authority and their right to make decisions in relation to individual children. Neither curriculum planning nor assessment can be seen as general features of playgroup provision, and indeed would not necessarily be consistent with aspects of the philosophy promoted through the Pre-school Playgroups Association (PPA). In this philosophy, parental involvement and a focus on the parent/child system are emphasized. Parents at sessions are not necessarily to be regarded as the helpers of the supervisor-in-charge. They may well be the employers of the supervisor to whom all decisions must ultimately be referred; some of them may have attended the same Foundation Course as the supervisor. This situation clearly constrains any decision-making and assessment functions associated with the role of the supervisor. Nursery school practice is therefore characterized by the ideologies, goals, professional training and forms of organization found elsewhere in the education system. Curriculum, assessment, and the status of the adult-in-charge as *in loco parentis* are largely absent from playgroups. It would be inadvisable to assume that their absence made no difference to the children's experience, or, at least a difference so slight that research work could proceed without taking it into account.

The study of Sylva et al. (1980) focused on ways in which children operated with materials in nursery schools and classes and in playgroups. The study by Blatchford et al. (1982) investigated the process of transition from home to 'pre-school'.

In both there are marginal references to differences between settings. In the Oxford study the short career of supervisors was noted and the relative lack of sustained child/child and adult/child interaction in playgroups. As the study was not designed to take account of differences in what Sylva et al. call 'ethos and organisation', the patterns of interaction remained largely a mystery. If, however, patterns of attendance, and the absence of, for example, curricular goals and individual assessment had been considered, the mystery might well have been illuminated. In the NFER work, Blatchford et al. found that although there was much overlap in practitioners' views of their purposes, supervisors tended to give a higher priority to social benefits and advantages to parents, while teachers emphasized cognitive skills, competence in the use of language and children's development. It was also found that supervisors were less likely to report children as 'upset' or having problems in 'settling'. One explanation offered for this kind of difference was a speculation that playgroups might offer a 'more informal atmosphere', though as other studies, including that by the Oxford team, report more adult-directed activity in playgroups than in nursery schools, the relative degrees of informality appear to be in doubt. However, if account is taken of the fact that most supervisors are not in the position of assessor, are not *in loco parentis*, and emphasize social rather than educational or developmental benefits, the lack of focus on individual children's less obvious problems is by no means surprising.

Although, as has been discussed, studies based on the essential similarity between 'pre-schools' sometimes nevertheless report differences, this evidence tends to occupy a somewhat peripheral position in the reports, rather than being regarded as of central importance. This leads to the most intriguing question of all: why, when with little difficulty, fundamental differences between forms of provision can be identified, do authoritative and prestigious research teams persist in the apparent assumption that as far as children are concerned one setting is much like another? These teams do not always make this assumption in relation to adults, and in particular to themselves. In an illuminating passage Smith and Connolly (1980) describe the appointment of a new supervisor for their experimental controlled setting, in which variables were to be manipulated one by one. Unlike the previous supervisor, she was experienced and trained in nursery school work, and this they judged to be 'important for the effective execution of the variations in regime which were planned'. The new supervisor was not intended as one of those variations in regime. Her experience, perspective and training seem to be important to the interaction between her and Smith and Connolly. That such attributes might also influence her relationships with the children is not considered. Underlying much research in the field of early childhood there appears to be a model of 'the child' who 'grows' or 'develops' or 'evolves' accordingly to a largely predetermined programme. Environmental conditions may encourage or distort or inhibit the gradual emergence of the model, but essentially the process takes place in much the same way, given reasonably favourable conditions, whatever the particular features of the social context. Given this underlying assumption, it is possible to design research programmes without considering the social context in which the children's behaviour occurs. It is further possible to miniaturize the goals of the research in such a way as to produce apparently objective, precise measurements of behaviour. When the research design does not allow for the study of 'ethos and organization' there seems to be no means of coding and interpreting information which might challenge the underlying assumption, which is, as a result, 'objectively' validated.

How, therefore, does it happen that there is a belief in some quarters that the progress of children in different 'pre-school' settings has been measured and has been found to be broadly similar? Jerome Bruner makes this suggestion in his introductory report to the Oxford Preschool Research Project (1980), and has been quoted by educational journalists such as Auriol Stevens (1981). Bruner bases his suggestion, however, not on his own work but on a study of playgroups of a rather special nature in Northern Ireland (Turner, 1977), a study which did not include any nursery schools or classes at all. Other studies, such as that by Woodhead (1976), are concerned not with day-to-day practice but with the effects of special compensatory language programmes. Examination of EPA reports, such as DES/SSRC (1975), yields no clear comparative data. As Bruner admits, such comparisons are usually considered to be invidious, and indeed there are strong grounds for objecting to them, especially when the process of evaluation ignores the overall purposes of each form of provision for children. Nevertheless, if comparisons are to be made there is clearly a need to be sure about what is being compared with what, and the process of clarification is unlikely to be assisted by unexamined assumptions and the use of vague terminology.

## 'UNDER ONE HEADING'

Perhaps the perspectives of research teams would be a matter of academic interest only, if the concept of the pre-school were confined to them. After all, as members of the Oxford research team complain, few practitioners study, digest and practise the insights and recommendations of psychologists. There is, however, a tendency among some local authorities to package different forms of non-maintained provision under one heading, so that a variety of styles, purposes and practices appear on social services department lists as 'playgroups'. In some authorities, playgroups are regarded as homogeneous when attendance for the sake of the child or the mother is recommended by social workers, doctors and health visitors. The global figures of provision quoted in the PPA book *Parents and Playgroups* give little indication of the standards and types of experience offered to children. Questions concerning the categorization, oversight, support and monitoring of non-maintained provision are particularly significant when it is remembered that it is not a small minority of children involved. The PPA 'facts and figures' for 1981 show that more than half a million children attended playgroups in England and Wales, compared to the 215 000 in nursery education in England (DES, 1981). It can be calculated that more than 50 per cent of children presently attending first or infant schools in England and Wales previously attended playgroups (Central Statistical Services, 1980). The issue therefore concerns the experience of early childhood provision of a high proportion of young children and their families, not to mention the significant number of older schoolchildren and other volunteers who help in playgroups for a variety of reasons.

## CONCLUSION

The 'pre-school' while mythically powerful is empirically non-existent. Children, however, do not learn in a vacuum; their learning experiences are rooted in particular social situations. The implications of the use of concepts such as pre-school are of concern not only to those who are engaged in providing for young children but also to educationalists in general. If, for example, it were the case that as far as children were concerned it really did not matter whether there was a curriculum, or what particular intentions, practices, relationships, organizations and attitudes were formed by the adults who catered for them, then there would be a major question to be faced by teachers, social scientists, policy-makers, parents and many others.

It is at least possible to hold the view that young children do respond to major differences between one setting and another, that they are involved in rule-making, the development of relationships, interpreting their surroundings and making sense of what happens to them. In other words, children are not separate from the patterns of social relations which make up the group, but participate in that pattern. They are not 'pre-schoolers', a word which is empty of reference to children as thinking individuals and members of families, communities and groups, and which defines them solely in terms of their present and future institutional statuses. As long as the study of young children and of provision for them is largely conducted through a screen of vague and misleading assumptions, the extent to which children, in common with other human beings, are active agents in their own socialization will remain a mystery.

## TOPICS FOR DISCUSSION

1. 'Underlying the concept ("pre-school") there is a stereotype of "the child" which does not reflect either the variety in children's needs or the active way in which children may participate in their social world.' Critically evaluate the author's arguments for making this statement.
2. Discuss the evidence which suggests that the great variety in pre-school provision has an important effect on styles of practice and on the ways in which practitioners regard the children in their care.
3. Discuss the various forms of pre-school provision mentioned by the author with respect to their differences in ethos and organization.

## SUGGESTIONS FOR FURTHER READING

1. Gipps, C. (1982) 'Nursery nurses and nursery teachers I: their assessment of children's verbal-social behaviour'. *Journal of Child Psychology and Psychiatry*, **23**, 3, 237–54.

   Gipps, C. (1982) 'Nursery nurses and nursery teachers II: their attitudes towards pre-school children and their parents'. *Journal of Child Psychology and Psychiatry*, **23**, 3, 255–65.
   The author's two studies formed part of the National Children's Bureau's evaluation of combined nursery centres (Ferri et al., 1981). Because of the very great differences between teachers and nursery nurses in terms of qualifications, training and role in the nursery, these two groups were asked to complete ratings of children's verbal-social behaviour in day nurseries, nursery schools and combined nursery centres. The ratings made by the various groups of staff were analysed separately in order to see whether they differed, while the validity of the ratings was assessed by comparing them with observations of the children's behaviour and their scores on two language tests (the English Picture Vocabulary Test (EPVT) (pre-school

version) and the Boehm Test of Basic Concepts). Combined nursery centres are a relatively new form of pre-school provision in which nursery education and day care are provided under one roof. They are usually staffed by a headteacher and matron assisted by teachers and nursery nurses. Gipps found that:

a. The two 'objective' measures used to validate the verbal-social ratings (the language tests and observations of children) did not support the higher verbal-social assessments which were assigned by nursery nurses in day nurseries. It appeared that the nursery nurses were rating directly observable verbal and social behaviour and that teachers were assessing a more complex reasoning skill. An alternative explanation might be, the author suggests, that the day nursery children, who had generally been in nurseries longer and had therefore had more exposure to pre-school provision, were, in fact, more socially mature.

b. There were considerable differences in ratings between the different professional groups working in the same type of pre-school provision, indicating a different underlying system of values and judgements.

In the second part of the study, Gipps examined nursery nurses' and nursery teachers' attitudes towards children and their parents, again finding clear differences between the professional groups. Day nursery nurses expressed more sympathetic attitudes towards both children and parents than did their colleagues in centres and schools, while teachers had more sympathetic attitudes than nursery nurses. Teachers' attitudes towards parents were not related to their attitudes towards children, while this was the case for nursery nurses. The difference between teachers and nursery nurses in their attitudes towards parents is discussed in relation to differences in educational levels, consequences and possible mediation strategies.

2. Clark, M.M. (1983) 'Early education: issues and evidence'. *Educational Review*, **35**, 2, 113–19.

Clark discusses recent developments in pre-school education, including possible implications of the non-mandatory nature of its provision. The author argues that a commitment made by the British Government in 1972 that by 1982 pre-school education would be available for all children whose parents wished to use it, has, because of the non-mandatory nature of such provision, been vulnerable to cuts in the education budgets as have been attempts at such expansion in the past. Starting school is the theme for the following section in which similarities and differences between pre- and first schools are explored. Clark raises a crucial issue in the current climate of opinion in early education by suggesting that it is perhaps important to consider the *balance* of activities which are termed 'work' and 'play' and to consider whether play as a learning strategy has a wider role in the reception class and beyond, likewise whether younger children are more capable of sustained 'work' and cognitively challenging activities than is sometimes appreciated – provided they see a purpose in the effort.

3. Lloyd, I. (1983) 'The aims of early childhood education'. *Educational Review*, **35**, 2, 121–26.

Of immediate relevance to Reading 2 is Lloyd's assertion that different aims of education arise largely from varying conceptions of value and that whatever those differences are, one's aims must be the same for *all stages* of education including early education. The author suggests that recent claims that the pre-compulsory years are critical for future learning seem well established and that educationists should be bold enough to conclude that there is at least a *prima facie* case for making all the years of early education compulsory.

## Reading 3
# RACISM AND THE UNDER-FIVES
## *J. Durrant*

# UNDER-FIVES
## *J. Kidner*

## INTRODUCTION

Over the past decade there has been increasing recognition of and interest in pre-school provision. The changing role and status of women, the increase in the numbers of single-parent families, and the economic, environmental and social pressures that impinge upon the quality of family life have all contributed to push the provision of services for small children and their families to the forefront of public debate.

Despite the relatively recent arrival of day care within social services departments as part of Seebohm reorganization, such provision has changed considerably in many parts of Britain. It had developed from being a service concentrating on children's health and hygiene to one that supposedly focuses on all aspects of a small child's development and acknowledges the family, community and environmental factors that influence care. Social services departments, particularly in the inner cities, are increasingly acknowledging the positive contribution that day-care provision can make. This is in supporting families in their parenting tasks, providing small children with an enriching and stimulating pre-school experience, and contributing as part of a wider social work strategy to preventive work with vulnerable families.

Such developments have potentially a considerable impact on Britain's ethnic minority communities, concentrated as they are in urban areas where day-care provision has expanded most significantly. Although there are

Durrant, J. (1986) 'Racism and the under-fives', in Coombe, V. and Little, A. (eds) (1986) *Race and Social Work: A Guide to Training.* London, Tavistock Publications, chap. 12, pp. 128–36.
Kidner, J. (1980) 'Under-fives'. *Multi-Ethnic Education Review*, 5, 2, 4–6, ILEA.

common needs for all people, black and white, black families suffer disproportionately from unemployment, under-employment, low wages and the
effects of poor housing (Commission for Racial Equality, 1978). All of these
factors have a major impact on a family's ability to maintain itself without
supportive day care. Black people also have particular needs that stem from
their minority position. These might relate more generally to language,
cultural and religious norms, or to the insidious and long-term effect of
racism. It is not surprising that disproportionately large numbers of black
children and their families require day-care provision. This is particularly
true within council day nurseries; and two neighbouring south London
boroughs recently estimated that between 50 and 80 per cent of the children
receiving day care in the statutory sector were black.

## IDENTITY NEEDS

Like all other aspects of social services provision, day care has been
developed almost exclusively by white policy-makers, and therefore inevitably from a white perspective. This viewpoint has defined notions of 'good'
child care, appropriate patterns and forms of family life, problematic
behaviour in young children, and acceptable forms of stimulation and play.
Such ideas continue to be reinforced by the major form of training acquired
by most day-care employees and through the practices currently operating in
most social services agencies. However, all this has largely ignored the
development of a child's cultural and racial identity and the impact of racism
on the provision of day-care services and those who receive them. We
cannot realistically stress the importance of the pre-school years on a child's
physical, intellectual and emotional development whilst ignoring the importance of those years on the development of racial attitudes in both black
and white children.

A common misconception is that small children do not have a racial or
cultural awareness, and that because most small black children have now
been born in Britain they do not have any particular needs in this area.
Research has shown that not only do small children as young as three and
four notice colour, but they ascribe certain values and status to it. David
Milner found that black children (particularly those of Afro-Caribbean
origin) significantly undervalued their own group and showed a strong
preference for their white peer group (Milner, 1975, 1983). Unlike the white
children, who always correctly identified themselves, the black children
often refused to acknowledge that they were black at all. For young children
to reject and be embarrassed by what they are has implications for future
self-esteem and mental health.

Racism and its powerful and debilitating effects are a major issue in our society, and those who work within and provide the pre-school service cannot isolate themselves from such a debate. A positive sense of identity is not something acquired at a prescribed age but subtly developed from birth. The role of childminders and pre-school workers is both to value the child as part of a wider family and community and to meet the individual and group needs of the children in their care. It is not possible to do this without acknowledging the skills and self-assurance that a black child needs to cope positively with being black in a white majority society, or without acknowledging the effects of racism that have shaped her or his parents' experience. The colour of a person's skin is significant, and for carers to pretend otherwise is both harmful and false. Children, however young, are not 'all the same'. The pre-school worker has a crucial role in helping the young child during his or her formative years to develop a positive self-identity, to feel proud of being black and having a rich cultural heritage, and to help equip the children with the skills and confidence they will need when facing racist comments and attitudes.

The process of a child feeling comfortable and positive about her or his colour is one that white people take for granted; no special efforts are considered necessary. For a black British child it is a much more difficult process. Black people are largely invisible within the mass media, magazines and books, cards, etc. – all of which tend to ignore the multiracial nature of British society. Where black people are portrayed this is frequently in marginalized or stereotyped ways (in sport, as musicians, or nurses, say), whilst their other talents, occupations and aspirations are ignored. The majority of people in positions of power and influence are white; heroes of childhood are presented as white; so small black children are denied the range of role models available to their white peers.

White children systematically learn to value their whiteness through the process of socialization and the structure of British society. Black children are denied this same opportunity; and the support that their parents, families and communities provide is frequently undermined. Britain's historical and colonial past, and present practices, ensure that positive attitudes towards black people will not occur by chance or good luck, but must be actively and consciously developed.

If a small child and her or his parent(s) see that the nursery or childminder actively values their colour, experiences, culture and lifestyle, that child is helped to start to value him/herself more. If the differences between people and races are understood, enjoyed and valued – with being black not seen as second best, problematic or irrelevant – children, as well as feeling good about themselves, will interact more positively with others.

Such an approach is also important for developing anti-racist views amongst white children. Small children inevitably absorb the values and prejudices of those around them. If white under-fives are presented with a purely ethnocentric service, there is a danger that they will see white values as the 'norm' and devalue and disregard alternative views and experiences. If we wish the next generation of young adults to challenge racism and develop strategies to eradicate it, we first have to acknowledge its existence openly, and then ensure that we do not compound past mistakes with a 'colour-blind' approach.

## ANTI-RACIST STRATEGY

Moving towards an anti-racist strategy cannot start from workers adopting a 'neutral' stance. Whilst the vast majority of nursery workers and carers would no doubt be abhorred at individual acts of aggression towards the black community, many collude with the more covert forms of institutional racism by inaction, apathy and fear. Day care will never be a truly effective service for small children and their families unless workers in the field move from a neutral position to one that actively challenges their own and other institutional practices. It is not sufficient purely to strive to understand more about black culture or to devise compensatory experiences to 'disadvantaged' groups without acknowledging that white racism perpetuates those disadvantages in the first place, and as such is an issue that white people have to acknowledge and tackle.

An anti-racist dimension needs to be integrated into all aspects of service delivery and not 'tagged on' in a tokenistic and piecemeal way. If adults in the pre-school field are genuine in their commitment to offer a high-quality service, it should be possible to walk into any unit and see an integrated multiracial perspective being put into practice.

## AFFIRMATIVE ACTION
### Teaching materials

Teaching materials that portray all cultures and peoples in a positive way should be provided. Care should be taken to avoid books portraying black people in stereotyped ways (e.g. doing only the manual jobs) or marginalizing them (e.g. one black child hidden in the background) or their experiences. As well as material showing both black and white children in everyday situations in Britain, other books and stories from the Caribbean, from Asia, from Africa, and elsewhere should also be used; and these will provide a welcome addition to the usual range of fairytales. Where children in a group are learning English as a second language, libraries can be asked to supply books in the appropriate mother tongue for children and parents to enjoy and share.

Pictures are also a useful source of discussion and presentation. They should not, however, portray simply a 'travel brochure' image of Africa, Asia and the Caribbean; nor, like those used by some charitable organizations, should they reinforce the stereotype of the 'impoverished Third World' without acknowledging the cultural richness and vitality of such countries. Pictures do not need to be bought. In the streets of any main town or city there are everyday scenes that can provide material for art work and collages. These include market-places, street life, children's playgrounds, and train journeys, all of which can be adapted to give an affirmative multiracial perspective. Collages made by children on particular themes, e.g. 'shades of black', 'shades of white', 'friends come in all different colours'; discussions and work on different hair textures; displays and collages of different fruits, vegetables and sweets; all such activities can be used to acknowledge and celebrate the differences as well as the similarities between children.

## Toys and games

Musical instruments, records and songs from a variety of countries, multiracial jigsaw puzzles, and dolls that look like real black people (not white-featured dolls 'blacked up') all provide children with activities that acknowledge and delight in the reality of a multiracial society. In nurseries, the dressing-up box should include saris, kimonos, shalwars, and other kinds of national dress – regardless of whether there are any children in the group whose families originally came from that culture. The 'home corner' also needs to reflect the fact that there is no standard 'home', and that some of the differences will be cultural ones.

The removal of golliwogs, Black Sambo books and any material that degrades, insults or patronizes black people is essential. That some black people might not object is not an argument for their retention. Full-time pre-school provision is so scarce that many parents may not wish to complain for fear of losing their place; whilst others might be unsure of their stance and will not want to question or criticize institutional practices. It is not for white people to seek to defend such material; they need to listen to what black people are telling them about their perception and experiences. Sufficient black people have been vocal enough in their abhorrence of such material for workers to act.

# Festivals

The major festivals of other religions and cultures should be celebrated. These provide useful topics and themes for discussion as well as visibly demonstrating that a multiracial society provides an enrichment for the nursery year. It is also important to ensure that a multiracial perspective is integrated into Christian festivals. No one race has a monopoly on Christianity, yet frequently Christmas is presented as an all-white affair with the token black king and/or angel, regardless of the make-up of the nursery group or surrounding community.

# Food

Children who receive full day care (whether in nurseries or childminders' homes) have a considerable number of their meals away from the family base. It is therefore important that careful consideration is given to the type and range of food provided. Meals should take account of not only religious needs but also cultural ones. This will relate not just to the food eaten, but also to the way in which it is consumed (fingers, spoon, fork, etc.).

Food has a greater significance than simply its nutritional value, especially for small children; and the ranges of food that children eat at home should be provided in the nursery. Traditional 'English fare' tends to be bland and, when provided in institutions, often rather tasteless, especially to people who are used to hot and more highly flavoured foods. Many children are labelled as 'poor eaters' when in fact they are simply not used to, and even dislike, much of the food they are given.

Although many nurseries and childminders are careful to ensure that children do not eat certain meats that for religious reasons are forbidden, few provide an appropriate alternative. Where *halal* meat is not served at all, many children are simply presented day after day with a lump of cheese or an egg, along with their mashed potato or rice and vegetables. As well as this being totally unappetizing and boring, the children are left with the feeling of being 'different' or inferior, and see their culture's dietary norms as stopping them enjoying the same foods as their peers. Cooks of West Indian, African, Asian and Chinese origin frequently have to learn to cook 'English' food. There is no reason why, with the appropriate guidance from the relevant staff, parents and community, the same cannot apply in reverse.

All children, regardless of country of origin, are citizens of this country. They therefore must have and be seen to have the right to eat and enjoy familiar, properly cooked food, without those foods being labelled 'funny', 'a nuisance', 'too expensive' or an irrelevance. If we cannot cater for even the more basic needs of our young, our claims to be a 'caring profession' must be suspect.

## Clothes, skin and hair

Another basic need often overlooked is physical care. Good grooming is an essential part of demonstrating care and affection for many families, and this should be recognized and supported by pre-school carers. Too many adults are quick to be critical of parents for putting children into what staff might see as 'inappropriate clothes for play', without positively acknowledging the love and attention that have gone into ensuring that the child is well presented.

In the same way that the skin of white children needs special attention (before exposure to the sun), black children's skin can become dry and patchy if not properly creamed. This should be done by carers after sand and water play activities, and after exposure to the sun to maintain the skin in peak condition. Hair care needs similar attention. Every effort should be taken – by providing hats and supervising the activity – to ensure that, as far as possible, children are not sent home with sand in their hair. When such accidents occur it is important for workers not to be dismissive of parental complaints, as this devalues the time and effort it takes to remove sand, particularly from Afro hair, and restore it to its original oiled, braided and well-groomed condition.

## POLICY ISSUES

Any of the initiatives outlined above will be irrelevant unless staff, carers and policy-makers are prepared to examine their own attitudes and change their behaviour accordingly. If the basic structure of the services and the values on which they are based remain unaltered, little that is worth while will have been achieved.

Much modern-day care prides itself on its increasing ability to respond to the family as well as the child; all too frequently, however, it is the parents who are expected to adapt to an unknown set of values and assumptions. There is no universal agreement on the virtues of free play versus more structured learning; on appropriate ages to wean and toilet-train; on standards and styles of family life and of discipline. Nevertheless, such issues are frequently presented as though there were consensus, with the task of the worker or minder being to 'persuade' or teach parents the 'right' way to care. This approach totally disregards variations of class and, more profoundly, of culture. Many referrals for council day care are made in this light, with reports talking of 'understimulated children', 'parents who do not provide appropriate toys', and children who are supposedly linguistically delayed and deprived even when fluent in their mother tongue. This creates not only undue stress for a small child having to contend with two widely differing sets of expectations and adult behaviour, but also an environment that clearly does not welcome and accept parents on their own terms.

It is always easier to justify the need for change and the development of anti-racist strategies in other individuals, other establishments and other agencies, and much more painful and difficult to identify that same need within ourselves and our place of work. Even where a local authority has a clearly defined 'equal opportunities policy', there is still an urgent need for establishments and individuals clearly to think through such a policy's meaning for their own unit and job role if it is to have any relevance for practice.

Day care is a labour-intensive activity, and therefore its most expensive and potentially valuable resource is its staff group. An anti-racist approach inevitably has implications for staffing and also for training. When staff are selected, their ability not just to work with children but to work with, understand and develop the identity and respect of black children and parents is crucial and should be demonstrated before appointment. Staff should be selected who have a genuine desire and commitment to work within a multiracial society and fully understand its implications for practice. Managers also need to be clear about how they wish the service to develop, and about the skills, knowledge and attitudes that staff will need in order to realize this.

## Training

The identification of appropriate staff and such a strategy cannot possibly develop without the active involvement of black people as staff, managers, parents and community representatives. Their presence does not diminish the responsibility of other staff to challenge racism, nor does their employment mean that a non-discriminating service has been achieved. Their presence does, however, provide positive role models for both children and parents, and ensures that a more genuine dialogue can take place about service development with people who have personal experience of racism rather than a purely intellectual concern with it.

Black pre-school workers, like all black people, have a unique contribution to make. It might seem obvious to state that black people bring into the work the experience of contending daily with the powerful and painful effects of racism; but to have survived and stayed 'whole' gives black workers a strength, understanding, experience and humanity that white colleagues, however sensitive, can never fully share. The experiences and skills they bring must be seen as equally valid to those acquired by most white staff through the traditional forms of training.

This is particularly pertinent to day-care practice, which depends so heavily on one form of training (the NNEB) geared to an age group of students (16 to 18 years) who, regardless of their future potential, can hardly be expected to deal with the complexities that day care raises. Despite some individual initiatives by particular colleges, the national syllabus remains rooted in outdated assumptions and ethnocentric norms – for example, regarding the role of women, 'appropriate' child-rearing practices and the 'problems' of ethnic minorities. These traditional prejudices appear to compound for too many staff rigid, conservative and insensitive attitudes, particularly towards parents. As the majority of NNEB trainees go into private nannying, it is impossible to argue that a course serving the needs of this group will also equip young people with the range of skills required for day care in multiracial inner-city areas. A training course does not qualify staff to work with children if it systematically ignores or marginalizes the reality of Britain as a multiracial society; there therefore appears to be no justification for such a course being a prerequisite to social services day-care practice.

As many authorities still refuse to recruit people without an NNEB certificate, local people with roots and commitment are frequently excluded from employment, despite the fact that their experiences might be more relevant to the changing nature of day-care practice. NNEB qualifiers should not be discriminated *against*, but they should have to compete with others to demonstrate a full range of skills, as defined by black practitioners as well as white.

It will be difficult for many staff to challenge established practices and their own behaviour and responses towards ethnic minority parents and children. So all staff need continued opportunities to learn, evaluate and question their own and others' actions, and to develop appropriate support systems to effect change.

## CONCLUSION

Because they are in their formative years, the children who receive care in homes and nurseries are highly vulnerable. Therefore those who develop and implement policy have a responsibility to ensure that a child's racial and cultural needs are given the same degree of attention as her or his physical, intellectual and emotional needs. This cannot be done by denying either the existence of racism or the experiences of black people, who daily contend with its effects.

An anti-racist strategy is an ongoing process. It has constantly to be reviewed and challenged by all who profess to care about the well-being of small children and their families. Such a strategy needs to be integrated into all aspects of provision, play, staffing, admissions, discipline and assessments. If we fail to do so we fail all of our children and continue to contribute to the pain that racism causes. For black people in the pre-school world, the debate has gone on for long enough: now is the time for action.

## SUGGESTIONS AND EXERCISES

Some day-care staff still persist in the view that it is 'prejudiced' to notice differences in colour, and argue that they do not know how many ethnic minority children they have in their care. It is essential that staff know and recognize the origins of their children. To help them to overcome this difficulty it is useful to get course participants to complete the following project prior to coming to the session.

### Project work

1. Find out the origins of the children in your nursery; they will probably all have been born in Britain.
2. Can you identify areas of conflict in child rearing between home and day care for ethnic minority children? How are these resolved?
3. Do ethnic minority children present you with difficulties?
4. How does your centre cope with any dietary differences amongst ethnic minority children?
5. What are the forms of discipline in operation where you work?
6. Do they conflict with those exercised by parents?
7. In what ways are ethnic minority parents involved in the activities of the centre?
8. Does your establishment have any particular role for its ethnic minority staff?
9. Do you use multiracial materials in your centre, e.g. pictures, books, music, toys?
10. What major festivals are celebrated in your centre?

For this session members should have the answers to their project with them on paper. These are the *objectives*:

1. To identify areas of concern for workers with under-fives of minority groups.

2. To outline the identity needs of under-fives in day-care settings.
3. To show how their physical needs can be catered for in a centre.
4. To consider the language needs of ethnic minority under-fives.
5. To discuss ways in which parents can be involved in day care.
6. To examine family and child-rearing practices in different communities.
7. To discuss how an anti-racist strategy may be devised in day care.
8. To make suggestions for developing anti-racist views amongst children in day care.

To achieve the objectives, trainers should spend about 15 minutes outlining some of the salient points made by Durrant in the foregoing chapter. If you have used the video *Colourblind?* in a previous session, mention some of the points made there about under-fives. Members should then be divided into small groups of about six or eight to discuss the following statements:

(a) 'Young children do not notice people's colour.'
(b) 'The ethos of a day-care centre is determined by management. The role of staff is to implement the policies of the agency.'
(c) 'It is unrealistic to expect staff to cater for all the ethnic groups in their centres adequately.'

Each group should discuss a different issue bearing these points in mind:

- Do participants agree with the statement?
- What reasons do they have for supporting the view?
- On what basis do they disagree with the view quoted?

Each group should spend about 45 minutes in discussion and then come together for a reporting-back session (about 30 minutes). After this it might be sensible to have a short break.

On resumption each participant should then be given 10 minutes to present a project report. Participants should be prepared to answer questions from colleagues; and the tutor should be able, at the end of presentations, to summarize findings. The tutor may also wish to collect and collate the material to produce a picture of practice in an area: Is it uniform? Is it good? Where are the gaps? This picture could be used to influence policy.

The *key points* to remember are:

1. Some minority communities have a high percentage of women at work and children needing day-care provision.
2. Physical care of black children is often different from that of white children.
3. Attention needs to be paid to the language needs of ethnic minority children.
4. Different child-rearing patterns in minority communities need to be recognized and care taken to avoid conflict between home and day-care setting.

5. Day centres should reflect the multiracial nature of society, not simply with play materials but also by having ethnic minority staff.
6. The involvement of parents in day care is difficult to achieve but is very important where the ethos of the nursery or home is different from that of the child's home background.
7. Workers have to move away from a 'neutral' stance and towards an anti-racist strategy.

*Timing:* 3 hours should be allocated.

## UNDER-FIVES

Multiculturalism and anti-racism, as educational processes, are often contrasted and descriptions proposed of the relationship between the two. It may be that the two in practice are recognized by superficial features, features that do not probe into teachers' aims. Sarees and samosas may be tokenistic – on the other hand, they may be genuinely aimed at white parents to convey a message about the nursery, or at minority group parents to suggest ways in which their knowledge and expertise can be brought into the nursery setting.

I wish to explore in this article what is good anti-racist practice in a nursery. I would like to emphasize from the outset that anti-racist practice may not *look* anti-racist, it may look multicultural, or it may look neutral. There are strategies that may be used by many teachers who do not realize the anti-racist significance of that aspect of their practice.

## LOOKING FOR RACISM IN THE NURSERY

The first issue to raise here is whether adults are prepared to look at their own situation with some degree of objectivity. A preliminary and most important study should look at whether the nursery roll reflects the composition of the local under-fives community (including the allocation of morning and afternoon places, the full-time places . . . ). If it does not, then urgent changes will be needed. We also need to look objectively at practices within the nursery. If we want to provide an education for equality we must be prepared to criticize our own and each other's behaviour and reactions to children and parents and to events and ideas. Many classroom researchers have found that only relatively objective observations have revealed the full extent of discrimination (for example, Dale Spender found that she spent more time on boys than on girls *even* when she thought she was doing the opposite!).

One of the most important issues for adults to look at is the degree to which different groups of children have access to different curricular content. For example, do bilingual children get grouped with the younger children for a story that's simpler in content and form? If that is the case then they will be missing out on a cognitive need for a more complex story. Are bilingual children given very simple matching games (for instance, colour matching or matching simple objects) which are cognitively very easy for them just because the English vocabulary of the game (red/blue/green or house/sun/dog) is deemed necessary? Similarly, Afro-Caribbean boys may be left to play outside for long periods because it is thought that they have energy to work off, or that they 'can't settle' to a craft activity. Situations more subtle than these may go unnoticed unless the staff have made a commitment to monitoring themselves systematically. All too often adults undertake long and complex 'assessments' of individual children and fail to 'assess' themselves and their effect on whole groups.

In order to move away from the sorts of restrictions mentioned, it is important for nursery staff to establish communication with parents and invite parents to comment on how the nursery is run, and how this affects *their* child(ren) (for example, through the curriculum, organization, mealtimes, toilet facilities . . . ). The children must be able to bring their own language and knowledge into the nursery. This means that nursery staff need to respond positively to children and parents in ways that show clearly that their language and culture are welcome.

The children, parents, workers and visitors to a nursery may not have understood what an anti-racist policy involves in terms of their behaviour, so workers must talk together about how racist incidents are to be handled. Adults sometimes hide their racist views by implying that they treat all children equally. But nursery children are very young and are sensitive to an adult's real feelings and probably very vulnerable. Such adults may need to be confronted with situations where their views are made explicit and then tackled. This may lead to conflict in the short term but may well be better in the long term. Workers in an all-white nursery will have to think particularly carefully about how their children's views of black people are being formed, and ensure that the children have opportunities to explore their ideas and opinions.

## NEW POSSIBILITIES
## THROUGH THE CURRICULUM

Nursery workers are necessarily involved in responding to children's immediate demands, requests and explorations and must prepare themselves to tackle issues of inequality in this way. However, we also have to plan and organize our materials and activities in advance. The nursery curriculum has to change in ways that encourage all children to explore new behaviours and develop better understandings of cultural and linguistic diversity. All children need to know that things like khurta-pyjama, chop sticks and cane row are day-to-day, not special, strange or exotic objects – and that bilingualism is natural. This will not in itself end racism, of course, but it will open up possibilities for all the children that otherwise might not have existed.

Name cards, books, notices and letters should be available in different languages and scripts as a matter of course. Even very young children will learn to recognize the scripts that have significance for them, and the expectation of biliterate development will have been established.

Nurseries can use many different starting points for themes which extend children's understanding of different lifestyles. Any such multicultural theme must be introduced in a way that acknowledges and confronts racist attitudes, that avoids stereotypes, that involves parents, and that ensures that all children are benefiting. Insights from any particular activity, event or theme must be reworked into the day-to-day running of the centre. If, for example, children's experiences of different tastes in food have been extended through a class theme on cooking then every effort should be made to extend the range and availability of items on the nursery lunch menu.

The options open to children can also be extended through the provision of books and stories which break away from conventional role models. For instance, *Wagon wheels* shows a black family travelling West, being helped by indigenous Americans, an eleven-year-old boy caring for a three-year-old brother, and so on. This true story has the power to engage children and the power to open their eyes to the sorts of stereotypes that are all too prevalent even at this age.

Stories can be used to encourage non-stereotyped play in the home corner, out of doors or with Lego, and so on. The story can be told using the equipment – for example, the baby doll, the bikes or the Lego car. The children can be involved in acting out the events with the adult in this 'story-telling' situation and will then take on the ideas in their free play. When this type of activity becomes a regular feature of the nursery curriculum it will be picked up and reflected in the children's response. Similarly, if the children's home play area always includes a wide range of cooking utensils and dressing-up clothes they will find ways of building these items into their play. In interaction with each other, and with adults, the children will come to an increased understanding of different styles of cooking and dressing.

Craft activities can be developed using a variety of media. Textiles produced and decorated in various ways from many parts of the world can be explored and examined carefully: Peruvian weaving and knitting, mirror-work from India and the Middle East, cottons batiked, tie-dyed or printed. Wherever possible experts should be brought in to explain and demonstrate their skills to the children. The children can then use a range of materials, velvets and cottons, threads and sequins, tiny mirrors, wools, dyes and printing inks. It is important for children and adults to appreciate the *approach* to the craft as well as the end product. Children could then, for example, be encouraged to attempt a simple task with great care rather than to try an immature version of the finished item. Music and songs from different cultures can be used in a similar way – exposing children to a wide variety of styles and then encouraging the children to respond, singing along with a tape, dancing or clapping, or creating their own tunes, rhythms or sounds.

## HOW MUCH CAN THE UNDER-FIVES UNDERSTAND ABOUT RACISM?

These activities are readily recognizable as multicultural, and adults who have consciously adopted an anti-racist stance will, through such activities, events and themes, be firmly supporting and validating the experiences of minority group children and parents. The degree to which this has really been achieved will be best measured by the parents. They will have received the nursery workers' true message whether it be pure multicultural tokenism or a genuine attempt to unpick the ethnocentric curriculum.

Now, if the staff of a nursery have closely examined their own immediate responses to the children and have planned for an extended multicultural curriculum, they still need to consider a third level of anti-racist practice. This is to examine for themselves the real nature of racism on a worldwide scale, and then to apply to the nursery situation insights from their own strategies for understanding racism. Our three-year-olds today must eventually come to understand the full extent of racism. We need to examine what are the basic concepts that three-year-olds can develop which will help them at a later stage to build a clear picture of how racism operates.

Take a simple example. One aim of an anti-racist teacher will be that children should develop a critical approach to books and their contents. To a young child a book is no more 'right' or 'wrong' than, say, a tree. Both are objects in the child's life. It is only as children come to an understanding that a book is made by people, and that people have opinions and that those opinions can be right or wrong, that they will realize that they have a right to criticize, to disagree with the author, to question the truth as presented in the book.

So, for the nursery worker, the appropriate activity will be to find ways of helping children to establish the concepts of authorship and book production. This may involve writing to the children's dictation, typing up and photocopying their stories, finding books which include photos of the authors and biographical details, inviting authors to visit the nursery, writing books for the children featuring events and people they know . . . These activities may not *look* anti-racist but they would be important strategies in a longer-term anti-racist campaign (and of course infant and junior teachers should build on these important beginnings).

A similar long-term aim will be for children to adopt a critical approach to visual media (television, posters, and so on). A first step would be to examine photographs and drawings closely. Who took the picture and why? Why was this subject chosen? What's included and what's missing? What is the overall impact? At the nursery stage children can be involved in such critical activities using very familiar pictures and scenes. If there are two angles on the same person or event how do they compare? Why has an illustrator used this colour or technique? The content may not be 'racial', but the process will be part of an anti-racist strategy.

Children will need to perceive at a later stage the way in which land and labour are exploited at a multinational level. Concepts such as the division of labour, the use of capital, and international communications will need to be explored. In the nursery we must lay the foundation for such an understanding, so nursery workers must face the challenge and create appropriate activities. This might mean following the school-keeper or secretary for a morning to see how their jobs are crucial to the smooth running of the establishment. Then find out who does what in each child's home and what would happen if one person went on strike. Are all the participants benefiting equally from their role in the equation? What about international communications? Which children have been on an aeroplane and where to? Can you arrange to send or receive letters from Nigeria or Bangladesh or . . . ?

Following the secretary certainly won't look multicultural or anti-racist, but it will be helping children to understand how crucial jobs are often given lower pay and status. The implications will need to be explored over a long time-scale but the sooner a start is made, the better.

Many aspects of racism are extremely complex and a mathematical interpretation of events is crucial, yet many children are put off maths in school and are never made aware of its power and importance in relation to the social rather than just to the physical environment. Children in nurseries play with plastic shapes and explore weight, length and time. They are encouraged to sort objects by attributes like colour, shape and size, but are rarely encouraged to sort events and ideas. Nursery workers can help children to realize the power of mathematical thinking by looking for real situations where sorting is required or where ordering or comparing are essential. Organizing the nursery spaces (for instance, the home corner or book corner) can become a mathematical activity for a group of children rather than a late-night chore for an adult. Photographs can help children to compare events over time – for example, who has what for dinner on successive days or do the vegetarian children get sufficient variety in their menu?

Nursery workers have a challenge to meet. The challenge is threefold and all three facets must be tackled. It's all too easy to opt for something that looks good or for something that responds to blatant bad behaviour. Our children deserve something more. They deserve adults who are prepared to look objectively at their own practice to see how it affects different groups of children. They deserve a curriculum that values a range of cultures, languages and lifestyles and is supportive of their own, *and* they need to be exploring concepts and ideas which will eventually be consolidated into an understanding of racism and other forms of oppression.

## TOPICS FOR DISCUSSION

1. 'Like all other aspects of social services provision, day care has been developed almost exclusively by white policy-makers, and therefore inevitably from a white perspective.' Discuss the implications of this statement for teachers of young children in multi-ethnic communities.
2. 'An anti-racist dimension needs to be integrated into all aspects of service delivery and not "tagged on" in a tokenistic and piecemeal way.' Discuss.
3. What factors are crucial to the establishment of effective anti-racist practices in the education of young children?

## SUGGESTIONS FOR FURTHER READING

1. Browne, N. and France, P. (eds) (1986) 'Unclouded minds saw unclouded visions: visual images in the nursery', in *Untying the Apron Strings: Anti-sexist Provision for the Under-fives*. Milton Keynes, Open University Press, chap. 8, pp. 120–42.

This important chapter begins with the authors' assertion that 'we have become increasingly aware of just how much (young children) notice differences between people and how perceptive they are about the way people are depicted' (p. 121). Yet it is commonplace to hear those working with the under-fives claim that the very young child cannot be sexist, racist or otherwise discriminatory. The authors review and evaluate recently published nursery resources and suggest strategies for producing more positive material and for talking about 'the images on offer in the nursery' (p. 122). They argue that it is of paramount importance to provide resources that accurately and sensitively reflect the diversity in children's lives and proceed to a more detailed description of the review of resources they themselves undertook. Finally, they offer strategies for extending, adapting or replacing visual material to ensure the provision of more positive images. The chapter provides a succinct rebuttal of the widely held view that all children are treated equally – with the implicit assumption that nothing needs to be changed since all children are receiving an 'equal education'. In brief, the authors pose the question, 'Is the (assumed) equal treatment approach not merely a cover-up for a reluctance to counter the over-generalized differences prevalent in sex and race stereotyping and for a similar reluctance to adopt an anti-sexist, anti-racist approach, which is considered to be too political?' (p. 124).

2. Houlton, D. (1986) 'Teachers and diversity', in *Cultural Diversity in the Primary School*. London, Batsford, chap. 3, pp. 50–77.

Houlton reviews a number of studies which suggest that teachers are inclined to form expectations of children on the basis of ethnic and social stereotypes, and he summarizes some of the evidence which demonstrates how teachers' expectations are likely to influence their classroom behaviour and, as a result, affect children's attitudes and performance in school (the self-fulfilling prophecy). The author refers to a number of recent investigations which suggest that in multicultural schools, despite a growing awareness of the need for a diversity-based approach to learning, assimilationist beliefs continue to exist among teachers. He argues, again from research studies, that the prevailing atmosphere in all-white schools is one of indifference, even hostility, towards the idea of a multicultural curriculum for their pupils, and offers a framework which suggests the main areas of knowledge and interpersonal and professional skills that teachers need to be developing.

3. Cohen, L. and Cohen, A. (eds) (1986) *Multicultural Education: A Sourcebook for Teachers*. London, Harper & Row.

The sourcebook provides an up-to-date set of readings and suggestions for further reading that are representative of the range of issues and emphases in current debates about multicultural education. *Multicultural education* is not a unitary concept; it subsumes a variety of beliefs, policies and practices in educational provision in multiracial Britain. The selected readings in the sourcebook reflect something of the present diversity in ideology and practice in multicultural education and examine changing perspectives that underpin thinking and practice in educational provision at both governmental and local level over the past 20 or so years. The debate on multicultural education has shifted considerably during the past few years and is now beginning to reflect greater concern for the role that education can play in countering the pernicious effects of racism both within schools and in society at large. Of particular relevance to Reading 3 is the chapter by L. Cohen and L. Manion, 'Under-achievement: some differing perspectives' (pp. 242–61).

Reading 4

# A FIRST-CLASS ENVIRONMENT? WORKING-CLASS PLAYGROUPS AS PRE-SCHOOL EXPERIENCE

## J. Finch

## PLAYGROUPS AND THE WORKING CLASSES

The voluntary playgroup movement has been the major growth area in the pre-school scene since the mid-1960s.[1] Although in one sense playgroups provide a form of day care (albeit very limited), there are several reasons why they should also be seen in the context of pre-school education. They developed initially as a middle-class response to the lack of nursery school places, for which they were designed as self-help substitutes. Further, Lady Plowden has subsequently questioned the wisdom of the Plowden Report's recommendation that nursery education should be expanded, arguing that she sees voluntary playgroups as the preferred alternative.[2]

How far can voluntary playgroups be seen as providing a form of pre-school education comparable with, even superior to, nursery schools? This question becomes particularly pertinent in the light of the expansion of playgroups beyond the middle-class areas where they originated. This article will offer an evaluation of the voluntary playgroup as pre-school experience, drawing upon material from a small study of playgroups in predominantly working-class areas, run on a voluntary basis by local women.

Pre-school education for the working classes has usually made its appearance in the literature of education and of social policy as part of various compensatory strategies. Pre-school intervention was central to the Plowden strategy and to several of the EPA (Educational Priority Area) projects. The compensatory rationale, which emphasizes the need to begin early to counteract alleged defects in the child's home, has remained strong in the literature on pre-schools, despite well-known moral objections to the implied devaluing of working-class culture, not to mention the ambiguous evidence about whether intervention at the pre-school stage actually 'works' as a long-term strategy. Meanwhile, the active encouragement of voluntary playgroups became a part of central government policy from 1968 onwards,

Finch, J. (1984) 'A first-class environment? Working-class playgroups as pre-school experience'. *British Educational Research Journal*, **10**, 1, 3–17.

in the wake of the effective withdrawal of funding from the nursery education (indeed the whole pre-school) sector, despite the commitment to meet the Plowden targets for nursery school places (contained in the 1972 education White Paper).[3] A major consideration quite clearly was cost. Speaking in 1976 about pre-school services, David Owen (in his capacity as a DHSS minister) said, 'The theme is low cost. We did not meet to discuss the desirable; we want to grapple with the attainable' (DHSS/DES, 1976, p. 1).

Playgroups provide a very convenient answer in the quest for 'low-cost solutions', to which successive governments have been commited. Not surprisingly, they now form a major part of pre-school provision.[4] Working-class as well as middle-class children are unlikely to have access to alternative forms of provision, unless their families seem so disorderly or unsatisfactory as to attract the attention of the social services department, or other welfare agency.

Despite the PPA's claim that playgroups have now moved well beyond their middle-class origins, very little is known about playgroups run on the self-help principle by working-class women, with catchment areas such as inner cities or council estates. Most of the literature on playgroups in such areas concerns 'provided' groups, sponsored and funded by organizations such as Save the Children Fund, NSPCC or the local social services department. Although these often attempt to incorporate mothers on a voluntary basis, they are far removed from the principle of self-help, being much more like a variation on the compensatory theme. This indeed is not surprising, as provided playgroups have been seen as an appropriate part of such strategies, at least since Sir Keith Joseph made his famous 'cycle of deprivation' speech to an annual conference of the PPA (Pre-School Playgroups Association, 1972).

If pre-school provision for working-class children is seen as a form of compensatory education, there is a rather obvious tension between that rationale and the principle of self-help. The tension is particularly acute if one envisages self-help provision by those sectors of the working classes who would be considered most 'disadvantaged'. To express this crudely, if you want pre-school experience to counteract a child's home, you can hardly let mothers do it themselves; conversely, if you do foster self-help among the working classes, you may get a form of pre-school provision which reinforces rather than counteracts the 'undesirable' home setting. This raises some very important questions about current pre-school policies, to which I return at the end of this article.

## WORKING-CLASS PLAYGROUPS
## AND MOTHERS' ASPIRATIONS

Whatever the intentions of policy-makers, what do working-class mothers themselves want from a playgroup? I shall attempt to answer this question in relation to the mothers interviewed in connection with my study of playgroups. This study was small scale and longitudinal, and was carried out between 1978 and 1981.[5] Five playgroups, in various parts of one northern county, were identified at the beginning of this period, with a view to undertaking regular observational visits for two years, followed by interviews with the groups' leaders and some mothers who used them. Four of the five were as close as possible to 'genuine' working-class self-help groups, and a fifth group was added as a middle-class comparison. The criteria used to identify the 'working-class' groups were: catchment areas consisting of inner urban areas or council estates; groups run by local women; all or most of the group leaders to be women with minimal educational background and training.[6]

In the event one of the groups, Seafield, never really got started, and two other working-class groups closed before the end of the study: Greenall closed about six months after the observational visits began, and Skyways closed towards the end of the observational period. Interviews were conducted in Skyways and in the two groups which remained open: Manchester Avenue and Bankside, the comparison group.[7] Most of the detailed data in this article are taken from Skyways and Manchester Avenue, the two working-class groups which I was able to observe over an extended period.

In interviews with mothers who used the working-class groups, it became clear that what they wanted from a playgroup was that their child should receive some preparation for school.

Although most of the mothers interviewed would not have been able to evaluate directly what the playgroups were providing (since mostly they were not present during sessions), in general terms almost all said that the playgroup experience should prepare their child for school, not in the sense of beginning formal teaching, but rather by familiarizing the child with the institutional atmosphere, with school routines and with relating to other children and adults in those settings. Points emphasized were: learning to be with people other than the child's mother; learning to sit, concentrate, listen and take orders; learning to share. Fairly characteristic comments were,

> I think it's . . . before they go to school it's a help if they're taught part of the time to sit down and do something, make something. It's not such a shock when they get to school. (Skyways, 1.3)

To be with people more. Not to be learning anything, but just to learn to share. 'Cos he does get rather selfish . . . I want them to learn him to be that way inclined 'cos I can't. I try you know, but I can't. (Skyways, 1.14)

It prepares them for school you know. Like my little boy, he'd been going only a couple of months before he went to school and he was terrified when he went to school. But little girl, she'd been going a long while before she went to school. She weren't bothered you know. (Manchester Avenue, 1.5)

Thus, despite the stereotypical middle-class interest in education, the evidence of my study bears out Tizard's (1975) observation that 'working class women are just as likely as middle-class ones to want education as well as day-care services for their children' (p. 216). The working-class women in my study were very clear that they wanted to locate playgroup experience firmly in the context of formal schooling. They seem well aware of how crucial is schooling to their children's future. Their use of playgroups could be seen as an attempt to play the middle-class game, and to give them a good start in the education system through which they most likely had in fact been designated failures. Most of the women in the working-class groups, both leaders and mothers, had left school at the earliest opportunity: only 3 out of 16 at Skyways and 4 out of 18 at Manchester Avenue had undergone any form of full-time education after school, mostly NNEB or SEN training.[8] A common theme was that they wanted their children to gain more from education than they had themselves. This is illustrated by the following extracts, including one from a woman who had left school without learning to read or write.

I'd like them to learn at school which I weren't interested in doing, you know. I know that myself. (Manchester Avenue, 1.3)

To be quite truthful I'm not educated enough. I'm rather a bit of an illiterate with reading and writing . . . My eldest girl, she's rather clever and I'm rather proud of her. Like when I was her age, I was never at school. I was always sneaking off and she knows this. 'Cos she's been off school for two weeks with tonsillitis and I couldn't write a letter for her to go back to school with. (Skyways, 1.14)

Typically they blamed themselves rather than the educational system for their own failure, and displayed a strong faith in the ability of schools to develop their children's talents.

So the women who ran and used these groups characteristically had been educational 'failures' themselves. Their experience of employment was mostly of unskilled or semi-skilled manual work, as was their husband's. The areas in which most lived consisted of poor-quality housing. Although the more general term 'working-class' is used in this article to describe the playgroups, many of their clientele might well be more accurately called the urban poor – certainly they were mostly drawn from that section of the working class who have often formed the target for compensatory pre-school provision.

Their own desire for a playgroup to prepare their children for school provides an additional reason for evaluating playgroups as pre-school education. Despite the fact that the PPA has now specifically rejected the 'substitute nursery school' rationale (Pre-School Playgroups Association, 1980), these mothers wanted a playgroup to be precisely that. How far are groups run in these areas, on a self-help basis, likely to be able to meet such aspirations?

## DOES THE WORKING-CLASS PLAYGROUP HAVE A DISTINCTIVE CHARACTER?

Although it is obvious that playgroups vary considerably in character, in organization and in the experiences they provide, within the playgroup movement, there is a clear sense of what a good playgroup 'ought' to be like. This is well expressed in the following statement, taken from Crowe's (1973) book on playgroups, and produced in poster form, to be used for display purposes, inside the PPA's monthly magazine in November 1981. It carried the title, *E is for Excellence.*

> A good playgroup provides a first class environment where, in a happy, busy atmosphere, children are painting, experimenting with wet and dry sand, water, clay, dough, bricks, wood-work, climbing apparatus and a wide variety of table toys; playing imaginatively in the home corner (or on improvised ships and buses); listening to stories, looking at books, enjoying music, chatting with interested adults about anything and everything. There will be ample opportunity for the children to respond to beauty in many forms.
>
> They will be stimulated to curiosity, wonder, reflection, discovery and thought. There will be the security that comes from community rules, kept out of consideration for others. In this security the children will know freedom-with-responsibility. In such an atmosphere the children can feel fearless, confident and happy and grow towards their full stature. (*Contact*, November 1981, p. 26)

Of course many playgroups diverge from this ideal, but some groups described by other authors are quite recognizable reflections of it. Not surprisingly, in my study, Bankside, the middle-class group, was closest to this model; although it did not fit perfectly, being rather more adult directed than the model would imply, as are many other playgroups in middle-class areas.

Crowe's statement, recently endorsed by the PPA as an account of an excellent playgroup, providing a 'first-class environment', will be used as the model with which to compare the working-class groups in my study; not to imply that they are 'worse' or 'better', but in order to specify their distinctive character. Even to contemplate applying such a description to a working-class group makes it immediately apparent that many features of the 'excellent' playgroup seem peculiarly characteristic of middle-class culture. The 'busy atmosphere', the 'chatting with interested adults', the 'security of community rules' and the 'freedom-with-responsibility' do not immediately conjure up images of childhood experience in the inner city or the run-down council estate. In practice, the working-class groups in my study diverged considerably from the PPA model, but in somewhat different directions. That was clearest in the two groups which I was able to follow through for the full period.

Of the two, Manchester Avenue, the group which remained open, more closely resembled the ideal model. The leaders set out the large church hall in which they met with a range of activities from which the children could choose, including both large and small items. As I recorded on one visit,

> The hall was set out with a variety of activities and the children moved between them in 'free play' style. Large equipment (e.g. climbing frame, tyres, two rocking horses) was in the middle of the hall and the quieter activities around the edges (e.g. Wendy house, sand, shop). The children did appear to play at one activity for a while and then move to the next. (Manchester Avenue, Fieldnotes, 13.3.79)

After a few visits I realized that most activities provided were the same on each occasion. However, each session entailed a 'special' activity and this provided the major focus for the morning. It seemed always to involve making those kind of objects which one comes to recognize as the characteristic playgroup product: variations on the theme of coloured paper, glue and toilet roll holders. I observed that all children were sent to this special activity at some stage during the morning, whether they chose it or not, and that the playgroup leaders concentrated their own efforts upon it. This activity was often the only obvious location of adult–child interaction during the session, commanded the complete attention of at least one leader, and almost always had entailed considerable preparation the previous evening.

So at Manchester Avenue, there was something of a tension between the ideology of 'free play' (which they espoused to a degree), and of 'production'; that is, the demonstration of what each child had achieved during the morning by ensuring that all had some object to take home. I noted some ambivalence on these issues when I attended a committee meeting quite early in the research. Mrs Gordon, the playgroup's non-participating chairman (*sic*), led the following discussion:

> While playgroup activities were being discussed, Mrs Gordon set up a discussion, rather obviously for my benefit, by asking, 'You still let them do mostly the free-range type of play do you?', to which they answered yes, although it was quite difficult to get the children to go out into the kitchen to do baking when there were other activities going on. I felt that they have taken the free play ideology on board, but not completely. There was a lot of interest in the 'work' that the children had produced (e.g. clowns made from paper plates) and a desire to 'display' it at the Christmas fair. In particular, Mrs McIver produced a collage of Jack and Jill, which looked as if it had never had a child anywhere near it; the pieces of material were stuck on very evenly inside neatly drawn lines. This sort of thing was obviously very much approved of. (Manchester Avenue, Fieldnotes, 2.10.81)

So Manchester Avenue diverges from the PPA model in two important respects: the degree of freedom of choice and of expression offered to the children, and the incidence of one-to-one interaction between children and adults. Both are restricted at least partly in the interests of ensuring that children produce suitable 'work' at the playgroup.

The case of Skyways was somewhat different. They had a smaller range of equipment and virtually no large items; nor would they have been able to set these out so as to allow children to move freely between them, since they met in youth club premises. Even given these constraints, opinions varied about the adequacy of their equipment. The leaders mostly said that they had eventually been able to buy what they needed and could use, but the mothers tended to be more critical. Most thought that they had insufficient toys, or toys of the wrong sort.

> They used to have a lot of toys but not enough – you know, there was just like ornament type of toys I call them. Not a lot to do with, once they'd had a shake or a pull, or all this kind of thing. Not enough to get their imagination going. (Skyways, I.2)

> I thought to myself, Oh these kids must be absolutely sick of playing with these toys over and over again. Cos there was sort of plasticine and these

puzzles you sort of fit in and that. And God every time, I thought, there's the same thing stuck out. No wonder they got up and ran around and carried on. (Skyways, I.3)

My own observation was that in Skyways, whether through lack of toys or the way the play was organized or a combination of both, the children did not seem at all engaged by the activities offered, and it is quite correct to say that they 'ran around and carried on'. Although there had been some signs of more organized activities while Linda Richardson, the first supervisor, was there, once she moved out of the area and left the playgroup it became very clear that, as I noted on one visit, 'the children are more or less just left to play'.

The hall looked particularly tatty today – perhaps the decorations have deteriorated significantly, or maybe I just took my perception of it from the general atmosphere of the playgroup. The playgroup activities seemed to be scattered around rather than put out, and on this occasion I got the distinct feeling that the playgroup is an activity which takes place around the pool tables, around which the children were chasing each other. They were not being organised from the centre at all, until they were gathered together at the end. (Skyways, Fieldnotes, 13.11.79)

The mothers mostly were very dissatisfied with what went on in sessions, and words like 'disorganized' and 'rowdy' were used frequently.[9] I recorded the following notes after a conversation with two mothers jointly:

The thing they emphasised most of all was that the playgroup wasn't organised. They came back to that comment on numerous occasions. They said that the leaders weren't organised about the kind of activities they provided, about making decisions, and that they weren't even organised about handling the children. (Skyways, I.8)

The most damning criticism came from one mother who called this playgroup 'an absolute waste of time':

There was one woman who did have the intention of trying to do something but I think even she gave up in the end and just left the children . . . You know, there was no–nothing at all. I just thought that was an absolute waste of time. (Skyways, I.5)

The same theme of lack of organization was reiterated by the leaders themselves who, reflecting on the group after it had closed, felt that they should probably have been doing something different, but they did not know exactly what. As one of the mothers described it, 'Sometimes Marjorie used to say, "We'll really have to knuckle down and play with them a bit won't we?" That kind of thing.' Marjorie expressed the same concern in a conversation I had with her:

> She said that we didn't really organise enough for the children. There was a bit too much of letting them get on with their own thing. This was mostly because we didn't really know what they could do. (Skyways, I.1)

The leaders, it seems, were genuinely puzzled about what they could have been doing differently whilst also feeling, as several said in interview, that they were doing their best. As one mother put it, 'somehow they just didn't seem to have the answer' (Skyways, I.2). The exceptions to this general picture were special events such as the Christmas party, which were acknowledged by all concerned to be successful. I attended the Christmas party on two successive years, and noted that it followed what could be regarded as a traditional model with special Christmas food, traditional party games and a visit from Father Christmas.

Although sometimes dissatisfied with the playgroup, the leaders were clear that they were trying to do what 'ought' to be done by adopting the ideology of free play. Linda Richardson had begun the enterprise quite specifically committed to this, and the others went along with this apparently correct way to run a playgroup, without always feeling entirely comfortable about implementing it. In the PPA model, free play takes place within a clearly structured and adult-controlled environment, which allows freedom but also circumscribes it. At Skyways however, the implementation of the free-play ideology meant something rather different. Linda Richardson gave me the following account of how the approach had originally been evolved by the initial leadership group, which included two former teachers, who both left the district (and the playgroup) after only a few months:

> *Q* The decision to go for the free play kind of idea – was that basically your choosing or was it something that the four of you agreed?
> *A* Well, I think it was suggested and we agreed. I don't remember who suggested it. Em, I think we thought it would be easier on our behalf because obviously we didn't have any idea about running a playgroup. You know, none of us really knew what to do. I mean, Jean and Sandra were teachers, so they sort of had the organisation bit going. They knew, you know, about the advantages of sitting them all down and that . . .
> You found sometimes they did just sit down and play for ages, or they got fed up with it and moved on. So it's basically, they organise it themselves, the kiddies. Then there were charging around. Then of course we stopped at ten for their drinks. That was organised. They had to sit down for that

. . . But I think it was just suggested, and we said, right, you know, see how it went. And it went very well, so we carried on. (Skyways, I.11)

It is worth looking in detail at Linda's account of how they evolved their style of playgroup, because it clarifies several important points. First, the idea of free play seemed an attractive one to a group of women who 'didn't have any idea about running a playgroup' – it seemed relatively easy to implement. However, it was implemented in a way not likely to produce, in the words of the PPA poster, 'freedom-with-responsibility' in a 'happy, busy atmosphere', because at Skyways free play meant that 'basically they organise it themselves, the kiddies'. Thirdly, reflecting on the early days, Linda said that 'it went very well so we carried on'. In her eyes, a key part of it was the participation of the two former teachers, who 'had the organisation bit going'. Before the end of the first year, both had moved out of the district and a few months later Linda herself left. At that point, the other leaders and those who had become replacements, were left puzzled about what else they could be doing.

The particular style of playgroup which developed at Skyways can be seen as a product of seeing free play as the 'proper' way to run a playgroup, without setting it within the structure more likely to produce a group closer to the PPA model. Its character was given a further distinctive flavour by issues about the presence of adults in the playgroup. Towards the end, a group of mothers began to stay during sessions, although they did take an active part in running the playgroup. The leadership resented their presence enormously and said, 'It were just a morning out for them' (I.6), and 'They were just using it like a cafe' (I.4). Several mothers, for their part, told me that they stayed because the playgroup was badly run, and they feared for their children's safety:

They decided in the end that on most occasions at least one of them would stay because they were a bit worried about the way the playgroup was run. The thing that worried them particularly was safety. The cooker was always on in the corner and there was no way of guarding it against the children. The people running it weren't sufficiently bothered about safety and used to put hot drinks down on a low table so that the children could easily knock it over and get scalded. (Skyways, I.8)

The presence of these mothers, however desirable from their own point of view, meant that it became increasingly difficult for the Skyways leaders actually to run the group at all. First, the 'atmosphere' which their presence brought to the group was regarded as an unsuitable setting for children to play in, 'They used to just sit around a table and smoke all morning. Cos I know when I used to leave Karl, when I came back I used to walk in and the air was blue, you know, with smoke. An I used to think, Ooo' (Skyways, I.6).

Secondly, the unwelcome presence of these mothers seemed to make it almost impossible for the leaders to organize, and especially to discipline, their children. The most graphic description of the problems which this caused them was given by Marjorie:

> There was a really nice little girl, I think she was Indian or something, she was really forward . . . and she used to love to draw. You could just sit her down with a piece of paper and felt tip pens and she would draw all the time, but of course the other children wouldn't let her get on with it. I didn't really know what I could do to control the group. With all the mothers sitting there, you couldn't really tell off the children. (Skyways, I.1)

It would be all too easy to dismiss Skyways as a single and uncharacteristic example of a working-class, self-help playgroup. However, Greenall was similar in many ways, but the consequences there were less spectacular because it suffered from a lack of children throughout the time I was in contact with it. In my view Seafield, if it had ever opened, would have developed along rather similar lines to Skyways. On the evidence of the two groups discussed in detail here, it does seem that working-class playgroups can diverge significantly, and sometimes wildly, from the PPA model. Such variations, however, can take different forms: in Manchester Avenue in the direction of more rigid organization and more formalized activity, and in Skyways quite the reverse. In both cases, the claim that a playgroup provides a 'first-class environment' for children's learning looks rather thin.

## TWO MODELS OF THE
## WORKING-CLASS PLAYGROUP

These data on working-class playgroups might appear to invite the conclusion (especially in relation to Skyways) that working-class women are incompetent individuals who will produce entirely unsuitable forms of pre-school care if left to their own devices. Such a conclusion would be quite unjustified, in my view. To argue that working-class women are incapable of running 'proper' playgroups is to ignore important material and cultural features of these women's lives. I want to argue alternatively that these playgroups can be seen as entirely comprehensible outcomes of the material and cultural circumstances of working-class women, which find collective expression in the playgroup. Their own experiences offer familiar models which get translated into the running of the group: in particular two models, which derive from child-rearing practices, and from the workplace.

Skyways playgroup can be seen, par excellence, as an example of the collective and institutionalized expression of particular child-rearing practices. The Newsons' (Newson and Newson, 1968) classic study has documented the class-based nature of such practices for the pre-school age group, and a comparison of their study with the playgroup data reveals some remarkably close continuities. First, working with the broad categories of 'working class' and 'middle class', they demonstrate some fundamental differences in mothers' approach to their children's collective play. Whilst middle-class mothers organize the provision of suitable company for their children, and ensure that 'the child's whole sphere of interaction is supervised by a watchful adult' (p. 134), working-class mothers send their children out to play with a group of children whom they do not personally select, and whose activities they do not supervise. The effect, argue the Newsons, is to prepare children for the tough, competitive world outside the home. Later researchers have confirmed that the characteristic form of collective play for young children in inner-city areas is the 'unsupervised street playgroup'.

Skyways playgroup seems effectively to have been the equivalent of 'playing out'. This provided the culturally accessible model of children's collective play, and therefore it is not at all remarkable to find a group of mothers sat at one end of the hall drinking tea and talking while the children were left to their own devices – or indeed that the leaders tended to congregate in the kitchen area and only engage directly with the children at special times. In the early days, the presence of two former teachers modified this somewhat, but right from the beginning the approach had been, in Linda Richardson's words, 'basically they organise it themselves, the kiddies'. The children themselves responded in a way which again is entirely recognizable from the Newsons' account: they were rowdy, 'carried on' and ran around a lot, would not allow the 'nice little girl' to complete her drawing and did not readily respond to adult direction of their activities. The exception to all of this was parties, which were organized in a quite different way. These were occasions, it could be argued, on which an alternative cultural model of 'what to do' was available, and 'playing out' was temporarily suspended.

Secondly, class-based practices of intervention in children's play are also replicated in the institutionalized 'playing out' of the playgroup. For working-class mothers, the Newsons argue, the norm is minimal interference, except in cases of quarrelling which threatens to be sufficiently serious as to risk physical injury to one of the children (Newson and Newson, 1968,

p. 112). Such practices were certainly replicated in Skyways, where they adopted a non-interventionist stance, except *in extremis*. Furthermore, the lack of alternative cultural models for such interventions created acute problems once the unwelcome group of mothers began to stay. At this point, the leaders quite literally could not have intervened even minimally with the children: they had no way of doing so which would have been comprehensible, since disciplining another woman's child is, in working-class cultural practice, 'real dynamite' (p. 128). Hence the situation where effectively each mother intervened with her own child whenever that became necessary, and as one mother described it, 'The children didn't know who they had to take orders off. When the mothers were there, everybody was shouting at them to do this and do that. Well it just made them more rowdy than ever' (Skyways, I.9).

Thirdly, the way in which interventions (both positive and negative) in children's play are handled, is strongly class related. Pilling and Pringle (1978), reviewing the literature on this topic, contrast the style adopted by working-class mothers, who issue commands simply requiring obedience but offer no justification or explanation, with the handling of the middle-class child, who is given fewer specific instructions, a greater degree of personal discretion and the opportunity to learn 'techniques of self-justification' (p. 360). The PPA model playgroup can be seen as the collective representation of precisely these latter kinds of virtues offering, as it does, considerable choice within clearly defined limits and 'freedom-with-responsibility'. At Skyways, by contrast, adult–child interaction relied almost entirely upon specific instructions and allowed children little discretion. More positive aspects of intervention were almost entirely absent. Crowe's description of the 'excellent playgroup' in which 'children are chatting with interested adults about anything and everything' contrasts sharply with Skyways, where as one mother put it, 'There was no – you know – adult working with a child. The only time they ever came into contact with a child was when they gave them their drink or they read a story to them' (Skyways, I.5).

Manchester Avenue was rather similar in this respect: although their organization of the activities was closer to the PPA model, I observed little adult–child interaction designed to exploit children's questions and build on their interests. Manchester Avenue, however, was not based primarily on the model of the unsupervised street playgroup. Whilst their organizational practice made them closer to the model on which playgroups are overtly based, that is, the nursery school, the content of their activities made them closer to the model of the workplace. Thus the children 'work' in the playgroup and have to produce visible fruits of their labour. The role of adults is a supervisory one, which ensures that children are given the opportunity – if necessary, are obliged to take the opportunity – to engage in such production. As I noted on one of my visits,

> As before 'today's activity' was set out on tressle tables at the front of the hall. They were making cardboard animals out of toilet rolls and coloured paper. Several children had to be 'encouraged' to do this. I heard several times 'Who hasn't made one yet?', and I noted that when one mother collected her child at the end, Mrs Hawkes apologised because not everyone had made animals today. (Manchester Avenue, Fieldnotes, 4.12.79)

The children at Manchester Avenue were learning to labour in work settings where they produced uniform items under supervision, in a process over which they had little personal control. There were signs, in fact, that the 'production' model was latent in Skyways as well. When the leaders spoke about what they should have been doing, they implicitly used a supervisory model by talking about 'helping the kiddies'. It is possible that in other circumstances, this is a direction in which they might have moved. It is not surprising, of course, that working-class women effectively operationalize a model of the workplace rather than the nursery school, since the former is a setting with which they are familiar, whilst the latter is not.

To argue that the working-class playgroup diverges significantly from the PPA model of the 'excellent' playgroup is not to imply that all middle-class groups fit that model. In many groups, the 'class' lines are not so distinct. Further, there is evidence that very many playgroups do not fit the 'excellent' model. Watt (1977) has questioned whether *any* playgroup can offer an experience analogous to a good nursery school, and the evidence of Sylva et al. (1980) would tend to support this. 'Middle-class' playgroups, for their part, may well reproduce aspects of peculiarly middle-class culture, which might seem equally unattractive on other grounds. Kanter (1976) has argued that nursery schools in the United States effectively prepare children for life in organizational bureaucracies: it would be useful to see her arguments translated into an empirical study of middle-class playgroups in Britain. Certainly on the basis of this study of working-class groups, there seem to be grounds for seeing playgroups as the first step in differential cultural reproduction through education.

## WORKING-CLASS PLAYGROUPS AS PRE-SCHOOL EXPERIENCE

How far is the working-class playgroup likely to fulfil parental wishes that it will provide a preparation for school? Although my study did not attempt to evaluate the *actual* effects, it seems that such groups are unlikely to fulfil parental aspirations, because by definition they *cannot*. In so far as such groups replicate working-class child-rearing practices, they are operating precisely those control strategies, modes of communication and experiences offered, which have been shown to be negatively linked with school performance, from Bernstein onwards. The more 'supervised' version of the working-class playgroup, modelled on the workplace, is not necessarily superior to the 'unsupervised' model in this respect.

All this is very unfortunate for those who wish to promote low-cost provision, if compensatory education is also their aim. There is of course considerable debate about whether any playgroup, or indeed nursery school, can significantly alter the influence of the working-class home, especially of the more 'deprived' sort. The self-help version (to return to the crude formulation in the introduction to this article) does indeed seem to reinforce rather than to counteract the 'undesirable' child-rearing practices emanating from the home.

At this point, the argument begins to look rather like a revised version of the cycle of deprivation, providing further evidence of the incompetence of certain working-class mothers. As I have already suggested, this interpretation is both improper and naive: the reasons for this are threefold. First, these women are being asked to produce self-help nursery education, when material resources are seriously lacking. Each of the working-class groups in my study struggled with unsuitable premises, poor basic facilities and limited equipment. Watt (1977) has argued cogently that all playgroups try to do too much with too few resources precisely because they have modelled themselves on nursery schools. Her observation, that 'the expectation of what playgroups can do within the institutional model based on the nursery school may be unrealistic', has particular force for working-class playgroups (p. 84).

Secondly, to ask the women in my study to provide pre-school education for their own children is to ask them to provide preparation for an educational system which rejected them. It is precisely *because* they were 'failures' that they are eager to give their own children a good start. The self-help solution throws the onus straight back on to them.

Thirdly, the self-help solution ignores the constraints which these women are under and makes it insulting to throw the onus back on them. The reality of these women's lives is that it is a grim struggle in many cases. These are women whose lives are similar to those in Hobson's (1978) study, where she demonstrates powerfully how their isolation contributes to their oppression. They are also a group particularly at risk to clinical depression. Rather than telling them to run playgroups themselves, it seems more appropriate to offer them a break from their children and the opportunity for some paid work. Playgroups, however, fit into the assumption that pre-school provision should be on a very limited part-time basis, drawing on the ideology that young children ought to be at home with their mothers.

To see working-class women's conduct of playgroups as evidence of their individual or collective incompetence is to continue the process whereby women have various expectations laid on them, and then are labelled as inadequate if they do not fulfil them. As Smith and James (1975) have argued in relation to pre-school intervention, different patterns of child rearing cannot be seen purely as a product of 'cultural' differences, but as a necessary response to harsh realities, in which the 'disadvantaged' are in fact those who have lost out systematically in the struggle for scarce resources. Working-class mothers are of course doubly 'disadvantaged': by their class and by their gender.

It has been no part of this study to evaluate alternative strategies for pre-school provision. But the focus on working-class, voluntary playgroups does suggest that the arguments about pre-school intervention which characterized the late 1960s and the 1970s, have by no means been settled by the emphasis on self-help, despite the confidence and the undoubted achievements of the playgroup movement.

In terms of compensatory education, one possible response is to modify self-help with an injection of professional skills and more material resources. It has of course been characteristic of many compensatory programmes that parents have been involved so that skills could be shared. However, this approach implies the supremacy of professional values and a devaluing of working-class culture by aiming to teach mothers how to 'get it right'. An alternative approach is to throw the onus upon schools, whose 'aims, climate, vocabulary and all the rest of it tend, however sympathetic and gifted the teachers, to align most fluently with the middle-class home' (Midwinter, 1974, p. 3).

These debates have been well rehearsed, and remain unresolved. Meanwhile, one is left with the desire of working-class parents for good pre-school education: precisely the kind of 'first-class environment' which self-help playgroups cannot provide for them. One does not necessarily have to espouse a 'deficit' model of compensation to acknowledge that it is legitimate for working-class mothers to demand, from state resources, *good* nursery education for their children.

## ACKNOWLEDGEMENTS

I would like to thank the following people for comment and constructive criticism on a draft of this paper: Alan Cohen, Sue Duxbury, Felicity Harrison, Helen Roberts.

## NOTES

1. Although the word 'playgroup' can apply to a range of different types of provision (from full-time facilities provided on a commercial basis to small groups meeting in someone's home), the term here is used to refer only to the most common form, that is the group run on a voluntary non-profit-making basis, usually for two or three sessions a week. Such groups are referred to as 'community' playgroups, and regarded as the most desirable form, by the Pre-school Playgroups Association (PPA, 1980). This is the national body to which many, but not all, such groups belong. More than 12 000 groups belonged to the PPA in 1982.
2. Presidential address to the Pre-school Playgroups Association, April 1982. See also, 'We didn't know then what we know now', *The Times Educational Supplement*, 2 April 1982.
3. The Plowden Report (Central Advisory Council for Education, 1967) recommended that nursery education should be expanded so as to provide places for 90 per cent of four-year-olds and 50 per cent of three-year-olds. The White Paper of 1972 (*Education: A Framework for Expansion*, Cmnd 5174) accepted these targets in principle.
4. The PPA estimates that 570 000 children were attending their member playgroups in 1981, as compared with 210 000 in state nursery schools and classes (*Times Educational Supplement*, 2 April 1982).
5. The interview stage of this study was carried out with financial support from the Social Science Research Council. I am also grateful to Felicity Harrison for assistance with the initial analysis of the data.
6. Having specified the criteria of selection, I shall subsequently refer to these as the 'working-class' playgroups. However, the use of the term 'working class' is never unproblematic, especially when it refers to women. In fact this study also raised some interesting questions about women's class position, and these are explored in a paper entitled 'Dividing the rough and the respectable: working-class women and pre-school playgroups', presented at the annual conference of the British Sociological Association, April 1982.
7. A total of 48 people were interviewed in the three groups. The criteria for selection were: anyone who had ever been a leader or a regular helper; anyone who was currently a committee member, whether or not they had ever helped in the group; a cross-section of mothers currently using the group. This yielded the following interviews:
   Bankside: 4 leaders, 11 mothers.
   Manchester Avenue: 9 leaders and/or committee members, 9 mothers.
   Skyways: 5 leaders, 11 mothers.
8. The exceptions to this were: at Skyways, one graduate who lived in the area for a few months only, and one trained teacher, who also helped briefly but was not in the interview sample; at Manchester Avenue, two trained teachers, one of whom had trained as a mature student and the other did not live on the council estate.
9. The Skyways mothers were interviewed after the playgroup had closed and therefore probably referred particularly to what it had been like in its final stages.

## TOPICS FOR DISCUSSION

1. Critically evaluate the author's evidence which questions the notion that play-groups provide a very convenient answer in the quest for 'low-cost solutions' for pre-school provision.
2. 'If you want pre-school experience to counteract a child's home, you can hardly let mothers do it themselves; conversely, if you do foster self-help among the working classes, you may get a form of pre-school provision which reinforces rather than counteracts the "undesirable" home setting.' Discuss.
3. 'The working-class women in my study were very clear that they wanted to locate playgroup experience firmly in the context of formal schooling.' Why?

## SUGGESTIONS FOR FURTHER READING

1. Henderson, A. and Lucas, J. (1981) *Pre-School Playgroups: A Handbook.* London, George Allen and Unwin.

The authors provide a detailed and practical guide to many of the issues concerned with the starting, organization and running of a playgroup. The initial discussions (chap. 1–5, 'Families today' and chap. 6–8, 'The developing child') are useful accounts of children in today's society, the effects of geographical and social mobility, the problems of one-parent families, the father's role, and a consideration of pre-school provision in its various forms in the 1980s. There is also a very readable description of the growth of the child in the early years, the child's status in the family, and a valuable examination of the problem of young children with special difficulties. The concluding sections of the book provide a theoretical discussion of, and practical implications for, the importance of play in the playgroup together with an account of activities which introduce music and books, imaginative play, and science, language and mathematics.

2. Shipman, M. (1980) 'The limits of positive discrimination', in Marland, M. (ed.) *Education for the Inner City.* London, Heinemann, chap. 5, pp. 69–92.

In Reading 4 Finch makes the point (p. 67) that 'certainly on the basis of this study of working-class groups, there seem to be grounds for seeing playgroups as the first step in differential cultural reproduction through education'. Shipman's paper echoes and enlarges on this theme. For example, he affirms that 'Parents may have seemed ignorant in denying the immutability of intelligence, in emphasizing the importance of actually teaching the basic subjects, or organizing children's work sequentially, and in demanding order in schools as a basis for learning, but their observations of their own children have usually turned out to be a better basis for action than theories of intelligence or learning. But parents also see the tough world beyond the school and mistrust the liberal romanticism that denies their children the skills that are being drilled into the children of just those professionals who seem to be responsible for the innovations to which they object. These parents only want what the more fortunate among us can choose or buy' (p. 82). (See 'Suggestions for further reading', no. 3, Reading 3, for a brief account of Shipman's paper.)

3. Davie, C.E., Hutt, S.J., Vincent, E. and Mason, M. (1984) 'A comparison of home and pre-school', chap. 10, pp. 166–76, and 'Summary and conclusions', chap. 11, pp. 176–86, in *The Young Child at Home.* Windsor, NFER/Nelson. Chapter 10 presents a comparison between children's home experiences and their

experiences at nursery school, nursery class, playgroup and day nursery. The study is of particular relevance to a theme echoed by working-class mothers cited in Reading 4. Finch reports that the mothers 'typically blamed themselves rather than the educational system for their own "educational failure" and displayed a strong faith in the ability of schools to develop their children's talents' (p. 57). Davie et al. report that in their study, extended conversation, which requires lengthy attention to an individual child with an adult who has drawn on a wide variety of 'shared' experiences, is rarely found in the pre-school context, where nursery staff have to cope with a large group of competing children. The free-flowing adult–child conversation in pre-school education is, in effect, a very rare event (Hutt et al., 1982; Thomas, 1973; Sylva et al., 1980; Tizard et al., 1980, 1982, 1983). Indeed, Tizard et al. (1982) remark that, 'As we expected, the talk of nursery teachers contained a much higher proportion of cognitive demands and "testing" demands than the talk of either working-class or middle-class mothers. However, because there was so much more adult–child talk at home, the children received about twice as many cognitive demands and testing demands in an hour at home as in the same period at school (p. 112). Thus, the widely held view that pre-school staff are providing a more enabling verbal climate compared with *most* working-class children's experience at home is open to serious doubt. It is equally the case that many working-class mothers grossly underestimate their very positive influence on their children's cognitive growth. Davie et al. provide a fascinating account of the comparison of time spent in different forms of activity at home and in the various pre-school provisions investigated, together with an analysis of specific types of adult speech (explanations, approbation, option, rebuke) to the child as a percentage of the total adult speech to the child, again comparing home and school. Chapter 11, 'Summary and conclusions', provides a 'digest' of the whole study. The findings and discussion have important implications for teachers of young children.

# SECTION TWO

## PRE-SCHOOL CHILDREN

# INTRODUCTION

Section Two of the sourcebook is largely devoted to an account of various aspects of the growth and development of the young child. Reading 5 examines the stages of development in childhood from the standpoint of 'transitions' and 'consolidations', thereby emphasizing that the process of development is made up of alternating periods of rapid growth (accompanied by disruption or disequilibrium) and periods of relative calm or consolidation. The authors show how major physiological development, or a change in role or status, is accompanied by the development of major cognitive or language skills in the young child. There is a very useful and comprehensive discussion of individual differences in development and a summary of sex differences in development in childhood. The suggested further readings examine the evidence which suggests that the environment in which the child is reared has a major impact on the rate of development and possibly on the final level the child achieves. The paper by Graham (1985) provides a wealth of evidence to show how social adversity in childhood leads to later ill health.

In Reading 6, Bryant presents scholarly analysis of some of the central tenets of Piagetian theory. He affirms that 'Piaget . . . thought that teachers played an insignificant role in children's cognitive development, and yet, paradoxically and almost perversely, the teachers responded to his neglect of them by trying to use his ideas to foster that development' (p. 92). In examining the question of whether teachers were justified in pursuing Piaget's ideas, Bryant reaches the conclusion that there are sound reasons for applying Piaget's work to the consideration of how children should be taught, but 'that some clear and critical thinking is needed before the jump from his theory to the classroom is made' (p. 92).

Reading 5
# THE DEVELOPING CHILD
## *H.L. Bee and S.K. Mitchell*

## STAGES OF DEVELOPMENT IN CHILDHOOD
### Transitions and consolidations

The process of development is made up of alternating periods of rapid growth (accompanied by disruption or disequilibrium) and periods of relative calm or consolidation. Change is obviously going on all the time, from conception throughout childhood (and adulthood, too). However, we are persuaded that there are particular times when the changes pile up or when one central change affects the entire system. This might be a major physiological development, or a change from one status to another (baby to toddler, for example), or from one role to another (such as at-home child to going-to-school child). Frequently, these role or status changes are accompanied by the development of major cognitive or language skills, too. These pile-ups of change often seem to result in the child's coming unglued for a while. The old patterns of relationships, of thinking and of talking don't work very well any more, and it takes a while to work out new patterns.

Erikson frequently uses the word 'dilemma' to label these periods. Klaus Riegel (1975) once suggested the phrase 'developmental leaps', which conveys nicely the sense of excitement and blooming opportunity that often accompanies these pivotal periods. We will use the term 'transition' to describe the times of change and upheaval and the term 'consolidation' to describe the in-between times, when change is more gradual.

### From birth to 18 months

We have summarized the many changes of infancy in Table 5.1. As you can see in the Table, we think there are really three subperiods here, with one transition point at about 2 months and another at 8 months.

The overriding impression one gets of the newborn infant – for all her remarkable skills and capacities – is that she is very much on automatic pilot. There seem to be built-in rules or schemes that govern the way the infant looks, listens, explores the world and relates to others.

Bee, H.L. and Mitchell, S.K. (1984) 'The developing child', in *The Developing Person: A Life Span Approach*, 2nd ed. Reprinted by permission of New York, Harper and Row Publishers, Inc., pp. 282–99.

Table 5.1 Summary of development from birth to 18 months

| Age | Physical and perceptual development | Cognitive development | Language development | Social development |
|---|---|---|---|---|
| 0–2 months | Major neurological change at about 6 to 8 weeks. Activity mostly controlled by primitive portion of brain before that point. Built-in schemes control | Child's built-in schemes, primarily reflexive actions, dominate his interactions with the environment | Crying and a few pleasure noises are the prelinguistic vocalizations | Child comes equipped with good proximity eliciting attachment behaviours and can discriminate between others to some degree on the basis of smell and feel. No clear-cut attachment to a single individual, however |
| 2–8 months | Major neurological change leads to more voluntary control by child: can sit up and reach for things; examines objects for *what* they are, not just *where* they are. Vision improves; can see parent at a distance | Infant explores and examines objects and people more systematically, repeats interesting actions; develops early steps of the object concept | Cooing and babbling sounds dominate; child seems to play with sounds; discriminates among many sounds, including those not in the language being heard | The first central attachment is formed. Child now shows preference for one or more adults over others. Still little interest in other infants |
| 8–18 months | Child learns to crawl, then walk during this period. Neurological development largely complete by 18 months | Child completes sensorimotor period; can represent things to himself internally; experiments more systematically with objects; uses chains of actions to gain desired outcome | First words and beginning two-word sentences for most children. Many overextensions of early words | First attachment spreads to other care-givers, plus major increase in interest in other children. Attachment behaviours now include moving towards as well as eliciting care-giving. Attachment behaviours less often displayed, however. Child more independent |

One of the really remarkable things about these rules is how well designed they are to lead both the child and the care-givers into the dance of interaction and attachment. Think of an infant being breast-fed. The baby has the needed rooting, sucking and swallowing reflexes to take in the milk; in this position, the mother's face is at just about the optimum distance from the baby's eyes for the infant's best focusing; the mother's facial features – eyes and mouth, particularly – are just the sort of visual stimuli that capture the baby's attention; the baby is most sensitive to sounds that are at the upper end of human voice frequencies, so the higher-pitched, lilting voice most mothers use is easily heard by the infant; and during breast feeding, the release of a hormone called 'cortisol' in the mother has the effect of relaxing her and making her more alert to the baby's signals. Both the adult and the infant are thus primed to interact with one another.

Sometime around 6 to 8 weeks of age, however, there are several changes in the system. Perhaps because of the child's early explorations and perhaps because of simple physical maturation, the child's actions and perceptual examinations of the world seem to switch into a different gear, one controlled much more by the cortex and less by the primitive portions of the brain. The child now looks at objects differently, begins to discriminate one face from another, smiles more, sleeps through the night, and generally becomes a more responsive creature.

Because of these changes in the baby, and also because it takes most mothers six to eight weeks to recover physically from the delivery, there are big changes in mother–infant interaction patterns as well. The need for routine care-taking continues, of course (ah, the joys of diapers), but as the child stays awake for longer periods, smiles and makes eye contact more, there are more playful and smoother-paced exchanges between parent and child.

During the period of consolidation from 2 to 8 months, change continues steadily. There are gradual neurological changes, with the motor and perceptual areas of the cortex continuing to develop. The child is also exploring the world around him in an active way, which seems to be essential for the development of the object concept and other changes in cognitive skill. The child is busy assimilating new experiences and accommodating old strategies to handle the new information.

Somewhere around 6 to 8 months, two changes bring about a brief disequilibrium (transition point): (1) the child forms a strong central attachment and may start to show distress or fear with strangers, and (2) the child learns how to crawl. The combination of these two changes – one motor and one social/cognitive – requires a new adaptation both by the child and by the parents.

The period from 8 to 18 months is a time of intense activity and change. Social relationships are dominated by the central attachments, language begins, the child learns to walk and move about more confidently. Cognitively there are rapid changes towards the eventual milestone of internal representation. Descriptively we can see all these things happening at the same time. What we still don't understand is how these several lines of development are linked together.

There are some suggestions that the early cognitive developments are a necessary underpinning for beginning word use: the child may develop the concept and then learn the word to attach to that concept. There is also a growing body of evidence linking the security of the child's first attachment with cognitive development. Securely attached children seem to explore more freely, to persist longer in their play, to develop the object concept more rapidly, and the like.

Such a link might exist because the securely attached child is simply more comfortable exploring the world around him and thus has a richer and more varied set of experiences to stimulate more rapid cognitive development. A second possible explanation is that the type of parent–child interaction that fosters a secure attachment may *also* be optimal for fostering language and cognitive skill. In particular, one of the magic ingredients seems to be *contingent responsiveness*. We have seen that parents who use contingent pacing have more securely attached children; we have seen that parents who respond contingently to their infant's vocalizations have infants who talk sooner; we have seen that responsive toys and responsive parents foster more complex play and more rapid development. Presumably most parents provide similar levels of contingent responsiveness in many domains, so that the rate of children's development on all three fronts will be similar.

## From 18 months to 6 years

The transition at 18 to 24 months is marked by the achievement of internal representation and by the development of more complex language. Children passing through this transition frequently show disruption of sleeping or eating habits as symptoms of the disequilibrium being experienced.

We have summarized the changes from 2 to 6 years of age in Table 5.2. We see this as a single period, without significant subperiods or transitions.

One way to think of this stretch of four years is as a long consolidation. The major breakthroughs in language and cognition at 18 to 24 months usher in entire collections of new skills and opportunities, and it takes the child three to four years to master the new skills completely.

Another way to look at the pre-schooler is in terms of his striving for

Table 5.2 : Summary of development from 2 to 6 years

| Physical and perceptual development | Cognitive development | Language development | Social development |
|---|---|---|---|
| With major brain growth complete, there are no new major motor skills but considerable refinement of existing skills occurs. Coordination improves, particularly small muscle coordination; child begins to play games and use large game equipment, such as bats and balls | Preoperational stage of development according to Piaget. The child's logic is still fairly primitive, but he can use words or images to stand for things in his play, begins to be able to take other people's perspectives, becomes able to classify fairly skilfully, and develops a full gender concept | Child moves from Stage-1 to Stage-2 language, constructing more complex sentences. By age 6, language is used skilfully by most children. The meaning of words has come to match the meaning in the adult language fairly well | Primary attachments to parents are still present and visible, especially when the child is under stress. Child explores farther and farther from this safe base, however, and develops more relationships with peers. Primitive forms of early friendships are formed, and sharing and generosity as well as aggression can be seen. Play choice begins to be with the same sex and with sex-stereotyped toys and games |

independence. He can get around in the world much better than he could before, and he pushes for the freedom and opportunity to go his own way. It is this element of the period that Erikson emphasizes in his stages of autonomy versus shame and doubt and initiative versus guilt.

It seems to us that the advances in language and cognition and the push for independence are not separate from one another. Each makes the other possible to some degree. They also combine to influence the form of the child's attachment behaviour. When language is rudimentary and the child's locomotion is poor, then clinging, touching and holding, or crying are just about the only stress-related attachment behaviours available to the child. However, as language becomes more skilful, she becomes able to stay in touch with adults and peers in new ways; she can call to her mother, 'Mommy, are you still there?' or ask for attention, 'Daddy, look at my picture!' The attachment may be no less strong, but it can be maintained at greater physical distances.

These new skills also clearly affect the child's developing self-concept and sex-role identity. The child understands that there is a continuing self and begins to define the dimensions of that self–size, age, gender, and the like. He also now comprehends the things that other people say about him, and that information is also factored into the self-concept.

For most children, the next major transition occurs somewhere between 5 and 7. Again the cognitive shift is probably the critical experience, although the fact that most children start school at this time is clearly of importance as well. (It's not accidental that these two things occur together. Schooling is begun at about ages 5 to 7 in virtually every culture, presumably because of some recognition that children of that age are now cognitively and socially ready for the demands of formal schooling.)

Like the earlier transitions, this one is often marked by increases in problem behaviour, difficulties adjusting to school, loss of appetite, or other symptoms. But it is also frequently a time of excitement, even joy, for children. Whole new vistas open up. The child is more independent, more focused on the peer group and less on the parents, and is learning immensely powerful new cognitive and academic skills.

## From 6 to 12 years

We have summarized the changes that take place from ages 6 to 12 in Table 5.3. Freud called this the *latency period*, as if it were a period of waiting, with nothing very important happening. In one sense he was right; it appears to be a relatively calm period. Nonetheless, there is a great deal of change. Unlike the earlier periods we have talked about, though, in which there are

Table 5.3   Summary of development from 6 to 12 years

| Physical and perceptual development | Cognitive development | Language development | Social development |
|---|---|---|---|
| Physical growth continues at a steady pace without any major spurts until puberty. Among girls, puberty may begin during this time. Gross-motor skills continue to improve; the child can ride a bike, play ball, and perform other complex motor tasks. Adult levels of visual acuity are reached. | This is the period Piaget called *concrete operations*. The child's thinking becomes reversible; and she can use the operations, such as addition, subtraction and serial ordering. She is less tied to the physical features of objects, more able to perform actions in her head. She also grasps conservation. Inductive logic is now seen | Although the basic language skill has been acquired, the child normally learns to read and write in this period and becomes more skilful with advanced forms of sentence construction, such as passive sentences | Freud called this the *latency period* because sexual interests seem to be largely submerged. Peers become very important, but nearly all peer groups are same-sex groups. Children are exploring and learning their sex roles partly through imitation of same-sex models. Attachments to parents are less visible but still present. Individual friendships become important, especially for girls |

significant changes in many areas – language, cognition, social and physical development – the changes from 6 to 12 seem to centre mostly in one area, cognition.

During the primary school years, the child's understanding of the world, and of people and relationships, shifts fundamentally from an egocentric to a more reciprocal view. We can see this in the quality of children's friendships, which move towards sharing and exchange; we see this in children's judgements of other people's actions, which shift to an emphasis on intentions rather than on consequences; we see this certainly in children's understanding of the lawful relationships among objects. The school-aged child is no longer tied down by what things look like on the outside; she can understand that there are constancies – qualities of people, of friendships, of objects – that remain the same even when they appear to be different.

We do not want to leave the impression that social relationships are unimportant at this age. They are vitally important. Whether a child has friends at this age, for example, is one of the few things about childhood that predicts emotionally stable or unstable adulthood. But the most striking characteristic of this period is the development of more complex mental abilities, which in turn affect a wide range of behaviours and relationships.

## THE ROLE OF THE ENVIRONMENT

Some of the patterns of developmental change we have described are obviously strongly influenced by maturation: motor development, early language, possibly cognitive development as well. But no development is purely maturational. At the very least, expression of any physiologically programmed development requires a minimally supportive environment. Infants need to spend time on their stomachs if they are to learn to crawl at the normal time; toddlers need to be exposed to language if they are to develop language themselves. There are many other examples.

For some kinds of development, and possibly for some periods of development, the range of acceptable environments may be quite broad. For example, several respected theorists have recently suggested that cognitive development in the first 12 to 18 months of life is highly *canalized*. That is, the path or sequence of early development is very powerful (a narrow canal), and nearly all basic child-rearing environments provide enough support for it to proceed normally. Furthermore, infants seem to have excellent 'self-righting' tendencies: if the child is deflected from the underlying pathway because of some inadequacy of the environment or some accidental occurrence, the power of the underlying developmental system is such that the child can often recover later. A child who is ill in the early years, for example, may show slower development during the illness but then later largely catches up to her healthier peers. Beyond infancy, however, canalization seems to be much weaker. Optimum development seems to demand much more specific input, so that a narrower range of environments provides sufficient support.

Despite such apparent built-in directionality, however, and despite differences in specific heredity, the environment in which a child is reared clearly has a *major* impact on the rate of development and possibly on the final level the child achieves. We've mentioned such environmental effects as we have gone along, but let us summarize:

1. Physical development is affected perhaps least by the environment, though diet has a significant effect on the rate of growth, on final height, and on the development of brain cells. Children who have been deprived of adequate diets prenatally and in the early years frequently also show intellectual deficits, and these deficits may remain even if the diet later improves.

2. Both the rate of development of cognitive structures, and the level of cognitive power (as measured by IQ tests, primarily) are affected by the richness and variety of the objects available to the child, by the regularity and predictability of experiences, by the amount of encouragement for exploration, and by the amount of parental support and involvement. Comparisons of children from middle-class and poverty-level families (who differ on many of these dimensions) show that by age 3, children from middle-class families have IQs that are 15 to 20 points higher, on the average, than children from working-class families. Some of that difference *may* be genetic. Current research suggests, though, that much of the effect is environmental.

3. Language development appears to move along with only basic environmental support – mainly exposure to language from adults. But as we've already pointed out, parents who talk more to their children, and who respond contingently to their child's language efforts, have children who develop language more rapidly. Such children also show higher IQ scores.

4. The influence of the environment seems to be especially strong in the area of social and emotional development. Attachment behaviours in the early months may well be instinctive, as Bowlby suggests, but the security of the attachment seems to be largely a function of the child's experience with the major care-givers. In older children, behaviour disorders and problems with relationships with others seem to be a function of both the security of the early attachment and the level of stress or support in the family environment.

We can illustrate the degree of the potential impact of the environment quite clearly by looking at the results from a fascinating intervention study by Rick Heber and his colleagues (Heber, 1978). Heber selected a group of 20 infants born into poverty circumstances to mothers with IQs below 75. Without intervention, such children are also likely to end up with very low IQ scores. Heber wanted to find out if that probable retardation could be prevented if the infants were given a massive dose of a well-designed, stimulating environment – one that embodied all the optimal features we have just listed. The intervention began in the first weeks of life and continued to school age. It included five-day-a-week, all-day day care for the infants and vocational and educational rehabilitation for the mothers.

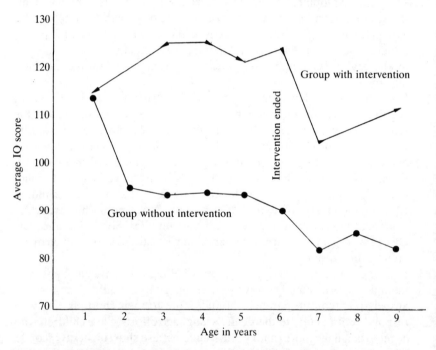

Figure 5.1   In Heber's study, 20 children received massive intervention, including enriched day care for the infant and educational training for the mother. Twenty children from equivalently impoverished families received no such intervention. The figure shows the IQ scores of these two groups of children over time. The treated group's IQ does drop when the intervention stops but continues to be more than 20 points above the IQ of the non-treated group. (*Source:* Heber, 1978, p. 59, combination of Figures 4 and 5.)

Figure 5.1 shows the IQ scores of these 20 children compared to another group of 20 from the same kinds of families who did not receive the special

Table 5.4  Summary of sex differences in development in childhood

| | |
|---|---|
| **Physical development:** | |
| Rate of maturation | Girls seem to be on a bit faster developmental timetable with slightly more advanced development at birth and with earlier puberty |
| Quality of maturation | Girls' physical growth is more regular and predictable with fewer uneven spurts |
| Strength and speed | Little difference in the early years |
| Fat tissue | Girls have a thicker layer of fat tissue, just below the skin, from birth onward |
| **Perceptual development:** | |
| Sensitivity to pain | Boys appear to have a greater tolerance for pain, but the sex difference is small |
| Responsiveness to taste | Girls appear to be somewhat more responsive to taste stimuli |
| Perceptual style | Girls are more likely to be field dependent; boys are more likely to be field independent |
| **Cognitive development:** | |
| Cognitive structure | No sex differences on any measure of structure during childhood is found consistently |
| Cognitive power: IQ | No sex differences on total IQ scores is found |
| Verbal skill | Girls slightly better at some verbal skills, particularly in the early months of life and again in late elementary school |
| Maths skill | No difference in this age period, except that girls are sometimes better at computation |
| Spatial skills | No difference in spatial visualization skill at this age |
| **Social development:** | |
| Aggression | Boys are more aggressive on nearly all measures, beginning in toddlerhood |
| Competitiveness | Boys show more competitiveness than girls, although this difference does not appear as early as the aggression difference |
| Dominance | Boys again show more dominance in play with other children |
| Nurturance | No clear sex difference found in this age period |
| Sociability | Girls typically have fewer but closer friendships; boys have more, but less intimate, friendships |
| Compliance | Girls appear to be somewhat more compliant to adult requests, especially in early childhood |

care. As you can see, this rich environment did, in fact, prevent intellectual retardation for this group of children. The fact that the children were still above average even three years after the intervention stopped suggests that the effect may be permanent.

We should emphasize that Heber's study does not prove that all mental retardation could be 'cured' with appropriate environmental interventions. Heber did not include in his group any children with known brain damage or other physical abnormality – either of which might cause lasting retardation. What his study does show is that for those children who have the environmental deck stacked against them, changing the environment greatly alters the outcome. Since briefer or less massive interventions attempted by other researchers have resulted in somewhat smaller intellectual gains, the case for the importance of the environment is further strengthened.

# INDIVIDUAL DIFFERENCES IN DEVELOPMENT

We have been talking right along about differences in rate of development and about some of the explanations of those differences. But there is one aspect of individual differences that we have sidestepped a bit, namely, sex differences. Do boys and girls develop in the same way, at the same rate?

## Sex differences

Table 5.4 summarizes the major sex differences in development during childhood that have been reasonably well established. Two points are worth making about these differences.

First, even where the difference is very clear, such as with aggressiveness, *the actual magnitude of the difference is small* and the two distributions (male and female) overlap almost completely. That is, *within* each sex there is almost a full range of performance or skill on each of the dimensions listed in the Table. (Many boys have fast maturation, or low tolerance for pain, or low levels of aggression, or poor maths skill; many girls are competitive, or non-compliant, or field independent, or good at spatial visualization tasks.) It is only when we look at the average scores for the two sexes that we see a difference. It is worthwhile to try to explain such differences, but it is important to keep in mind that the actual impact of gender on behaviour is really very small.

Second, both biological and environmental causes seem to be at work in producing the differences we do see. The difference in aggressiveness seems to have biological roots, such as varying hormone patterns, but parental treatment may well magnify the biological effect. Similarly, differences in early language skill may be partly biological (varying maturational rates) and partly caused by differing amounts of exposure to language. We realize that it is not popular (at least not within the women's movement) to look for *any* biological causes of sex differences. However, the evidence we have at the moment compels us to accept the plausibility of some biological effects interacting with environmental shaping.

# SOME LINGERING UNANSWERED QUESTIONS

We cannot leave this summary without talking at least briefly about some of the questions and issues about development in childhood that are currently being discussed. The field of developmental psychology is presently in a state of considerable theoretical ferment. Old assumptions are being questioned right and left, and new theoretical paradigms have not yet emerged. Two questions, in particular, are the focus of present debates.

## Are there really stages?

[. . .] Is there any *synchrony* in development, any pattern of connectedness or overall organization that characterizes each of a series of ages? We often talk as if there is, such as in the discussion of the period from ages 6 to 12 that you read a few pages back. However, many psychologists are now asking whether development is really a set of largely unrelated sequences or whether there are overriding characteristics at particular ages that affect all the child's behaviour. There is evidence on both sides, and the argument will no doubt continue.

## Is early experience really more important than later experience?

The assumption that experience in the first years is more important, more formative, than later experience has been around a long time. Obviously, Freud believed it, as do Erikson and many others. One way to get a handle on this issue is to use an analogy suggested by A.D.B. Clarke (1968; Clarke and Clarke, 1976): when we construct a house, does the shape of the foundation determine the final structure completely, or does it partially influence the final structure, or can many final structures be built on the original foundation? Perhaps even more important, if there are flaws or weaknesses in the original foundation, are the weaknesses permanent, or can they be corrected later, after the house is completed?

Put more precisely, we are asking whether the early years of life (infancy, or even childhood as a whole) are a *critical period* in development – a period during which a particular experience or set of experiences has a lasting effect that cannot be undone later. Current theorists also talk about the *resiliency* of children. Are they resilient enough to recover from deprivation or abuse if they are later placed in better circumstances?

Again, there are data on both sides. Some prenatal influences are permanent, such as the effect of rubella in the early months of pregnancy.

Some effects of poor diet in the early years do not seem to be outgrown, and some effects of early cognitive impoverishment may also be very long lasting, as may the effect of abuse or neglect or insecure attachment.

At the same time, there is evidence that children can and do recover from many such early experiences. Many preterm infants, and others who suffered from prenatal trauma, seem to turn out quite normally if they are later reared in supportive environments; longitudinal researchers who have hunted for permanent effects of early experiences frequently have not found them (Kagan, 1979); and [. . .] those who experienced poor early childhoods may sometimes be 'healed' by particular relationships or experiences in adult life.

Our own conclusion at the moment is that children (and adults) are probably considerably more resilient than many of us had thought a decade ago. But we think there is a danger that the theoretical pendulum is now swinging too far towards the *resilience* side of the argument. Alan Sroufe has stated the middle ground well:

> There is reason to doubt that children are infinitely resilient, even given the flexibility of our species. . . . What children experience, early and later, makes a difference. We cannot assume that early experiences will somehow be canceled out by later experience. Lasting consequences of early inadequate experience may be subtle and complex, taking the form of increased vulnerability to certain kinds of stress, for example, or becoming manifest only when the individual attempts to establish intimate adult relationships or engage in parenting. But there will be consequences. (Sroufe, 1979, p. 840)

When we talk about continuity and discontinuity in development or individual consistency or inconsistency over time, we are really raising variations on these same two fundamental themes. We will meet these questions again as we explore development in adolescence and adulthood.

## KEY TERMS

*Consolidation*   The term used to refer to those periods in development between transitions when the child is expanding and consolidating major gains or changes made at transition points.

*Developmental leaps*   Term used by Klaus Riegel to describe points of transition in development, when the child appears to shift into a different gear.

*Dilemma*   Term used by Erikson and others to describe the central task on which the child (or adult) is focused in each of several periods or stages of development.

*Transition*   The term used to refer to those periods in development when major changes in cognitive skill, social interaction pattern or physical development appear to disturb the equilibrium of the previous consolidation period and require a new equilibration process.

## TOPICS FOR DISCUSSION

1. Is there any *synchrony* in development, any pattern of connectedness or overall organization that characterizes each of a series of ages?
2. Discuss the viewpoint that the early years of life (infancy, or even early childhood as a whole) are a *critical period* in development, a period during which a particular experience or set of experiences has a lasting effect that cannot be undone later.
3. What evidence is there to suggest that the environment in which a child is reared has a *major* impact on the rate of development and possibly on the final level the child achieves?

## SUGGESTIONS FOR FURTHER READING

1. Graham, P. (1985) 'Psychology and the health of children'. *Journal of Child Psychology and Psychiatry,* **26**, 3, 333–47.

Inappropriate behaviour and adverse social circumstances in childhood are responsible for a high proportion of physical morbidity and mortality not only in childhood itself but also in later life. Graham provides a wealth of evidence to support this statement and traces the processes whereby social adversity in childhood leads to later ill health. The author reviews recent evidence which suggests that, contrary to popular belief, health promotion in childhood *could* substantially reduce the prevalence of physical morbidity. Emphasis is placed on the part played by methods of approach based on cognitive-behavioural techniques in the recent more successful examples of health promotion.

2. Quinton, D. (1980) 'Family life in the inner-city: myth and reality', in Marland, M. (ed.) *Education for the Inner City.* London, Heinemann, chap. 4, pp. 45–67.

It is a truism that statistics persistently and consistently point out that there are higher concentrations of adverse and debilitating living conditions in urban areas – more crime, vandalism and delinquency; more low-status and single-parent families; more psychiatric disorder, and so on. There is also a wealth of evidence to show a relationship between these factors and various educational and behavioural problems in children. Low social status, large family size and overcrowded conditions have consistently been shown to relate to delinquency, to poor attainment and to behavioural difficulties. But the relationships between various disadvantages and the behaviour and development of children are not as straightforward as they sometimes seem. Quinton asserts that families with problems are not necessarily problem families, that disadvantaged areas do not necessarily have high rates of delinquency, and that schools in similar catchment areas can have markedly different amounts of difficulty. Thus, the accumulation of statistics sometimes leads to a stereotype of a city family, and the author warns that we need to be careful about our assumptions concerning the connection between disadvantage and children's difficulties or capabilities. We may wrongly blame social disadvantages for school problems when on occasions the blame should lie within the school. We may expect poor attainment from children from disadvantaged homes, and we may presume that adverse effects may ensue from setting our expectations for these children too high – or too low! The research project which Quinton describes compared one inner London borough and the Isle of Wight. The study was designed to examine family, social and environmental factors associated with children's behaviour problems in school and with psychiatric disorder, the two areas being chosen because they were radically different environments: the one, part of a 'decaying' inner city; the other, a settled area of small towns.

The findings of the study highlight the differences between 'myth' and 'reality' and at the same time demonstrate the limitations of conclusions that can be drawn from area-based statistics. Thus, both official statistics and data from the study confirmed that the London borough had more of the adverse characteristics associated with family disadvantage – more low-status, one-parent, large and overcrowded families; more children in care; more immigrants from outside the United Kingdom; much less home ownership and many more homeless families. Consistent with expectations arising from this concentration of social disadvantage, the case *would appear* to seem clear – more social problems, more children with disorders. Paradoxically, however, differences between the areas were not strongly reflected in a large range of family patterns which were investigated. To summarize:

1. Within the family there were no differences in the frequency of parent–child interaction or communication, no differences in maternal warmth towards the children, no differences in the amount of control parents exerted over their children. (p. 49)
2. The similarities in marital relationships and family patterns between the two areas were much more striking than were the differences.
3. The amount of contact with, or support from, relatives was exactly the same in both areas, the majority of mothers having supportive relationships with relatives or friends or both.
4. There was no evidence that selective in- or out-migration was directly responsible for the increased rates of children's problems.
5. The patterns of family relationships in both areas were remarkably similar yet the children in the London area had more educational and behavioural problems.

The author suggests that we need to explain the nature of the connection between area indicators of disadvantage, family life and children's development, for although we know a good deal about the general correlations between multiple disadvantage and the various problems, we know much less about the processes linking particular disadvantages with the various difficulties of children. An important conclusion of the analysis, then, is that behaviour problems in primary school children can be largely explained by certain adverse factors operating through the family and, conversely, these factors have *similar implications* in other reputedly more favourable environments. Quinton concludes his paper with a consideration of the role of the school in attenuating the effects of social disadvantage, and emphasizes the point that many social disadvantages do not always, indeed *do not usually*, imply that homes lack warmth or supportive relationships – rather they lack skills and resources to help facilitate cognitive and intellectual development. Further, it is the job of the schools and their claim for special status that they are able to develop skills in children; it is their responsibility to find ways of doing so.

3. Williams, T. (1985) 'Health education and the school-community interface: towards a model of school–community interaction', in Campbell, G. (ed.) *New

*Directions in Health Education.* London, Falmer Press, pp. 7–16.

The author argues that because the health-related behaviours of young people are largely practised outside the classroom in the wider school and community environment, it follows that the teaching of health education should seek to link these areas of operation more closely together. The paper offers a number of basic concepts as a frame of reference for a model of school–community interaction which Williams considers essential to a personal construct of health education. His suggestions translate, in a very practical way, some of the points raised by Graham in the 'Suggestions for further reading' (no. 1).

# Reading 6
# PIAGET, TEACHERS AND PSYCHOLOGISTS
## *P.E. Bryant*

One of the most obvious and at the same time most surprising things about Piaget's work is the great interest in it shown by people concerned with education. There are two reasons for wondering at their enthusiasm.

One is that Piaget himself was not particularly interested in their subject. True, he directed the Institut des Sciences de l'Education in Geneva and true, too, he wrote a book about education. But the name of his department was misleading, since its subject was really Psychology or at any rate Child Psychology, and one book only among such a prodigious output is really very small beer. Piaget himself often expressed disdain for the most obvious and the least sophisticated educational question to be expressed about the intellectual development he charted so meticulously – which was how to hurry this development on. He called it 'the American question', and that was not meant as a compliment.

But of course interests can go one way and not the other. The fact that Piaget paid little attention to educational questions does not mean that there was nothing of interest in his theory to educationalists. There is, however, a more serious reason for wondering why his impact on education has been so great, and that concerns his view of language.

A teacher talks to children and spends a lot of time telling them how to do things. One way and another his or her work is based on the idea that someone, who has knowledge and skills, can transmit them to others who

Bryant, P.E. (1984) 'Piaget, teachers and psychologists'. *Oxford Review of Education*, **10**, 3, 251–9.

have less of them or do not have them at all. Yet in Piaget's view this sort of activity had virtually nothing to do with children's intellectual development.

Language seemed to him to depend on cognitive development and to follow it. The child, he argued, learns to express various concepts verbally only as a result of conquering these concepts first. The idea that intellectual development was the product of some direct communication from adult to child was anathema to Piaget and his colleagues. He thought it entirely inadequate on its own: it would only work, he argued, if the child had somehow managed to arm himself with the necessary intellectual structures first. 'In a word, whenever it is a question of speech or verbal instruction, we tend to start off from the implicit postulate that this educational transmission supplies the child with the instruments of assimilation as such simultaneously with the knowledge to be assimilated, forgetting that such instruments cannot be acquired except by means of internal activity, and that all assimilation is a restructuration or a reinvention'.

Where does that leave the teacher? Does it not mean that the teacher is doomed to be peripheral at best and ineffective at worst? I still find it hard to find a plausible answer to this question and I suspect that at bottom Piaget had little respect for the teacher's business. Yet if you look at almost any new programme for teaching science or mathematics to young children, there Piaget tangibly is. His work is cited as justification for many of the new methods and for some old ones too. His influence pervaded many of the *Head Start* programmes and now it even reaches, via Seymour Papert and his turtle, into some of the most interesting recent attempts to use computers to help children learn (Papert, 1980). Piaget, it seems to me, thought that teachers played an insignificant role in children's cognitive development, and yet, paradoxically and almost perversely, the teachers responded to his neglect of them by trying to use his ideas to foster that development.

Were they justified? My view is that there are grounds for applying Piaget's work to the question of how children should be taught, but that some clear and critical thinking is needed before the jump from his theory to the classroom is made. One useful starting point for these thoughts is a distinction which seems obvious and important and yet has not, as far as I know, been applied with any rigour to the question of Piaget and education.

Any theory about child development contains two related but entirely separable elements. One is about the nature of developmental changes. We try to chart the exact ways in which children change as they grow older – what skills they gain and what new psychological structures they build up between birth and late adolescence. This is not, as it may sound, a purely descriptive exercise. To say that the typical five-year-old has one psychological structure which affects the way that he responds in a particular task and that the typical seven-year-old has another, is to make a theoretical statement. One is trying to explain the behaviour of both lots of children in terms of underlying psychological mechanisms. In fact, in this case one has two theories, one about five-year-old and the other about seven-year-old children.

Piaget happens to be a case in point: not only did he produce some provocative ideas about the illogicality of young children and the striking growth of logical skill with age, but he also went to some lengths to explain what underlying psychological structures were responsible, first for the absence of logic and then, when the structures had changed, for its presence. It was his claim about the early lack of logic which had most impact and which even now dominates a substantial portion of current research on children's intellectual abilities. He argued that young children cannot make logical inferences, could not understand the principles of invariance of quantity, were unable to realize that other people have different points of view (socially and spatially) from themselves, were severely limited in the way they classified things in their environment, found measurement impossible, and were quite unable to understand that numbers or any other kinds of quantity could be arranged in an ordered series. One could go on: the list of things which, Piaget tried to persuade us, young children could not manage is long indeed. But the point here is that it is not just a list. He also had a theory – and rather a simple one at that – about the reason for these astonishing intellectual gaps.

His ideas centred around the notion of irreversibility and perceptual domination in young children. They were, he thought, rooted to their immediate perception and were unable to change it around or to link different perceptual inputs in any systematic way. So, for example, they could not work out what a room would look like from another angle, because that would involve turning their perceptual image of the room round, so to speak, in their heads. Piaget managed to use this idea as an explanation of all the various incapacities which I have already mentioned. It was an ingenious way to link an apparently heterogeneous set of things with one simple notion. But it did not of course explain why children eventually do manage to solve Piaget's various tasks as they grow older. Nor was it meant to.

The answer to that question is to be found in the causal part of his theory. Indeed the second element to be found in all accounts of children's development deals with the question of what makes them change as they grow older. Piaget's own ideas about the causes of development are extremely well known. They centre around the notion of equilibrium and disequilibrium, and of the effects of internal cognitive conflicts. Children, Piaget claimed, can for most of the time find a consistent explanation for what happens to them and for what they see happening around them, and when they do this they are, according to Piaget, in a happy state of cognitive equilibrium and are quite content with their own interpretations of the world around them. However, from time to time children will experience some kind of 'conflict'. They will find that they have two mutually contradictory ways of explaining the same event. According to Piaget this raises some uncomfortable doubts in the children concerned, who as a result are now plunged into a state of cognitive disequilibrium. This state, being an uncomfortable one, then provides the motivation for change. The child reorganizes his psychological mechanisms – the underlying structures – in such a way that he resolves the original conflict and now explains the hitherto puzzling events to himself in an entirely consistent and satisfactory manner. These changes are usually, so to speak, for the better. When they happen the child's intellectual processes improve.

Let us return now to teachers and ask which of these two sides of Piaget's theory should interest them more. At first sight the answer seems clear enough: it should be the second. After all, if we are looking for new and better ways of teaching children we need to know the way to improve their intellectual skills, and that takes us to the causal side of any developmental theory. So much is indisputable. But that does not mean that Piaget's claims about the extraordinary logical incapacities of young children should be neglected by teachers, and indeed they have not been.

We can turn to these first. The obvious broad implication of Piaget's suggestions about these glaring logical gaps in the intellectual repertoire of young schoolchildren is that there is a warning here for the teacher to keep off various topics until the children can actually understand what he or she is talking about. We can take two examples from the long list of incapacities which I have already given. One is the question of measurement, and the other of the understanding of number.

Measurement is a good example of the immediate practical implications of many of Piaget's experiments on logic in young children. The very first work that Piaget did with children involved asking them to make transitive inferences, which means linking two direct pieces of information A>B and B>C in order to draw the indirect inference that A>C. 'Bob is taller than Fred, and Fred is taller than Sam. Who is taller Bob or Sam?' is an example of a problem which can be solved by making a transitive inference, and Piaget was so struck with the evident difficulties of children as old as nine years with problems of this sort that he decided to pursue the question of the development of intelligence very widely.

There is no doubt that young children do have the sort of difficulty with problems of this sort, when they are given in the way that I have described, which Piaget originally claimed that they have. He and his colleagues were quick to point out that this suggested that the same children should have problems too with measurement. This was their argument. If children cannot link the quantities A and C through the common measure B, they are illogical but not only that: they also must have no idea about how to measure, since measurement also involves comparing two quantities which cannot be compared directly by taking a measure, first to one and then to the other. Piaget and his colleagues tested this hypothesis by setting up an experiment on measurement, in which children were asked to compare two towers of bricks, one which they had to build themselves to the same height as another which the experimenters provided. There were various measures (rods and strips of paper) around and the question was whether the children would use these to compare the two towers which were difficult to compare directly since they were placed on tables of different heights.

As the experimenters expected, the young children were reluctant to use the measures. Instead they resorted to comparing the towers directly, which was a risky operation and one which usually produced the wrong answer. So Piaget and his colleagues concluded that children up to the age of roughly eight years do not and indeed cannot measure, an incapacity which they thought should be traced directly back to the children's failure to make a transitive inference.

What is the message for the teacher? As far as I can see it is a pretty bleak one. Don't bother with measurement when the child first comes to school, seems to me to be the only practical implication. We must now consider whether this is justified. In fact subsequent work both on transitive inferences and on measurement manages to throw considerable doubt on whether it can be justified.

The question of children and transitive inferences is controversial. In 1971 Tom Trabasso and I (Bryant and Trabasso, 1971) pointed out that the original A>B, B>C, A>C experiments were extremely badly designed. For one thing they did not check that children actually remembered the premises when they were asked the inferential question, and that meant that the original failure need not have been a logical one. It could as well have been a failure to remember the original two comparisons AB and BC which the child was being asked to combine. But we found another thing wrong with the traditional Piagetian experiment, which was that it left open the possibility of getting to the right answer in an entirely non-logical manner. When the child is originally given the first two premises he is told and is often shown too that A is 'larger' than B, and also that C is 'smaller' than B. So the label 'larger' is attached to A and 'smaller' to C. By simply remembering these labels and repeating them when asked the 'inferential' question about A compared to C the child could produce the right answer, which is that A is the larger and C the smaller of the two. The child can produce the right answer to the inferential question without in fact making any inference.

There is a simple enough solution to these problems which is to design an experiment in which care is taken to ensure that children remember the premises when they are asked the inferential question, and in which the correct answer cannot be reached by merely repeating labels picked up in the first part of the task. Tom Trabasso and I set about doing just this. We made the children very familiar with the premises which they had to combine, before ever posing the inferential question. At the time that we did pose it we also checked that the children could remember that original information. In order to avoid children solving the 'inference' by repeating labels we increased the number of quantities involved in the original judgements. The children had to deal with five quantities and were originally shown that A>B, B>C, C>D, and D>E.

This meant that three of the quantities B, C and D were given two labels at first, 'larger' and 'smaller', and thus that any inferential question involving just these quantities could not be solved just by repeating a single label.

In this experiment four-, five- and six-year-old children succeeded triumphantly. They seemed to be able to combine the information in the four original judgements with consistent success. We concluded that we had demonstrated that the original claim by Piaget that young children cannot make inferences was quite unfounded.

There are, I think, two things to be said about our argument and our experiment. The first is that our criticisms of the original tests of transitive inferences are not in doubt. The second is that our conclusion that young children do make inferences is still a matter of some debate (de Boysson-Bardies and O'Regan, 1973; Thayer and Collyer, 1978; Breslow, 1981; Russell, 1981). This is an issue which is not settled yet.

But the educational side of the question, which is the supposed inability of young children to measure, is very much clearer. There were two obvious features to the results of Piaget's tower measuring experiment. One was what the children did not do: they did not measure. The other was what they did do, which was to make a direct comparison by looking from one tower to another. Is it not possible that the young children could in principle measure but did not, because they did not realize that a direct comparison was a risky business? So the experiment might not after all demonstrate either a logical gap or a complete inability to measure.

Hanka Kopytynska and I (Bryant and Kopytynska, 1976) have shown that five-year-old children do use an intervening measure when they have no chance of making a direct comparison between the two quantities which they have to compare. Our innovation was to give them wooden blocks with holes in the middle and to ask them to compare the depths of these holes. Since there was no way of seeing to the end of the holes a direct comparison was out of the question.

In this task the children did use a stick, and they did so on the whole without any prompting, in order to compare the two quantities. It seems that children can measure, but do not always do so when they should.

We have then to make a distinction between the possession of a logical ability on the one hand and on the other hand the way that this ability is deployed. Children or indeed adults must not only be able to make a particular logical move: they must also recognize when that move is needed. The children fail to measure in Piaget's task not because they lack the ability to do so, but because they do not realize that they would be helped by doing so.

It seems to me that this distinction between the possession and the deployment of a logical skill makes the whole question of intellectual development a much more interesting one as far as the teacher is concerned. After all Piaget's message to the teacher is a negative one. 'Do not launch into measuring straight away because the child will not understand what you are on about' is not an inspiring message. Surely teachers should be far more interested in the idea, which I am putting forward, that children can measure but need to know more about when it is right and helpful to do so.

This is not an isolated instance. In fact every one of the many claims that Piaget made for some glaring logical gap in young children is now hotly disputed, and in every case some evidence has been produced which appears to show that young children can manage the logical move in question in some circumstances though not in others. I shall take one other example which is the famous conservation experiment. This comes in many forms, but I shall stick to the experiments which deal with number. Here the child is shown two identical rows of counters arranged side by side like two ranks of soldiers. He is asked to compare them and usually judges that they are equal in number. Next he sees the experimenter changing one row either by spreading it out or by bunching it up. Then he is asked to compare the two rows again. At this stage children of six years or less usually say that the two rows are not equal and that there are more counters in the longer of the two rows. Piaget concluded from this that they do not have a proper understanding of number. They do not realize that only adding and subtracting will alter a row's number and they actually think that lengthening it or shortening it changes its number too.

Again this is a result with serious educational implications, for, if a child thinks that, he will not really know what number is. Piaget himself pressed this point with some vigour, and once again his message to the teacher was bleakly negative. Take care, he seems to be saying, not to force the child into experiences with number when he simply cannot understand what those numbers mean.

But is this conclusion justified? It has been criticized by many people. We can start with the most famous of all the criticisms, made by Margaret Donaldson (1978). She argued that the whole experiment was an unfortunate misunderstanding between the adult experimenter and child. The child, she claimed, really does understand the principle of the invariance of number but is persuaded to give the wrong answer by the actions of the experimenter. The child sees a strange and important adult who first asks a question about the two numbers, then deliberately makes what seems an important change to one of the quantities and finally poses the question once again. It was Donaldson's view that this strange routine which centred on the deliberate transformation of one of the quantities led the child to think that since the experimenter had made an important change and had then immediately posed another question, his (the child's) answer should change too. Hence the different answer after the transformation than before it.

She had the results of her experiment with Jim McGarrigle (McGarrigle and Donaldson, 1974) to support her argument. Instead of a serious adult changing one of the two rows, now the change was made, apparently as an accident, by a marauding and out of control teddy bear. When this happened the children – even four-year-old children – were much less likely to change their judgements after the transformation; they tended to maintain that the two rows had the same quantities despite the fact that one was now much longer than the other.

This was a provocative experiment and it had its critics. One was Scott Miller (1982), who produced some experimental results which seem to go flat against Donaldson's hypothesis. If Donaldson is right about the children being unintentionally misled by the experimenter doing the transformation, then they should not be at all misled if the transformation occurs quite naturally. So Miller conjured up a number of situations where one row of objects became longer than another as though it happened quite naturally and without the experimenter's intervention. In one case there were two rows of boats, one row of which floated apart, and in another two rows of crickets, one row of which escaped, so to speak, from their moorings and spread apart. Apart from the unusual nature of the material the procedure in Miller's experiment was exactly as in other conservation experiments.

As it turned out the results were the same too. The children made the same amount of errors when no adult was involved in making the transformation as when one was. It made not the slightest difference that the boats and crickets spread apart without the apparent help of any adult. Even then the children made Piaget's mistake.

What is the reason for these apparently contradictory results? One possible explanation is that the McGarrigle and Donaldson results were in fact misleading, and that the children were so taken with the bizarre activities of the miscreant teddy bear that they never paid much attention to the transformation or to the change in the length of one row. In Miller's experiment, on the other hand, the transformation was more interesting and when the children paid some attention to it they made the conservation error. In that case Miller's results, which certainly support Piaget's argument, would be nearer the truth than Donaldson's.

So Piaget might be right. Indeed that is what one would have to conclude were it not for another set of experiments which make Piaget's argument about conservation much less secure. These began with the work of Rose and Blank (1974) who took much the same line as Donaldson about children being misled, but who tested this idea in an entirely different way. They simply decided to omit the first question in the conservation task. They, like Donaldson, argued that the child might be misled by the experimenter solemnly asking the same question twice, and making an apparently important change in between the two questions, and they rightly argued that the simplest way to test this was to stop including both questions in the experiment. In fact the first question – the one before the transformation – is redundant, and so in one condition they left it out. They simply showed the children the two rows, and then transformed one, and then for the first time asked the children to compare the two rows. This turned out to be the more successful condition: children made many less errors in it than they did in the normal conservation procedure. Rose and Blank's experiment was with six-year-olds, but we have shown recently that their results hold true with five- and seven-year-olds as well, and with other materials too (Samuel and Bryant, 1984).

It looks as though the repeated questioning in the traditional form of the conservation experiment does mislead children who in principle do understand the rules of invariance, but who in practice are easily diverted from using them. Once again we are faced with the phenomenon of children being able to produce the correct answer in one situation, but not in closely similar circumstances.

These two examples demonstrate clearly enough that the original depressingly negative message to teachers which emerged from Piaget's theories about young children's logical incapacities is almost certainly unjustified. Again and again it has turned out that Piaget told only half the story. He was right to point out that young children make some surprising mistakes, but wrong to conclude that each mistake signalled some great logical gap. He did not seem to accept that it is possible to be illogical sometimes and yet to be able in principle to make the necessary logical moves. Surely this is a more attractive conclusion for teachers. It certainly makes their job more interesting. It means that they do not simply have to wait until the relevant ability develops. They have instead to show children the value and power of the already considerable skills which they bring with them when they first come to school.

I think that there can be no question that the implications of Piaget's theories about children's logical skills is, as far as teachers are concerned, restrictive and negative. But this is plainly not true of the other side – the causal side – of his theory as well. Here is an entirely positive picture of the way in which a child constructs the world for himself. The child explains things to himself, and when through some conflict he finds these explanations inadequate he adjusts them until they work.

It is not a story in which the teacher plays much part, as I have pointed out already, but it is exciting and it did fit in with many of the new ideas which have been current in primary education since the 1930s. It would be wrong to say that Piaget invented discovery learning or child-centred education, but it is easy to see why his causal ideas fit in so well with these educational notions.

Two problems haunt Piaget's causal hypothesis. One is the lack of serious evidence for it. Piaget himself produced none. He did not even make it easy for other people to do so for him, because he never provided any really concrete examples of the internal conflicts which he thought to be the basic causes of intellectual growth. He simply stated his hypothesis and left it at that.

That really is not good enough, especially since the ideas have had a considerable impact on teaching practices. It is true that some of Piaget's colleagues tried to fill the gap, but their experiments were poorly designed (Bryant, 1982) and anyway the sort of 'conflict' that they looked at was not conflict in Piaget's sense of the word at all. He was talking about the child having two mutually contradictory explanations for the same set of events. They, on the other hand, looked at what happens when a child predicts one thing and then sees something else happening. That may be a conflict, but it is not Piaget's conflict. More recently some of Piaget's colleagues (Doise and Mugny, 1979; Perret-Clermont, 1980) have looked at the possibility that social conflicts bring about intellectual change. These are interesting studies, but again the conflict that they deal with is not the sort that Piaget wrote about.

The second problem is even more worrying. There are strong *a priori* objections to Piaget's theory about conflict. It is wholly inadequate in terms of cognitive change. The trouble is that when a child is in conflict in Piaget's sense of the word, all that he can know is that he is at least partly wrong. He has two views. One of them, he now knows, is wrong (but which one?): or perhaps both are. He has no way of knowing which is the wrong one or whether both are, and there is nothing in the conflict which is going to tell him what is right. In other words the conflict may be a way of telling a child that his intellectual system is not working perfectly, but it is not a way of producing intellectual improvement. In the end Piaget never explains how it is that the child finds the solution and thus reaches the next stage of intellectual development. One is forced back to the notion of blind trial and error, and that certainly is ironic since Piaget himself always pooh-poohed the idea of trial and error having any importance at all.

Is there an alternative? I have suggested another idea recently which happens to be the opposite of Piaget's. It is that children learn that a particular strategy is right when they see that it produces the same results as another strategy. My evidence (Bryant, 1982) comes from experiments on measurement which showed that children were more likely to measure when they saw that measuring two things produced the same answer as comparing them directly when the direct comparison is a safe one, and also from experiments on subtraction and multiplication in which children began to be more willing to multiply or to subtract when they saw that the results of these activities were the same as those of others such as counting.

So my idea is that it is agreement, and not conflict, between the various intellectual strategies used by children that is the spur for intellectual development. Again this seems to me to be an explanation which is of some interest to teachers because it gives them a more important part to play. Surely teachers can do much to make the child's world more coherent by showing him the links between activities which may seem quite separate to him.

To disagree with Piaget and to argue against the usual lessons which are drawn about education from his work is not to dispute the significance of his contribution. He, far more than anyone else showed how it is possible through simple but ingenious experiments to reach conclusions which might have far-reaching implications for what goes on in the classroom. If he was wrong about children's logical abilities and inabilities, he was only half wrong. Children do make surprising mistakes and those mistakes are important. They do not in my view mean that the teacher has to treat various topics like measurement as out of bounds. On the contrary these mistakes are a useful sign of when children fail to take advantage of their own impressive capacities and they should be treated as such by teachers as well as by psychologists.

It is much the same with his causal ideas. The notion of conflict may be untested and even untestable, and it may well be true that the idea simply could not work anyway. But Piaget did us all a great service by pointing out that children may grow intellectually by constructing their intellectual world for themselves. It is encouraging to know that teachers can help children to do so.

## TOPICS FOR DISCUSSION

1. 'A teacher talks to children and spends a lot of time telling them how to do things. One way and another his or her work is based on the idea that someone, who has knowledge and skills, can transmit them to others who have less of them or do not have them at all. Yet in Piaget's view this sort of activity had virtually nothing to do with children's intellectual development.' Discuss with reference to the role of the teacher.
2. Critically evaluate the arguments and evidence which lead Bryant to remark that 'our conclusion that young children do make inferences is still a matter of some debate'.
3. Discuss Bryant's viewpoint that 'it is agreement, and not conflict, between the various intellectual strategies used by children that is the spur for intellectual development'.

## SUGGESTIONS FOR FURTHER READING

1. Sylva, K. and Lunt, I. (1982) 'Piaget's research into the minds of children', in *Child Development: A First Course.* Oxford, Basil Blackwell, pp. 91–116.
   This very readable account outlines the main features of Piaget's theory of the development of logical thinking in the young child, emphasizing his fundamental proposition that children actively construct their understanding of the world by interacting with it, and that at different stages of their development 'they are capable of different kinds of *interaction* and arrive at different kinds of *understanding*'. The authors consider the various stages (or 'periods') – the sensorimotor period, the preoperational period, the period of concrete operations and the period of formal operations – showing how the process of assimilation enables the young child to 'take in' information about the environment and then act on and accommodate to this information. Of particular relevance to Reading 6 is the section in the chapter which evaluates Piaget's work. The authors detail a number of methodological problems inherent in Piaget's experimental procedures, illustrating their arguments with reference to a number of later studies which demonstrate that children can solve logical problems and are capable of logical thinking at much earlier ages than Piaget supposes.

2. Hobson, R.P. (1985) 'Piaget: on the ways of knowing in childhood', in Rutter, M. and Hersov, L. (eds) *Child and Adolescent Psychiatry: Modern Approaches,* 2nd ed. Oxford, Blackwell Scientific Publications, chap. 11, pp. 191–203.

This very comprehensive account begins with the details of a number of particular observations and experiments conducted and recorded by Piaget, and discusses the inferences that he drew in each case. Hobson writes that 'in every instance, it will be important to distinguish between that which Piaget observed, and the way he interpreted his findings. Piaget's observations are sound, but what they signify for the nature of children's thinking is very much a matter of dispute' (p. 191). The author reviews a number of Piaget's observations on the child's growing awareness of 'object permanence' during the sensorimotor period of infancy, and later in the chapter evaluates the observations to illustrate ways in which Piaget's work has been subject to critical scrutiny. In a later section Hobson discusses Piaget's approach to child development, asserting that 'Piaget was little concerned with issues related to the child's personality, or emotions, or even "behaviour". His interest lay in the developing structure of the mind' (p. 194), and his aim was to tease out the patterns and structures that underpin the child's behaviour and experience. Hobson produces a powerful critique of the inferences which Piaget drew from his often sound, relevant empirical data, claiming that many of the inferences are often profoundly suspect. The author discusses the coherence of Piaget's concept of 'stages' of development, concluding that empirical studies have generally not found as much 'chronological synchrony or concurrence among same-stage acquisitions as Piaget's stage theory predicts' (p. 197). Furthermore, Hobson suggests that in Piaget's version of 'developmental stage' theory there are very serious disagreements about the criteria which are considered adequate to assess whether a child has 'reached' a particular cognitive structure, and the author concludes that 'Piaget has probably underestimated the significance of variety within intelligence, especially the variety of ways in which intelligence is acquired and applied' (p. 201).

3. Meadows, S. (1986) 'Perceiving and understanding', in *Understanding Child Development*. London, Hutchinson, chap. 2, pp. 33–66.

This very useful chapter provides the student of child development with a wide perspective of the complexity of factors involved in the growth of the young child's ability to perceive and understand. The author discusses cognitive development from the perspective of Piagetian theory, concentrating on the notions of cognition as adaptation. She concludes that 'as far as what *does* develop during cognitive development . . . Piaget suggested that there was a move during childhood from thinking that was fragmented, partial and closely tied to experience, to thinking that was at least capable of being logical, abstract and very flexible, by adolescence' (p. 34). Meadows considers Piaget's model of *how* cognitive development proceeds, examining the four factors he lists (organic growth, the role of exercise and of acquired experience in the actions performed upon objects, social interaction and transmission, and the final factor, equilibration, invoked to coordinate the diverse contributions of maturation and physical, social and logico-mathematical experiences). She discusses some of the problems inherent with the Piagetian model and goes on to look at 'logic' as a model for cognitive development and the major contribution that 'information-processing' approaches have made to the study of cognitive development. There follows a very detailed account of infants' perception and cognition and a discussion of brain organization and development.

# TEACHERS AND CHILDREN

# INTRODUCTION

Section Three of the sourcebook consists of six readings concerned with the interactions between teachers and children. Reading 7 is introduced with a detailed account of two opposing views of language and its acquisition, views that involve two quite different conceptions of language: language as *system* and language as *resource* (Halliday, 1978). The viewpoints differ in whether they attribute the main responsibility for what is acquired (learned) to the child or to the environment. Wells traces the development of language from its earliest stages emphasizing that 'the learning of language does not begin until the child starts to produce recognizable words with the deliberate intention to communicate particular meanings' (p. 111). Although 'cracking the code' may be the most difficult part of the process of language acquisition, the author stresses that before the child can begin this task he or she first has to discover that there is a code to be cracked (p. 111). This discovery is dependent on children having some way of establishing hypotheses about the meanings of 'communications' which are being addressed to them (p. 113). Wells discusses the relative contribution of child and environment to the process of discovering and cracking the linguistic code, concluding 'that what is most important in the behaviour of children's parents and other care-takers (in helping young children to acquire linguistic competence) is sensitivity to their current state – their level of communicative ability and their immediate interests – and to the meaning intentions they are endeavouring to communicate' (p. 119).

Reading 8 provides a fascinating comparison of the behaviours of difficult and well-adjusted children. The authors describe the work of Montagner (1978) and Manning et al. (1978) who were concerned with different styles of behaviour exhibited by nursery school children. The researchers appear to agree on three distinct styles: well-adjusted, aggressive and dependent. The authors produce comprehensive behaviour profiles of the children who conform to each style, noting particularly the behaviours, attitudes and reactions of peer groups and teachers to such children. They examine the friendship choices (or lack of), the various forms of interaction, the quality of interactions and peer relationships of children who conform to these three styles. Of particular importance in this reading is the discussion of the children's relationships with adults and the teachers' reactions to the various forms of behaviour which the different 'styles' seem to produce. The paper concludes with a useful discussion of the various theories on the origin of relationship difficulties.

In Reading 9 Hughes and Grieve consider the problem 'What happens when we ask a child a question?', arguing that although it is a commonplace procedure to ask children questions when studying cognitive and linguistic development, it is remarkable how little we understand of this interrogative process. Their paper reports fascinating information on one aspect of the process, for they found that when presented with a question by an adult, children will locate an answer for the adult's question *even if that question is conceptually ill formed*. The study describes what happens when bizarre (i.e. unanswerable as they stand) questions were presented to a number of children of different ages. The fact that children are not merely passive recipients of questions and instructions, but instead actively try to make sense of the situation they are in – however bizarre it may seem – has profound implications for those who rely on questioning as a means of developing children's linguistic abilities.

Reading 10 describes the development and evaluation of a method for introducing simple arithmetical symbolism to pre-school children. The author comments that the idea of pre-school children being introduced to arithmetical symbols runs directly counter to most current theory and practice in early mathematical education. For example, the most well-known and widely used infant school mathematics schemes do not introduce addition or subtraction until the children have experienced a wide range of activities designed to develop their general concept of number; even then, concrete objects are used to help children with problems of addition and subtraction before they are taught the appropriate formal symbolism. Current work on children's cognitive development casts doubt on Piaget's claim that until children achieve the stage of 'concrete operational thought' (around about seven years of age) they are unlikely to understand addition and subtraction. Indeed, Hughes argues that we have seriously under-estimated the numerical competence of very young children, and his findings suggest that 'providing young children with further concrete experiences of addition and subtraction may not be the most appropriate educational activity, for they are already relatively competent at the concrete level. Rather the educational problem is one of finding ways to help children free their thinking from the concrete, so that they can express the concepts they already possess in formal arithmetical symbolism' (p. 154). Parallel research undertaken by Bryant (1985) indicates that there is a difference between recognizing what kind of sum is needed to solve a mathematical problem on the one hand and doing the sum correctly on the other. His research illustrates and confirms that in mathematics, as in other cognitive problems, children sometimes do not take advantage of skills which they already possess.

Reading 11 is an account of a study of conversations between a teacher and some of her children in a nursery school. Dialogue is one of those activities which teachers of young children particularly would claim as a most important facet of their job. How valuable, then, to provide feedback to teachers about the nature and effects of their styles or strategies for achieving their own objectives, especially when their conversations take place in a context where very young children are developing their own linguistic and communicative competence. Wood and Wood have included in this study an exploratory investigation of the relationships between teachers' 'demanding' questions and the cognitive level of children's responses. Basically, the authors are asking whether one needs always to ask questions in order to receive back high-level responses from children.

Reading 12 explores the idea that the fantasy and sociodramatic play of young children can be thought of as the precursor of later imaginative story-writing or telling. The author offers examples of fantasy and sociodramatic play which, it is claimed, are fairly characteristic of young children in our society. The format and content of such activities are characterized by pretence, imagination and drama. Smith traces the developmental sequence of fantasy and sociodramatic play, showing how symbolic play is related to the acquisition of language. Although several studies have found *parallels* between the development of symbolic play and of language, the author stresses that these parallels do not necessarily mean that symbolic play and language influence each other *directly*, for they could both be aspects of a general symbolic or cognitive development (p. 187). Smith examines the structure and conventions in typical symbolic play episodes, describing the ways in which young children initiate fantasy play. Of particular importance is the discussion of the role of the adult in enriching a child's fantasy and in helping to develop and extend narrative structure. The suggested further readings extend the scope of this topic by reporting one study concerned with young children's resolution of distress through play, and another which examines how mothers' linguistic production during games episodes can be related to the young child's acquisition of language.

## Reading 7

# LANGUAGE AND LEARNING: AN INTERACTIONAL PERSPECTIVE

## G. Wells

### INTRODUCTION: OPPOSING VIEWS OF LANGUAGE AND ITS ACQUISITION

If one question more than any other has preoccupied students of language during the past 25 years it is 'where does language come from?' Clearly, language is learned, for each child grows up to speak the language of his or her surrounding community. But who has the greater responsibility for what is learned and the order in which learning takes place: the child or the people in his or her environment? Although the controversy goes back to classical times and perhaps even further, it was given new vitality in recent years by Skinner's (1957) behaviourist account of language learning and by Chomsky's (1959) innatist response. It was they who fired the opening shots, but the battle still continues today and neither side has yet won a clear victory.

One of the main reasons that the debate has continued so vigorously is that two quite different conceptions of language are involved: on the one hand, language as system and, on the other, language as resource. For Chomsky and those who follow him, the central and most essential characteristic of language is its grammar – the finite system of implicitly known rules that enables a speaker or hearer to produce and understand a potentially infinite number of different sentences. To learn a language on this account is to construct a grammar – a set of complex and abstract rules, which relate meanings to sounds. Since these rules are not made available to the child either through inspection of other people's utterances or through direct instruction, the learning of them is seen as inexplicable except in terms of innately given knowledge of the general principles underlying all human languages and a predisposition actively to construct and test hypotheses

Wells, G. (1985) 'Language and learning: an interactional perspective', in *Language, Learning and Education*. Windsor, NFER-Nelson, chap. 4, pp. 58–73.

about the organization of the particular language to which the child is exposed.

However, what is missing from this first account, as those who argue for the importance of the environment point out, is any recognition of the pragmatic dimension of language – the uses to which it is put. When people interact with each other through language, the production of grammatically well-formed sentences is not an end in itself, but a means for acting in the world in order to establish relationships with others, to communicate information and to engage with them in joint activities. Children are thus born into a community of language *users* and their learning of language forms part of their socialization as members of that community. Acquiring control of the complex patterns of their native language is, therefore, on this second account, a matter of learning how to do things with language – 'learning how to mean', as Halliday (1975) puts it. Through interacting with those in their environment, children thus both acquire the resources of the language of their community and learn how to make use of those resources in order to achieve a variety of purposes in relation to different people in different situations.

Both these accounts of language acquisition recognize that children must be equipped with the ability to learn a human language (in contrast to other species, which do not seem able to do so). Both also recognize that they will only learn if they grow up in a language-using environment. Where they differ is in whether they attribute the main responsibility for what is learned to the child or to the environment. In Chomsky's (1976) view, all that is required of the environment is the provision of instances of language in use in order to trigger the innate language acquisition device (LAD). To him, the fact that all normally functioning human beings learn their native language, despite wide differences in the nature of the 'primary linguistic data' to which they are exposed, makes it clear that the input plays little part in determining the particular course that development will take. In contrast, those who stress language as resource emphasize the interactional context in which language is learned and point to the wide variation between individuals in the degree of skill that is eventually acquired. Because language is concerned with the communication of meanings, they argue, it is essentially collaborative in nature. It is inconceivable, therefore, that children's experience of linguistic interaction should not have some influence on their learning. How important then, is the environment, or more specifically the experience of linguistic interaction with people in that environment, in determining what the child learns and the rate at which learning takes place? Since the answer to this question has far-reaching implications for the way in which we think about language and learning in school, the major part of this chapter will attempt an evaluation of the evidence bearing upon this issue which has emerged during the last quarter of a century.

# THE EVIDENCE FROM RESEARCH
## The precursors of language

From a strictly linguistic point of view, the learning of language does not begin until the child starts to produce recognizable words with the deliberate intention to communicate particular meanings. However, this ability does not emerge fully formed from nowhere. Rather it is just one step in a developmental progression that starts much earlier and continues well on into adolescence. 'Cracking the code' may be the most difficult part of the total process, but before the child can embark on that task he or she first has to discover that there is a code to be cracked. How this happens is now beginning to emerge from studies of infants in the earliest weeks of life. From the work of Trevarthen (1979) and Stern (1977), who observed and recorded infants interacting with their mothers, it appears that, long before they are able to interact with the physical world, infants are already behaving in ways that elicit responses from their parents and are thereby gaining feedback concerning the effects of their own behaviour. What both researchers noticed was that it is the infant who typically initiates the interaction and decides when it should end. However, it is the mother who, by the timing and aptness of her responses, gives continuity to the interaction in such a way that it looks as if the pair are engaging in something very like a conversation without words.

Initially, of course, it is most unlikely that the infant's gestures or vocalizations are intended to communicate. Nevertheless, as Newson (1978) puts it:

Whenever he is in the presence of another human being, the actions of a baby are not just being automatically reflected back to him in terms of their physical consequences. Instead, they are being processed through a subjective filter of human interpretation, according to which some, *but only some*, of his actions are judged to have coherence and relevance in human terms . . . It is thus only because mothers impute meaning to 'behaviours' elicited from infants that these eventually do come to constitute meaningful actions so far as the child himself is concerned. (p. 37)

In other words, infants come to be able to have and express communicative intentions by being treated as if they already had them. These early interactions are almost exclusively social – establishing the interpersonal relationship between 'I' and 'You', addresser and addressee, which forms the basis of communication. But, towards the middle of the first year, they begin to incorporate objects and events in the world that mother and infant share and, in this way, the 'It' is added and the triangle of communication is completed. This may happen in a number of ways; through the adult following the infant's line of regard and giving him the object he appears to be interested in; by drawing the infant's attention to potentially interesting objects or events; or by marking through gesture and speech the steps in familiar sequences of activity such as feeding, bathing, dressing, etc. What is important about these early experiences, it is suggested, is that, although the infants have no language yet themselves, these interactional episodes provide a framework within which they can discover some of the fundamental principles upon which language in use is based – the reciprocal exchange of signals, the sequential patterning of turns, and the assumption of intentionality. Since adult speech, often ritually repetitive in form, accompanies the focal points in many of these transactions, it seems reasonable to suppose that, by the later part of the first year, the child will also have formed a general hypothesis about the communicative significance of speech.

## First words

Treating speech as significant, however, is not the same thing as recognizing it to be meaningful. Perception of meaning entails the recognition that arbitrary but conventional patterns of sounds are intended, by virtue of that patterning, to bring about particular responses in the listener to aspects of the world that are shared with the speaker. To achieve this level of practical understanding the child has to be able to:

(a) analyse the situation in order to form hypotheses about the meaning intention that the speaker is expressing;
(b) analyse the stream of speech sounds in order to segment it into units and discover the relationships between them;
(c) construct hypotheses about the way in which meanings and sounds are related to each other.

Stated in this form the task seems formidably difficult. In considering how the child sets about it, therefore, it may be helpful to consider the strategies that archaeologists might use in attempting to decipher an inscription in an unknown language on an artefact that they have unearthed. Typically, they try to work out, from their reconstruction of the context in which the object was found, the probable intention in producing it and, from that, the probable 'content' of the message. Armed with hypotheses of this kind, they can then attempt to interpret any regularities of patterning they can discover in the written symbols. If they can find and decipher sufficient inscriptions of this kind, they may eventually be able to reconstruct the language in which the inscriptions were written. Note, however, that, in the early stages of such a task, the inferences are almost entirely from conjectured meaning to linguistic form. Without fairly rich hypotheses about the content of the inscription it will never be deciphered, however easy it may be to recognize repeated patterns in the symbols themselves.

The same seems to be true for young language learners. In order to crack the code, they must have some way of producing hypotheses about the meanings of utterances that are addressed to them. In considering the earlier stage of pre-verbal communication, we have already seen how the infant might form rather general hypotheses about the uses that language serves in interpersonal communication, and it does indeed seem to be this aspect of language that is first attended to. Of course, it is very difficult to know precisely what children understand at this early stage, but their own utter-ances give us some clues as to the sort of uses that they are aware of. Halliday (1975), for example, on the basis of a study of his own son's language development, suggests that by the second half of the first year a child has discovered that utterances may be used to communicate four very basic kinds of intention, which he characterizes as 'instrumental', 'regulatory', 'interactional' and 'personal'.

Most of the child's utterances that express these functions consist of a single word, sometimes based on an adult word, sometimes one of his or her own invention. In context, however, the child's parents or other care-takers can frequently infer the intention and so, if the child attempts to express such intentions, it seems reasonable to assume that similar generalized intentions are also attributed to the utterances of others.

Somewhat later, on Halliday's account, three further functions are added, the 'heuristic', 'imaginative' and 'informative', the last probably not emerg-ing until after the child has begun to produce multi-word utterances.

Although children's early utterances suggest that it is this pragmatic or interpersonal dimension of meaning that is paramount for them, quite early they begin to comprehend and produce utterances that also have a referen-tial function. Here, once again, it seems as if they may receive considerable help from the adults who interact with them. The 'naming game' is one that probably all children play with their parents or other care-takers, either in relation to real objects or, in Western cultures, in relation to representations of objects in picture books, magazines or mail order catalogues. From his studies of this particular interactional 'format', Bruner (Ninio and Bruner,

1978) concludes that the game has a repetitive and ritual character which renders the relationship between word and object salient. Equally, however, it appears that children must personally arrive at a hypothesis that there is a simple one-to-one relationship between single words and simple concepts, for otherwise how could they learn new words on the basis of a single hearing, as Carey (1978a) has shown that they can and frequently do?

Rosch (1977) suggests that, in organizing and storing our experience, we tend to operate with what she calls 'prototype' examples of concepts – that is to say, with particularly clear examples. It seems likely that young children also form prototypical concepts and that these usually map quite easily onto the words that adults choose to use when talking to them. Thus, for example, 'bird' is the word most commonly used by adults to refer to all the species that most children are likely to see, and children initially respond similarly to all particular birds as instances of the same prototypical category, referring to all of them by the same word, 'bird', or by their own version of this word.

To match words to meanings in comprehending adult utterances, however, the child must also be able to identify the boundaries of the words in question in the stream of speech in which they occur. To a certain extent, this task is made easier by the fact that, in naming objects, adults frequently produce the name in isolation. However, this will not explain how the child identifies other words, such as verbs, prepositions, etc., which occur in isolation much less frequently. One clue is provided by the kinds of words that children begin to produce themselves, both at the single word stage and when they begin to put words together. In some of their early work, Brown and his colleagues (Brown and Bellugi, 1964) remarked on the 'telegraphic' nature of early utterances, and suggested that the words used tended to be those that are stressed in normal speech. Children, therefore, may use word stress to help them segment the stream of speech. This point has been made again more recently by Wanner and Gleitman (1982), who point out that in stressed languages generally, it is the unstressed items that are omitted in early utterances. Stress alone cannot be sufficient, however. Although it may give global salience to particular words, it does not give unambiguous information about word boundaries (e.g. 'an/orange' or 'a/norange'). To determine precisely where boundaries occur, the child must also notice how words combine with other words in the context of larger structures (e.g. 'an orange', 'my orange', 'this orange', etc.). Weir's (1962) study of her child's pre-sleep monologues shows how some children systematically try out possible combinations of this kind in what looks very much like playful practice.

## First sentences

Many of the child's single-word utterances consist of words that seem to refer to objects in the environment and this, in combination with contrasts in intonation, gesture and voice quality, allows adults to interpret them in context as conveying pragmatic intentions of the kinds described by Halliday. However, if they were to remain limited to single-word utterances, children would have very restricted powers of communication, for central to language is its capacity to express relationships, such as actor–action ('the boy ran'), object–location ('Mummy is in the kitchen'), experiencer–state experienced ('I'm hungry') and so on. These relational meanings are typically realized grammatically – by word order, suffix or inflection – and are therefore not as transparent as those meanings that are lexicalized in individual words. Furthermore, there is rarely a direct, one-to-one relationship between meaning and formal realization. It is thus much more difficult for adults to attempt to teach the meaning–form relationships ostensively, as they frequently do with the names of familiar objects.

At this stage, therefore, children are much more heavily dependent on their own ability to form hypotheses about meanings and the ways in which these are related to the sequential patterns of morphemes that they can identify in the stream of speech. Where might such hypotheses come from?

Quite early in the post-Chomsky period of interest in language development, Donaldson (1966) suggested that the answer might be found in the cognitive schemata that the child has by this stage already constructed about the organization of the physical and social environment. Since then, a number of other researchers have pursued this line of investigation, often using Piaget's account of cognitive development as a basis for examining the relational meanings expressed in early utterances (and therefore also assumed to be understood). Brown (1973), for example, concluded from his analysis of his own and other researchers' data 'that the first sentences express the construction of reality which is the terminal achievement of sensori-motor intelligence' (p. 200); others have reached similar conclusions. However, although children certainly require the cognitive schemata which have already been acquired in order to construct hypotheses about the meanings that are expressed in the speech that they hear, this is not in itself sufficient. They still have to discover which of the possible cognitive schemata are actually encoded in the language being learned and how they are organized in relation to the grammar. In a recent article summarizing developmental studies across a wide variety of languages, Slobin (1981) suggests that the method used by the child is to pay attention to what, following Rosch, he calls 'prototypical situations' – situations, that is, that are particularly salient, such as the transitive situation of an agent causing a change in the state or location of an object (e.g. 'Daddy (agent) is painting (cause change of state) the door (object)'). Treating these as basic semantic categories, the child then looks for the 'canonical', or basic grammatical, forms in which they are encoded. Whether this or some other strategy is the one that is actually employed, it is clear that the major responsibility for carrying out the task of mapping meanings on to forms, must lie with the child. Since they cannot be taught, each child must reinvent them for himself. However, it is still possible that the conversational context may facilitate the task to some degree. And during the past 15 years or so there has been an increasing number of studies which have attempted to find out whether this is in fact the case.

## Modifications in adult speech to children

The first of these studies were designed to rebut Chomsky's (1964) characterization of the input as 'random and degenerate'. And they were remarkably successful. Snow (1977), reviewing studies by a number of researchers, showed that there is very considerable evidence that care-takers do generally adjust their speech when talking to young children and that they speak a recognizable register of baby talk, or 'motherese' as it has been called by some, which is characterized by formal simplicity, fluent and clear delivery and high redundancy in context.

Such characteristics certainly seem likely to facilitate the learner's task, but only in a rather general way. If one wanted to argue for a more specific effect of the input it would be necessary to demonstrate that it was, in addition, 'finely tuned' to the learner's current knowledge and progressively modified to present the child with precisely the information that he or she needed in order to take the next step. To some extent, adults do seem to behave in this way. Studies show that the frequency with which adults address utterances to their children of the polar interrogative type (in which the auxiliary verb occurs in first position) are associated with the rate at which the children learned the auxiliary verb system. Nevertheless, no other formal characteristics of adult utterances have consistently shown a similar association.

Evidence of a rather different kind, however, is provided by the Bristol Language Development study (Wells, 1985). This shows a remarkably close fit between the frequency with which particular sentence meanings, pronouns and auxiliary verbs occurred in the speech addressed to children and the order in which the items in these three systems emerged in the children's own utterances. Furthermore, the frequencies with which many of these items occurred at successive observations showed a sharp increase in the period immediately preceding the children's first recorded use of them. At first sight, therefore, it might appear that the adult input had the effect of determining the order in which the items were learned.

Nevertheless such a conclusion would be unwarranted, I believe. In the first place, for a fourth system investigated, that of utterance functions, the order of emergence was not significantly associated with the rank order of frequency of items in the input. On the other hand, when the effect of *complexity* was investigated – that is to say, the relative difficulty of particular items in terms of the number of semantic and syntactic distinctions involved and the level of cognitive functioning presumed to be required to cope with them – *all* of the linguistic systems examined showed a very substantial correlation between relative *complexity* and order of emergence, with the highest correlation occurring in relation to the system of utterance functions.

Complexity of what has to be learned, therefore, seems to be the main determinant of the order in which children's learning occurs, rather than the relative frequency with which the items are used in the speech that is addressed to them. Secondly, since the order in which learning occurs is remarkably similar across children, it would be necessary, if the main burden of explaining this order were to be placed on the frequency characteristics of the input, to attribute something like 'omniscience' to the adults who interacted with them. For they would not only have to know, in some sense, the order in which future learning would occur, but also be able to time the frequency with which they used particular items to anticipate the sequence of development. Although it is possible that some adults are able to do this, it seems most unlikely that all adults would be able to do so. A more plausible explanation would seem to be that the order in which learning occurs results from an interaction between learners who are pre-adapted to learn in a particular way and the relative complexity of the items in the language to which they are exposed.

The fact that, for some linguistic systems at least, there is also a close match between order of learning and input frequency can best be explained in terms of responsive behaviour by adults. As already noted, adults tend to simplify their speech in order to be comprehended by their children. They therefore tend not to use items that they find their children cannot understand. However, when an occasional use of a more difficult item to a child is responded to with apparent comprehension, they begin to use that item more frequently. And, since children soon begin to produce items which they have assimilated through comprehension of the speech of others, the emergence of an item in their own speech follows shortly after an increase in the frequency with which it is addressed to them. Thus it is the cues provided by the child that lead to changes in adult behaviour rather than vice versa.

## THE RELATIVE CONTRIBUTION OF CHILD AND ENVIRONMENT

Having surveyed a selection of the evidence available in relation to the main stages of discovering and cracking the linguistic code, we are now in a position to try to evaluate the relative contributions of the child and of the environment to the achievement of this complex task. To help us in this endeavour it may be useful to recall the initial distinction made between language as system and language as resource.

Viewed from the perspective of language as system, it is difficult, as Chomsky and others have argued, to see how the environment can have anything more than an enabling function. Speech addressed to the child provides instances of language in use, but the forming and testing of hypotheses about the relationship between language and experience and about the internal organization of the language system itself can only be carried out by the learner. Clearly, if the input were to be seriously impoverished as, for example, if it contained no instances of declarative sentences, this would certainly impede or distort the child's construction of the language system. On the other hand, above a certain fairly minimal threshold, the relative frequencies of items in the input do not, in themselves, appear strongly to influence the sequence of learning.

Furthermore, since all but the most seriously handicapped children succeed in constructing their knowledge of their native language in an almost identical sequence, despite quite wide variation in the amount and quality of the input, it seems reasonable to suppose that the sequence of learning is very largely controlled by the innate structure of the learner's mind. What this structure is, however, and whether it is specific to language or more generally involved in cognitive processing, is still far from clear.

Pressure to succeed in communicating may go some way towards explaining the motivation for the self-activated learning that takes place but, beyond that, there seems to be a built-in determination to master the system for its own sake – to regard language as 'an internal problem space per se'. It is only such a conceptualization of the child as language learner that can account for the well-known phenomenon of over-regularizations (e.g. 'goed', 'mouses', etc.) and the sorts of errors in older children's speech which have been carefully documented by Bowerman (1982), or explain their imperviousness to adult attempts to correct their speech. Models provided by others are only of use when children have reached the stage of being able to assimilate them to their own developing systems.

However, if the role of the environment in relation to the learning of language as system is restricted to the provision of primary linguistic data, such a limitation is very far from being the case when one adopts the perspective of language as resource. It is only from interaction with other people in particular situations that children can discover the appropriate ways of deploying their resources to achieve particular intentions – or indeed discover the existence of the linguistic code in the first place. Furthermore, in all these aspects of learning to be a language user, the quality of the child's interactional experience has been found to be significantly related to the rate at which learning takes place.

In the very early pre-linguistic stages, for example, Ainsworth et al. (1974) showed that mothers with the greatest responsive sensitivity to their infants during the first months were the ones with the most linguistically advanced children at the end of the first year. At the stage of early vocabulary learning in the second year, too, Nelson (1973) found that rapid acquisition of the first 50 words was associated with a maternal style that was both accepting of the child's contributions and non-directive of the inter-action.

By the end of the second year, when the child has already begun to construct a grammar, it is still the same sort of parental behaviour that is found to be associated with rapid progress. From the Bristol study (Barnes et al., 1983) comes evidence that such progress is associated with the frequency with which adults pick up and extend the meaning expressed in the child's previous utterance. Similarly, Cross (1978) found that a group of children selected because they were accelerated in their progress received a significantly greater number of sequences of adult speech which both expanded and extended their previous utterances than did a sample of children making normal progress. Even with some handicapped children, such as the deaf, it has been found that the same adult qualities of contingent responsiveness are the ones that most facilitate their linguistic development.

What these findings all suggest, then, is that what is most important in the behaviour of children's parents and other care-takers is sensitivity to their current state – their level of communicative ability and their immediate interests – and to the meaning intentions they are endeavouring to com-municate; also a desire to help and encourage them to participate in the interaction. To be a careful and sympathetic listener and to respond to the meaning intended by the speaker are qualities that characterize the be-haviour of conversationalists of any age, if they are genuinely concerned to achieve mutual understandings; such qualities are particularly important when interacting with a much less adept conversational partner.

In the very early stages of the child's development as a conversationalist, it is inevitable that the adult must take the major responsibility for managing the interaction but as Bruner (1981) remarks in his discussion of the 'Language Assistance System' (LAS):

> The first thing to note about the adult role in this system is the adult's willingness to share or even hand over control to the child once he has learned to fulfil the conditions on speech. However obvious this may seem, it is a *sine qua non* of the adult's role in the system. (p. 45)

Handing over control and being prepared to negotiate meanings and purposes are the characteristics that we have also noticed among facilitating adults in the Bristol data. The following example, in which three and a half-year-old Jonathan is helping his mother by polishing his wardrobe demonstrates this.

J:   Do you think this is lovely?
M:   I think it's a bit smeary
J:   Why do you think it's bit smeary?
M:   Because you put far too much polish on * * (inaudible)
M:   Right,
     Now you can put the things back on there (on the dresser)
     And I'll put the carpet-sweeper over the room
J:   Well why can't I put the carpet-sweeper over the room?
M:   Because that's my job OK?
J:   What is my job?
M:   You've done your job
     You've polished the furniture
     [a little later]
J:   It doesn't matter if that polish goes in your eyes does it?
M:   Oh it does yes
     It makes them sting
J:     * (inaudible)
M:   It makes them sting very badly
J:   Well just now some of that polish waved in my eye
M:   Did it?
J:   Yes
M:   Do they sting? (i.e. your eyes)
     Or did it miss?
     Don't rub them with the duster darling (v)
     The duster's all dirty
J:   Well how can that get out Mummy? (referring to polish)
M:   Why don't you go and wipe it with the flannel in the bathroom
     [J goes to bathroom]
J:   No I think I'll get it out with the towel
     Mummy I just have to see if I can get it out with this towel.
M:   All right.

It would seem, therefore, that adults like Jonathan's mother are intuitively aware that the major responsibility for actually mastering the resource of language rests with the child rather than with themselves and that their role is essentially one of sustaining and encouraging the child's self-activated learning.

## LANGUAGE AND LEARNING IN LATER CHILDHOOD

The emphasis so far has been on learning language rather than on learning through language. However, in practice, the two are to a very considerable extent co-extensive. Just as children learn the language system through experience of using it as a resource, so in increasing their control of the resources of language they also increase their understanding of the experiences that are encoded by those resources. The speech addressed to them not only provides evidence about the way in which the language system works but also about the world to which the system refers.

The significance of this parallelism is far-reaching for it implies that, in so far as the child's learning takes place through linguistic interaction with more mature members of his or her culture, the responsibility for what is learned should be shared between learner and teacher in the same kind of way that it was in the early stages of language acquisition: the child expressing an interest in some object or event and the adult sharing that interest and helping the child to take it further.

To a considerable extent this is what happens in the pre-school years at home, particularly for the children who make the most rapid progress. However, even in such homes, sustained discussion of a single topic is relatively rare and there is very little adult speech that looks like deliberate instruction. Most of the talk arises out of ongoing activity and takes on its significance from the purposes of those involved; at home, learning, like talking, is for the most part instrumental to the task in hand. As the example above shows, some of the richest opportunities for talking and learning occur when child and adult are engaged in collaborative activity, such as carrying out household tasks, like cooking or cleaning.

However, the most enriching experience of all for many children is probably the open-ended exploratory talk that arises from the reading of stories. Several investigators have noted how much more complex, semantically and syntactically, is the language that occurs in this context. It also has a particularly important contribution to make to the child's imaginative development. Furthermore, the frequency with which children are read to has been found to be a powerful predictor of later success at school.

The learning that takes place on such occasions is of particular significance, for not only does the discussion provide an opportunity for children to relate the characters and events of the imaginary world to their own first-hand experience, but it also introduces them to the potential that language has, particularly in the written mode, to create alternative 'possible worlds' through words. As Donaldson (1978) emphasizes, in order to meet the demands of formal education, the child needs to learn to disembed his or her thinking from the context of immediate activity and to operate upon experience, both real and hypothetical, through the medium of words alone. Stories, and the talk that arises from them, provide an important introduction to this intellectually powerful function of language.

Observation of children in their homes, then, shows that, as with the initial learning of language, the motivation to learn *through* language comes from within, as they actively seek to gain control of their environment and to make sense of their experience. Once the child can use his or her linguistic resources to operate on that experience, though, the contribution of other people increases enormously in importance. For it is through the power of language to symbolize 'possible worlds' that have not yet been directly experienced, that parents and, later, teachers can enable children to encounter new knowledge and skills and to make them their own.

In school, where classes consist of 30 or more children, the task is not an easy one. A teacher has to ensure that all children acquire the skills of literacy and numeracy and extend their knowledge in the areas prescribed by the curriculum, whilst at the same time respecting the sense-making strategies that each child has already developed and recognizing the individuality of the internal model of the world that each child has already constructed and the interests he or she has developed. As in learning to talk, however, the child will be helped most effectively by teacher strategies of guidance and contingent responsiveness – listening attentively in order to understand the child's meaning and then seeking to extend and develop it. This view of the teacher as essentially a facilitator of learning was strongly emphasized by Vygotsky, 50 years ago, in his discussion of the 'zone of proximal development'. As he put it, 'what the child can do today in cooperation, tomorrow he will be able to do alone' (trans. Sutton, 1977). The crucial word in that statement is 'cooperation'. A fuller understanding of the nature of linguistic interaction, whether at home or in the classroom, is leading us to recognize that, to be most effective, the relationship between teacher and learner must, at every stage of development, be collaborative. Teaching, thus seen, is not a didactic transmission of pre-formulated knowledge, but an attempt to negotiate shared meanings and understandings.

# TOPICS FOR DISCUSSION

1. 'Cracking the code may be the most difficult part of the total process (of language acquisition), but before the child can embark on that task he or she first has to discover that there is a code to be cracked.' Discuss the opposing views as to how children do this.

2. Discuss the relative contribution of 'child' and 'environment' in the acquisition of language from the perspective of (a) language as a system, and (b) language as a resource.

3. 'What is most important in the behaviour of children's parents and other care-takers is sensitivity to their current state – their level of communicative ability and their immediate interests – and to the meaning intentions they are endeavouring to communicate; also a desire to help and encourage them to participate in the interaction.' Discuss this statement with reference to the author's comment that 'models provided by others are only of use when children have reached the stage of being able to assimilate them to their own developing systems'.

# SUGGESTIONS FOR FURTHER READING

1. Katz, L.G. (1985) 'Fostering communicative competence in young children', in Clark, M.M. (ed.) *Helping Communication in Early Education. Educational Review*, chap. 7, pp. 60–8.

   Katz's valuable chapter addresses itself to the question of which educational practices facilitate or inhibit the development of communicative competence in young children, and as a corollary, how can practitioners acquire and strengthen facilitative practices or weaken inhibiting ones? The author suggests that contemporary research on the acquisition of language postulates at least four principles on which teachers might base the selection of educational practices. The deceptively simple first principle, that the development of communicative competence is facilitated by interaction, reminds us 'that mere exposure to language is not sufficient for children to acquire communicative competence . . . and stimulates us to examine what kinds of interactions might be most facilitating on the one hand, or inhibiting on the other' (p. 60). The second principle, which Katz suggests qualifies the first, is that interaction requires content, since communication cannot occur in a vacuum. This must lead us, she maintains, to consider carefully the content of interaction in early childhood settings – which leads to the third principle, that interaction is greatly facilitated 'when the content is ecologically valid to the participants' in the sense that it is either embedded in the context or is rich in associations for the children with respect to their own interests, perceptions and backgrounds. The fourth principle 'is that interpersonal as well as communicative competence is facilitated when the children experience others' responses to them as contingent upon their own', so that conversation, in this sense, 'which can be defined as strings of verbal responses in which each turn-taker's response is contingent upon the preceding one, is thus a model or a metaphor for the kinds of interactions required for the development of social and communicative competence' (p. 61).

   On the basis of the four principles outlined above, the author examines the two broad questions posed at the beginning of the chapter and describes, in a very practical way, those activities which facilitate communicative skills and, conversely, those practices which are likely to inhibit the growth of linguistic competence in the young child. She discusses also how practice can be improved, maintaining that efforts to change practice can be examined by asking what causes teachers to do what they do. This approach, she claims, seeks to derive theories of practice as opposed to the more usual approach which seeks to translate theory into practice.

2. Payne, G. (1985) 'Planning activities that will provide appropriate contexts to promote adult–child and child–child communications in the nursery unit', in Clark, M.M. (ed.) *Helping Communication in Early Education. Educational Review*, chap. 11, pp. 191–203.

The data used in Payne's study were collected as part of the research carried out by Clark, M.M., Barr, J.E. and Dewhirst, W. (1985) *Early Education of Children with Communication Problems: Particularly Those from Ethnic Minorities. Educational Review* Offset publication No. 3, Faculty of Education, University of Birmingham.

The research is addressed specifically to one aspect of the development of communication with and between young children in nursery settings. Payne's paper focuses on the problem of organizing and planning activities necessary to make full use of the invariably limited time available for oral communication. She considers the nursery experience first of all from the perspective of the child, discussing its implications for practice within the nursery setting. Further issues are considered with respect to the initial and in-service education and training of staff who work with young children. The research project followed a group of children from their nursery situations into their infant schools. Data were collected in four nursery schools in disadvantaged areas in the West Midlands. Each child's language (a sample of 10 boys and 10 girls from a variety of different ethnic backgrounds) was sampled in the free-play sessions in the nursery units, using a radio microphone. In addition an observer made relevant context notes (the type of activity taking place, the number of participants and whether they were adults or children, etc.). Transcripts were analysed in terms of the cognitive complexity of the language used and in terms of the activities that were represented. Payne comments: 'In order to meet the needs of the children with the wide range of ability (identified in this study), it is necessary to provide appropriate activities that will "stretch" the more able as well as help the less able. More able children need to be given opportunities to practise and develop their skills, communicating at all levels of cognitive complexity. They need opportunities to use language for reasoning, in arguing and predicting and to develop abstract concepts. Children with a more limited grasp of language also need opportunities to initiate and respond in dialogue so that they can develop the strategies that are needed to communicate meaning to others' (p. 43). The author describes those activities in the free-play sessions in the nurseries which seemed to be more effective than others in promoting conversation at different levels. She discusses also ways of encouraging the development of language skills and how to plan for language development.

See also Clark, M.M. (ed.) (1983) *Special Education Needs and Children Under Five. Educational Review* Occasional Publication No. 9, University of Birmingham, and Robson, B. (1983) 'Encouraging dialogue in pre-school units: the role of the pink pamfer'. *Educational Review*, **35**, 2, 141–8.

3. Sutton, W. (1985) 'Some factors in pre-school children of relevance to learning to

read', in Clark, M.M. (ed.) *New Directions in the Study of Reading*. London, Falmer Press.

Recent research on how children learn to read has demonstrated the importance of the child's ability to understand and to reason about the communicative functions of reading and writing. This ability, for some children, develops early – children who read before school, identified as 'early' or 'natural' readers. Sutton asserts that 'when considering ways in which reception class teachers can best approach the early stages of the teaching of reading, it is worth summarizing the personal qualities, abilities and environmental factors which are currently considered to be relevant to the process of learning to read (that is, those most often identified in studies of early, or "natural" readers' (p. 54). This very useful paper offers:

(a) a summary of personal qualities observed in studies of early readers;
(b) a summary of skills and abilities;
(c) a summary of environmental and social factors.

In the second part of her paper, Sutton considers the problem of 'whether it is best to put all children on to the same formal pre-reading and reading programme as soon as they start school, or whether there may be a range of relevant observations and assessments, albeit producing highly individual results, which should be used to determine *each child's* starting point, in terms of, for example, extending experience, involving parents and stimulating interest by the selection of subject matter' (p. 57). The author proposes a number of tests, questions and interview techniques which sample the level of those factors amenable to such quantification and which were used in her research with a group of young children (who had received no formal reading instruction and had not yet begun to read). Of particular interest is the technique of 'probe analysis' which Sutton describes in detail. See Lewis, G. (1983) 'Children's perception of dynamics in narrative prose'. *Midland Association for Linguistics Studies Journal*, **8**, 31–46.

Reading 8

# THE RELATIONSHIPS OF PROBLEM CHILDREN IN NURSERY SCHOOLS

## *M. Manning and J. Herrmann*

### A COMPARISON OF DIFFICULT AND WELL-ADJUSTED CHILDREN

The behaviour of a problem child often seems strangely unadaptive; he seems to be acting against his own interests as well as those of others. Yet it is likely that his behaviour makes some sense in its own terms. Even behaviour

Manning, M. and Herrmann, J. (1981) 'The relationships of problem children in nursery schools', in Duck, S. and Gilmour, R. (eds) *Personal Relationships 3: Personal Relationships in Disorder*. London, Academic Press, chap. 7, pp. 143–67.

which may be considered pathological, destructive and defeating its own ends, is likely to have its roots in forces and goals which are, in other circumstances, adaptive. To assess this, it is necessary to observe all the behaviour of a child and consider its implications in terms of goals and needs. Both Montagner (1978) and Manning et al. (1978) have considered different styles of behaviour in nursery school children; Roper and Hinde (1978) have analysed different types of social interaction; and Wolkind and Everett (1974) have considered clusters of behavioural characteristics and picked out two which suggest disturbance. The following account will refer to all these works as well as to recent unpublished observations directly comparing disturbed (Herrmann, 1978) or difficult (Manning and Sluckin, 1979, 1980) children with those well adjusted to the nursery.

It is not to be expected that all difficult children will be the same and the assortment of characteristics discussed above does not necessarily apply to each individual child. A number of different styles of behaviour have been described both by Montagner and by Manning, and among these descriptions there seems to be agreement upon three distinct styles.

The first is the *well-adjusted style.* Montagner calls children showing this profile 'leaders' or 'dominated but resembling leaders' according to their degree of self-assertion. Montagner stresses the non-verbal appeasement, soliciting, bonding acts shown by these children; offering, inclining the head, kissing, taking by the hand. Manning stresses their friendliness, their love of conversation and their limited employment of aggression mainly in disputes over specific problems (i.e. with evident purpose). Teachers also stress their cooperativeness, their willingness to talk, and their happiness in the nursery.

The second style may be called the *aggressive style.* Here there are few bonding acts (Montagner), much less friendly talk (Manning), and a tendency for spontaneous and unexpected aggression which may appear to be unrelated to the situation. Montagner distinguishes two types of child employing this style, the dominant aggressive and the dominated aggressive. Manning also separates two groups of teasers according to their relative assertiveness. The dominant aggressives are the children most commonly picked as problem children in nursery schools. They present management problems, frequently play rough games, seek to dominate others and use aggression to do so. They also tend to be defiant and may avoid teachers. Wolkind's cluster of 'management problems, temper tantrums, poor peer relationships, fears, worrying, bedwetting' would seem to fit here too.

The third style may be called the *dependent style.* Montagner calls it the timid dominated style and he describes such a child as dependent, often soliciting teachers, normally friendly, with some bonding acts but prone to unexpected outbreaks of violence. The behaviour is similar to that of Manning's 'games specialist' – timid and 'anxious to please', but prone to wild, uncontrolled behaviour in the more permissive atmosphere of a game. Wolkind's cluster of 'dependency, separation anxiety, fears, habits, worrying, bedwetting' may also be related. Teachers often complain that such children are demanding and want everything done for them.

Thus there appear to be two fairly distinct ways of being difficult in a nursery school and they will be considered separately here because these different styles affect relationships in different ways. It is likely that the constraints of the nursery situation make members of each group appear more similar than they are. However, Montagner (1978) stresses that many of the behavioural characteristics which he describes are recognizable from a very early age and he claims that he can distinguish potential leaders and potential dominant aggressives at 18–20 months. Hence they may not be styles of behaviour acquired at nursery school, but originate perhaps from very early relationships. However it may not be the styles themselves which are so persistent, but the needs or distortions which create them.

## Friends, games and interactions

It has already been stated that, in the view of teachers, difficult children fail to make many friends and do not adequately sample the resources of the nursery whereas, among well-adjusted children, type of play and friendship groupings tend to be linked. Vivienne Atkinson (1981) has shown that, at least in one nursery, those children who spend a great deal of time in fantasy play, and who develop elaborate fantasy games, tend to form tight, rather exclusive, groups of friends which may be quite large. Here the relationships are often complex but continuing and quite stable, the children tending to stay together even outside the fantasy situations, sitting together for snacks and so on. The children who like to spend more time doing quieter, more personal, constructive activities (e.g. puzzles, paintings, etc.) form looser groups and are more prepared to be friends with anyone. They like to talk about their activities and share their interests.

Difficult children, where games are concerned, tend to fall into two categories. Either they play wild, rough games most of the time, or they tend mainly to flit around, or to look on and sometimes to play wild games. In general, the aggressive type of child belongs to the first category and the dependent child to the second. The noisy rough games developed by both types are usually fantasy games of adventure, excitement and power although dependent children sometimes enjoy quieter fantasies too (in role-games as doctors, postmen or families in the Wendy house). In aggressive fantasies the children are Tarzans or Batmen or Daleks or witches with magic powers and they attack almost everyone, even bystanders or children engaged in other pursuits who have no part in their game. Usually aggressive children lead and dominate such games but dependent children, when they take part, are sometimes unexpectedly violent. Unlike similar games of well-adjusted children, these games are loosely organized and the relationships between the participants are unstable. Quarrels and temporary rejections are common. The aggressive children sometimes seem quite popular, for often they are inventive and their games are exciting even if they do not develop. Most children enjoy chasing, play fighting and monsters and they are attracted to them; indeed these emotionally charged fantasies seem to play an important part in normal development. However, when difficult children are involved, the games may become too frightening or too violent.

The dependent children appear often to be *trying* to play with other children but are not prepared to take the initiative themselves. They hover on the edge of a group, waiting to be invited, they come and stand silently at a sand-tray gazing, or more often glaring at the children playing together there. Sometimes they harass such groups, snatching their toys or challenging them, for example, by bringing up an opposing car or boat. One boy would submit to almost anything to get himself into a game with others: he would allow himself to be dragged along the floor, tied up or generally knocked around. These children are in general unpopular; usually they have little of interest to contribute to a game, for it seems enough for them simply to have got into one. Occasionally, however, they develop rather possessive relationships, usually with one other child. In such cases the difficult child may dominate the fantasies once they have started and it is typical that he or she will be reluctant to let the friend either go away or change the direction of the game. You may see such a child literally tugging another back into the Wendy house or hospital which the latter is trying to leave; or you may see her pursuing another pleading, 'You said we were friends, you said we'd be princesses and dress up together and get married'. If finally rejected such a child is likely to perform malicious acts of revenge. However, the pair 'make up' eventually. Clearly, there is some attraction between them although, again, the relationship is unstable. It is usually apparent that the difficult child is pursuing and seeking out the other, who occasionally tolerates, occasionally rejects.

One important similarity between these two types of child (and a difference perhaps of fundamental importance between them and well-adjusted children) lies in the apparent self-centredness of the way in which they play fantasy games, for often there are no roles for others. A well-adjusted child clearly wants to include others in his game. He will say 'I'll be the driver and you can be the guard' or he will indicate sharing by saying 'We'll make this our space ship, shall we?' A difficult child is more likely to say 'I'll be Tarzan' with no concern about his friends. Even when he develops quite elaborate fantasies, this tendency remains. One girl said, 'Let's pretend I am Father Christmas and I come up on a sleigh with lots of parcels and climb down the chimney'. In addition he or she is likely to make unacceptable rules concerning the activities of others. Simon perpetually cried, as others approached him, 'You can't come here. You're dead. I shot you' – although he himself had been repeatedly 'shot'. Colin, in a football game, organized others into specified places and then proceeded to kick the ball to and fro with his special friend. When others ran forward to intercept, he declared 'No, no you mustn't come up and try to get the ball. Go back to your place'.

Neil, a more well-adjusted child, by contrast, although doing a lot of ordering in an adventure game with carts was nevertheless assigning roles and jobs to others so that they felt part of the game. Thus Neil: 'No you run. You come in Stuart, give me your coat. Craig, we're the ones to keep the coats'. Because there are more roles in them, a well-adjusted child's games tend to develop because each participant contributes ideas. A train may have a driver, a guard, a ticket collector as well as passengers and each may suggest some happening on the journey. A difficult child will often oppose innovations, except those suggested by himself.

These self-centred tendencies in difficult children are of some interest since Chandler (1972, 1973) has demonstrated a link between poor role-taking skills and antisocial and delinquent behaviour in older children. However, it cannot be assumed that difficult nursery school children are necessarily 'egocentric' in Piagetian terms, i.e. that they are incapable of taking another's point of view. On occasions they show that they can do this perfectly well, as they also show they want and need to cooperate and be friendly with others. It seems that, for much of the time, other needs override these tendencies.

Observations regarding the tendency to interact at all and motivations underlying this, seem to support the idea of 'other needs'. Most workers investigating social participation have viewed it on a single scale: self-play, parallel play through to varying degrees of social participation in more elaborate games. There is a clear tendency, as would be expected, for social participation to increase with age, both in amount and complexity (Parten, 1932; Smith, 1973). However Roper and Hinde (1978) find that other dimensions are involved and that some children who play freely in groups, also play a lot alone. They also show that playing alone is not always associated with looking-on or being unoccupied. They suggest that to be playing alone does not necessarily imply that a child is lacking in sociability and they predict perhaps a more confident quality about the self-play of those who can also play in groups.

These conclusions are supported by other observational work which suggests that some of the other relevant dimensions concern the social adjustment of the child and his confidence in his ability to establish satisfactory relationships. The child who is equally happy at almost any 'stage' of social participation, seems to be the well-adjusted child who has no apparent problems about establishing easy and friendly relationships. Such children will sometimes be seen to be completely absorbed in a model or a painting, not to be distracted even by a fight proceeding close by. Alternatively they may be seen to be playing in parallel, at the sand or water, usually then making interesting comments about their own or others' activity. Yet on other occasions they will show themselves well able to participate in quite complex games.

On the other hand, difficult children come, in general, rather lower on the social participation scale (they rarely achieve complex integrated relationships) although their total amount of self-play may be variable. Most aggressive children play rather little alone, although they may occasionally be deserted by all their companions. Herrmann (1978), comparing two disturbed children with five normal ones, found that her disturbed boys were distinguished from other children in that they spent more of their time in a group and played very little alone. The figures are:

| % time in | Disturbed children | | Normal children |
|---|---|---|---|
| Group play | 68 | 41 | 41,29,28,21,17 |
| Alone | 20 | 21 | 22,30,36,43,68 |

Dependent children may play quite often alone but, with them, this tendency is highly associated with hovering and looking on. This is not the case for most well-adjusted children.

Moreover the self-play of difficult children, both aggressive and dependent, tends to be different from that of well-adjusted children in that long periods of interested, concentrated self-play are rarely seen. Aggressive children may concentrate for a short time on a painting, or perhaps on a sword or on a frightening mask for later display. More often, when alone, they will be seen to be displaying; perhaps hammering very loudly at the woodwork bench, painting with exaggerated flourishes of the paintbrush, dropping objects with a great splash into the water, shouting across the room to a friend or running across to tease (as described below). Dependent children will sometimes watch rather than try to attract attention, but they too will not be attending very closely to their own activities. One boy was often to be seen at the sand, letting sand trickle through his fingers (rather than do anything else with it) meanwhile looking longingly at an interacting group nearby. Herrmann (1978) found that her two disturbed children interacted more than normal children in most situations but especially in those where interactions are not so appropriate or expected (they came first and second in rank orders for time spent interacting in painting, manipulative play and transitional periods). In quiet activities, looking at books, playing with puzzles, making models or simply moving from one activity to another, normal children do not always seek to communicate but difficult children do. It is as if they are never really content not to be interacting. Normal children seem already to have developed a balance between self-sufficient and social play before nursery school age. Difficult children have not and their constant striving for social interaction suggests needs and anxieties which can only be satisfied therein.

## Quality of interactions and relationships with peers

It is revealing also to look at the quality of interactions and types of relationship achieved by difficult children. Herrmann (1978) found that her two disturbed children ranked fifth and seventh (out of seven) for the number of different peers with whom they were involved in friendly interactions although they came first and second as regards those interacted with in total. The figures are:

*No. of different peers interacted with per unit of observation time (x 100)*

|  | Disturbed children | Normal children |
|---|---|---|
| All peers per total time | 57,44 | 32,29,6,5,5 |
| Friendly peers per friendly interaction time | 9,19 | 12,20,22,25,30 |
| Dispute peers per dispute interaction time | 32,27 | 7,18,26,29,36 |

In other words, as described earlier, they are extremely interested in interacting but they can develop friendly relationships with only a few of their peers, although they dispute with many more. These relationships are sometimes intense but usually unstable. With others, and often with their friends too, their interactions are different in nature from those of well-adjusted children. Manning and Sluckin are investigating these differences further.

From what has already been said it is apparent that while the interactions of well-adjusted children seem to be concerned mainly with communicating, sharing and cooperating, those of difficult children only sometimes appear to have this goal; more often they are concerned with quite different, self-centred interests. This is not easily revealed by consideration of the form or even the function of speech and acts in isolation. It is necessary to assess their meaning in the context in which they occur.

Manning and Sluckin (1979, 1980) have developed categories which attempt to do this although in some cases they have to be defined in terms of the manner in which the relevant acts are normally received. Five main categories distinguish acts which are *friendly* (communicating, sharing, helping); *organizing* (attempting to make a child modify his immediate behaviour); *contrary* (in opposition to what is being done or is proposed); *annoying* (hurtful or against the interests of another child); or *submissive* (giving way against one's own interests).

Some of these categories are subdivided, especially *friendly*, which constitutes the major part of most children's speech, even the difficult ones. Friendly acts can be of very different natures and one of the most important subcategories is 'friendly adaptive', which indicates an appreciation of and concern for the interests of other children (by suggesting shared interests, offering roles or help or comfort, approving another's appearance or activities). This can be distinguished from, for example, friendly boasting; challenging ('I bet you can't do that'); claiming ('I'm the driver'); attention-seeking ('Watch this', 'See what I can do'); self- (comments about one's own appearance or activity) or defining relationships ('You're my friend'). In *organizing*, adaptive, positive, negative, demanding and physical sub-categories are similarly distinguished. A further qualification is that all utterances which contain additional material to make them more persuasive or interesting are marked by a (+) sign.

Although the results of this study are not yet complete, it is apparent that difficult children tend to show more contrary and annoying and less adaptive and (+) behaviour than well-adjusted children. Aggressive children score highly on attention-seeking, boasting, claiming and challenging among friendly acts and on negative, demanding and physical types of organizing. They seek to demonstrate their prowess, to compete, to control and to dominate. Dependent children often score highly on friendly claiming, and on defining relationships and on demanding types of organizing. They seek to be assured of friendship, attention, care, help and privilege. Thus while well-adjusted children usually enjoy developing cooperative interactions and treat all others as friends and partners in this (they seem able to take another's point of view from the start), difficult children more often appear to pursue other aims, which are centred on themselves and which involve the manipulatic ι of others in ways which they may well resent. Hence difficult children cannot treat their peers as equals, nor closely consider their point of view and they may well come to regard others as hostile. In games too, the relatively few (+)s in their records suggest that they are not concerned with attracting interest or developing the game. They are not in games for the games' sake as are the well-adjusted children.

This study also revealed a further feature of a difficult child's behaviour which has been commented upon by many observers. This concerns its unexpected and often inappropriate qualities when considered from the point of view of the situation and the behaviour of the other children. As already described, Montagner (1978) talks of hostility arising for no obvious reason and of gratuitous violence in his aggressives; he also talks of unexpected aggression in his timid-dominateds (dependents). Manning sees the aggressives as teasers showing 'out-of-the-blue' hostility, and the dependents as practising 'games hostility' mainly in a game context (Manning et al., 1978). In the former case it is the act itself which is unexpected. Teasing does not spring from a dispute or disagreement, often it seems like a sudden inspiration occurring to the child. He or she may dart from a solitary painting to tease another at the woodwork bench, splashing him with paint or tipping out his box of nails. Another may grab a toy in passing and flaunt it or hurl it to the ground. Herrmann also found that her two disturbed boys (unlike others) tended to be aggressive when alone or moving from place to place; their aggression was unpredictable and not related to any particular activity. Games hostility as practised by dependent children is unexpected often in its violence and roughness. Thus in a relatively friendly game of chasing between two loosely organized groups, one child may suddenly pounce on another, grip him round the neck and bang his head on the ground. Another may be unnecessarily intimidating in a game of monsters or robbers.

Bossy, organizing behaviour is likewise sometimes inappropriate both in its occurrence and in the intensity with which it is pursued. Thus Stephen outside, suddenly and for no apparent reason, insisted that Darren should put down the hood of his anorak and he hit him when he made a mild protest. The conversation went like this. 'Darren put your hood down.' 'No, I don't want to. It keeps me warm.' 'It's not raining or something.' Stephen then hits Darren. Montagner remarks that, in his 'leaders', behaviour is usually related to the situation in an appropriate way. Stephen's behaviour is not. It suggests that Stephen is pushed by some motive within himself that does not allow him to accept Darren's reasons.

This does not mean that incidents such as these bear no relationship to a past happening. Manning has shown that teasing in particular, is, in some children (usually aggressives), significantly related to past happenings, reprimands or organizing by teachers, opposition or organizing by peers. But the incidents are not simply reactions, often they occur sometime after the event, when the connection is sometimes made explicit by remarks such as 'You shouldn't have chucked me out of your game then'. Moreover it is not always just the original offender who is persecuted. It is as if these happenings merely activate already existing grievances. The same conclusion may be drawn from observations that difficult children have 'good' and 'bad' days and that often good days with peers are also good days with adults, as if there is a global effect.

A final facet of unexpectedness in aggression concerns the nature of attacks in rough and tumble games. This has been noted by both Manning and Montagner. Well-adjusted children enjoy rough and tumble play just as much as do difficult children, but it is apparent that well-adjusteds tend to display or challenge their adversary before an attack as if they desire the fight to be on equal terms. The difficult children, particularly the aggressive ones, will more often launch completely unexpected attacks, grappling or pulling from behind, or knocking to the ground without warning. Montagner (1978) describes how his dominant-aggressive children are not at all responsive to their peers; when they make a threat they do not wait for the victim's reply but pass straight to aggression.

These two descriptions then agree in contrasting the fights of difficult children with those of more normal children, where rituals and rules are deployed to communicate the need for cooperation and to limit the extent and damage of the fight. They are equivalent to those described by Sluckin (1981) in primary school boys and by Marsh et al. (1978) for adolescents on football terraces. It is difficult to escape the impression that these different types of children are in it for different reasons. To the well-adjusted children it is an opportunity to enjoy physical competitiveness and balanced trials of strength, to the difficult children it may represent new opportunities for power, control and perhaps revenge. Many of them get carried away by the exciting, chaotic and apparently permissive atmosphere of a fight so as to become virtually 'out of control'.

## Emotionalism

A marked feature of difficult children's behaviour concerns the emotionalism which they betray especially when opposed or frustrated. Well-adjusted children often cope with such occurrences with good humour and often much resourcefulness. Kate, returning after a diversion, to join her friend at the swing, found that the friend had been displaced by a much bigger girl. She quickly devised a new and more exciting game close by – which both children enjoyed immensely. Jennifer, whose friend did not immediately respond to her invitation to join in her 'building', persistently returned with a new fantasy until at last she attracted him. At first she said, 'Come on here. In the blue, blue car'. Then it was, 'I've got tickets on the bus'. Finally, she said, 'Yea, this is a house, eh? Now I'm going to cook the dinner'. This worked and her friend came in and said, 'Brrrr. I'm doing the washing machine'. And Graham, whose friend was trying to force him to push a cart (with him in it) that was too heavy, finally said: 'Well, I guess we're both tired. We'll have a rest'. His friend liked this idea and called the teacher. 'You know, Miss . . . we're window cleaners and we're having a rest'. Soon he helped carry the ladder.

These are all situations which would be likely to anger or distress difficult children, being pushed out of a favoured place, having one's invitation ignored, being ordered about. However, different types of difficult children tend to be angered at different circumstances and this seems to be an area in which one can most easily distinguish them. In general, aggressive, outgoing types seem most upset when their authority or leadership or general dominance is challenged. One became furious when a rival gang seized the football in a game that he was organizing; another stamped angrily out of a kicking game because his partner criticized his style of kicking and a third set up an intimidation episode to 'punish' a rival who claimed to have won in a race. First the claim was hotly denied, 'What do you mean you won? Don't you be so silly. You had to go over the bar, right?' (This was the first time the bar had been mentioned.) Then our boy grabbed his rival, glared at him and said, 'Don't just stand there and look at me. Tell me a question or I'll kill you'.

By contrast, the dependent children are more often upset when their friends leave them or when they feel no one will play with them. Their behaviour on such occasions has already been described. If active attempts to recall a companion fail, or sometimes after only minimal attempts, they may go to the teacher and say 'So and so won't play with me' or they will sit and sulk or complain they don't know what to do. It is often after such withdrawals that harassment occurs. Alternatively, they may obtain some favour, a sweet or a cake from the teacher or a friend and display it to those by whom they feel rejected.

Dependent children also tend to become angry with teachers if help, praise or assistance is not offered when they feel it is needed. Usually they seem to expect this of adults but not of their peers. Thus one girl was involved in prolonged, complicated attempts to put her coat on in the cloakroom. She laid it on the table, turned her back and tried to wriggle her way into it. She had little success but with her friends she joked about it with only an occasional 'Oh, I can't do this', half-serious complaint. But when a teacher appeared on the scene her behaviour changed. She became sullen and angry and thrust her coat at the teacher as if in protest that she hadn't received attention earlier. From the teacher's remark, 'Can't you do your coat? Are you getting cross about it again?' it would seem that such behaviour was not uncommon. Such children may also become quite hysterical if hurt even in a minor way. Again the appeal is to the teacher and if no attention is received the crying becomes increasingly angry and 'outraged'.

## Relationships with adults

Since nursery school teachers see difficult children as those who present management problems, the nature of the relationship of these children with their teachers is bound to be affected by this, and in many cases the most dominant aspect of that relationship is controlling. In a pilot study, Manning, investigating eight difficult children in the same nursery, found the following proportions of organizing acts out of the totals directed by any teacher to the child: 21, 33, 35, 48, 52, 52, 55 and 57 per cent. In a later study, when it had been suggested that teachers should show more friendly behaviour to difficult children, these proportions were reduced but they were still significantly higher than those for well-adjusted children, i.e.

Difficult children        14, 20, 22, 23, 26, 27, 33, 49        per cent;
Well-adjusted children 3, 8, 8, 14, 17, 19, 21, 35        per cent.

This is not always the teacher's fault. Some try very hard to have friendly conversations with difficult children but many of the latter do not respond well and often seek to avoid the teacher's company. This is especially true of aggressive children who tend also to be non-compliant, uncooperative and sometimes defiant. Herrmann (1978) observed the relationship between her subjects and their mothers when the latter spent some time in the nursery. She found that one of her disturbed children (A) headed the rank order for non-compliance to his mother's order. The other (E) headed the rank for disconfirmation (disregarding or contradicting the intentions of the mother) while (A) came third. Manning's observations also suggest that sometimes such children do not answer when teachers address a friendly remark to them. This is especially so when teachers try to 'teach' them by setting up discussions about things of general interest. Then they will 'dry up', refuse to answer or walk away.

Many of the actions of aggressive children relative to the teacher suggests a determination, sometimes explicit, not to be 'bossed around'. It has already been noted how aggressive or disruptive behaviour may follow upon teacher's reprimands or organizing. On other occasions such children may be openly defiant. An order to stop some exciting but disruptive behaviour, such as running wildly round the nursery or throwing sand, may be blandly ignored, as may an instruction to do some unwelcome act such as removing a coat. One boy even ran into the Wendy house and put his coat on again (in hiding) after the teacher had removed it for him.

In some moods difficult children may ignore any lead from a teacher however friendly. On one occasion, a teacher approached a group of boys who had been throwing stones down a drain. She talked to them about drains, how they worked and what happened if they were blocked. She did it well and most of the children were interested and asked questions, but the ring-leader spent his time on the outskirts of the group collecting more stones and awaiting the opportunity to resume his throwing.

Sometimes these acts seem to be personal affairs between the child and the teacher but sometimes there seems to be an attempt to get applause from onlookers. One boy, asked to carry a tape-recorder carefully and not switch it on, immediately operated the on-button, laughed excitedly and looked around for approval. In general, defiance of the teacher occurs very commonly in a situation where compliance means humiliation or loss of face. When, for example, a child is asked to apologize, for an act of teasing he or she may be very persistent and stubborn in refusal. If one interprets teasing as an attempt at 'one-upmanship' in the first place, the requirement to apologize may well be doubly humiliating.

For dependent children the situation may be different. It has been described how these children are demanding of teachers and how they become angry if the demands are not met. They also seek the company of teachers and are outwardly very affectionate and chatty, but one often sees contrary behaviour, which is nevertheless hidden under a cloak of friendliness. One girl played a lengthy 'game' of this sort with a teacher who was trying to persuade her to finish her painting so as to give others a turn at the easel. She kept coming away, washing her hands at length, then dirtying them again but always insisting that her picture was not yet finished. Throughout she was very friendly but adamant. Her behaviour was very reminiscent of that of an eight-year-old boy observed with his mother by Manning et al. (1978). The mother, taking part in a structured play session, was trying to get the boy to play a card game before the skittles game which he preferred. He ignored her reasons and persuasions and started the skittles game regardless. However, he maintained a friendly atmosphere throughout and kept reporting his score and prowess with such enthusiasm that the mother was eventually won over.

These children also seem to indulge in a number of acts which can be contrasted as mischievous, playful and slightly cheeky but not really difficult or defiant. A child may continue to stir a bowl or blow a trumpet after everyone has been told to stop, another may call a teacher by a playful name, tug or pull at her clothes or even slap her bottom. Yet all is done with a smile and in a friendly way as if no manner of offence is intended. This behaviour is often interpreted as 'limit testing', seeing how far one can go before being checked. It is assumed that this is part of some rule-making or ordering process of the child who will be happier once the limits are determined. While this may be true for well-adjusted children, nevertheless the children who tend to do this sort of thing most are always difficult or disturbed (not well adjusted) and it seems possible that they are trying to express a hostility that they feel towards adults but which they dare not show openly. It is not therefore certain that they will be happier if checked.

## Summary

The relationships of difficult children, both with peers and with adults, are often poor in just those elements which seem to be the essence of the relationships of well-adjusted children. What is missing is the delight in sharing experiences, in doing things together, in learning about and adapting to another's point of view. Occasionally these qualities appear, they are not totally missing, but when they do it is usually in special circumstances, perhaps in one-to-one relationships with one particular person. More often they are overlain with behaviour which seems to have quite different intentions. Aggressives aim to display power, superiority and dominance; dependents want to attract interest, friendship and care. In both cases the children seem to be pursuing self-centred goals and take no interest in others as individuals, indeed they show hostility towards them. Some of this hostility is in immediate response to opposition or frustration but much of it is spontaneous and unexpected. Both types of child may become angry or discontented especially when frustrated in their apparent aims. Both types seem always to be striving to interact and they cannot often settle to self-play.

Relationships with peers do not, in general, appear to be intimate or long-lasting. Those of aggressives are marked by quarrels and fights, those of dependents by tensions resulting from the difficult child's possessiveness. With adults, aggressives tend to be defiant and non-communicative, while dependents are demanding and contrary, although overtly friendly.

[. . .]

# TOPICS FOR DISCUSSION

1. What behaviour characteristics are associated with the three distinct styles identified by Montagner and Manning, and what particular problems do two of the styles present for nursery school teachers?
2. What are the two fairly distinct ways of being difficult in a nursery school? How do these different styles affect relationships in different ways?
3. In what ways do theories about the origin of relationship difficulties influence proposed remedies and treatments?

# SUGGESTIONS FOR FURTHER READING

1. Smith, P.K. and Connolly, K. (1981) *The Behavioural Ecology of the Pre-school.* Cambridge, Cambridge University Press.

    Smith and Connolly conducted a series of carefully controlled experimental investigations in a pre-school with two groups of three- and four-year-old boys and girls of mixed socioeconomic background. In their study, the Sheffield Project, they systematically varied the space, the size of the group, and the amount and kind of play equipment available to the young children. In general, the authors found that typical social play among pre-school children is both hardy and robust, and that when children interacted under a wide variety of physical conditions, the incidence of desirable or undesirable behaviour was not greatly influenced by simple changes in space, group size or equipment. There were two conditions, however, when the incidence of aggressive behaviour increased. One was extreme density. Thus, the reduction of space to less than 15 square feet per child led to greater aggression. The second condition was the combination of density with other sources of stress – for example, failure to increase the amount of play material when social density increased led to more aggressive behaviour. The authors stress the importance of considering physical factors in combination, and make the point of differentiating social variables that are often combined, distinguishing aggressive behaviour – intentional hurting or conflict – from rough-and-tumble play, which has no harmful intent. Smith and Connolly found that physical changes in the pre-school environment may not have identical effects on aggression and rough-and-tumble play, for under conditions of extreme density, aggressive behaviour increases but roughhouse type of behaviour decreases. Interestingly, in an earlier study (1977) Smith and Connolly looked at the social effects of limited play materials and resources. They found that limited supplies led to sharing of equipment, the spontaneous formation of relatively large subgroups, fewer 'loners' and increased competition, while plentiful equipment *reversed the pattern*. Thus, each of the environmental conditions would seem to involve advantages and disadvantages: plentiful equipment reduces conflict but creates less need for sharing, while limited equipment produces the reverse. Thus, decisions about physical arrangements should perhaps be made with an awareness of such findings and with consideration of the educational goals for a particular group.

2. Davie, R. (1984) 'Social development and social behaviour', in Fontana, D. (ed.) *The Education of the Young Child*, 2nd ed. Oxford, Basil Blackwell, chap. 7, pp. 113–27.

Davie stresses that social development, in some of its aspects, is virtually indisting-uishable from other, nominally separate, facets of development, and at all times it can be seen as a context for emerging intellectual, emotional and physical maturity. The author begins his account of social development by examining how the baby's first year of life is one of a developing awareness of the people around him or her and, in particular, of a growth in the baby's understanding of their significance for him or her. The quality of these early attachments and the security which young children derive from them provide a firm base for sound (or otherwise) emotional develop-ment as well as giving the children growing confidence to explore their environment – an essential requirement for enhancing their social development. Davie discusses the second year of life in the context of children's striving for some disengagement from those closest to them, seeing the relationship between children's need for attachment (love, security, etc.) and their need to disengage from their parents as mirroring important aspects of the socialization process. The author affirms that the areas of conflict which arise are not only inevitable but are essential for healthy development. He discusses the importance of the growth of language as one aspect of development which greatly facilitates social growth, particularly where language can lower the temperature in situations of potential conflict or can distract a child in order to avert a potential conflict. Davie traces the development of play and its importance in the social growth of the young child, seeing it, in one sense, as a rehearsal strategy in which the child unself-consciously practises new skills and consolidates older ones. The author provides some valuable insights into the maternal role, the paternal role and the impact of the family unit as a whole on the child's emotional and social development.

3. Stevenson, J., Richman, N. and Graham, P. (1985) 'Behaviour problems and language abilities at three years and behavioural deviance at eight years'. *Journal of Child Psychology and Psychiatry*, **26**, 2, 215–30.

The article investigates the significance of early behaviour problems in the identification of children with later disturbance. To determine their significance it is clearly important to determine the stability of behaviour problems within the pre-school period and how well early home-based measures of disturbance relate to later school behaviour. Previous studies investigating the relationship between parents' reports of problem behaviour and later disturbance in school have *not* found a strong association, and there has been little agreement between parents' and teachers' contemporaneous ratings of older children. Stevenson et al. undertook to establish whether continuities in problem behaviour could be identified between parents' and teachers' reports over a five-year period from age three to the first year of junior school. They aimed to establish whether early language development was also related to later behavioural deviance, since previous research has shown that behaviour problems and language delay at three years were strongly associated.

The authors followed a sample of 535 children from their third to their eighth birthdays. The mothers of all the children were interviewed for 1½ hours and data were obtained on the child's behaviour, development and family background. The interviews were conducted within one month of the child's third birthday. Behaviour problems were measured using a semi-structured interview concerning 12 items of behaviour. Three measures of language development were also used. At the age of eight, total score and individual items of the Rutter Teacher's Scale – a questionnaire designed to identify children with behaviour deviance – were obtained. The authors found that the rate of deviance for eight-year-old children living in an outer London borough was 22 per cent. Boys were found to show more antisocial deviance than girls, and manual social class and non-immigrant children showed significantly more neurotic deviance than children from non-manual and immigrant backgrounds respectively. Non-immigrant boys who showed behaviour problems at age three years showed more antisocial and neurotic deviance at age eight than did boys without such problems at the age of three. The overall association between behaviour problems at age three and increased rates of deviance at age eight was found within both social class groups for non-immigrant children. In the analysis of the predictive nature of early language development the research team found that children with low language structure scores at three years within each social class and within both sexes had significantly higher rates of neurotic deviance than children with high structure scores. Sex differences in deviant behaviour seemed to become apparent around the age of five years, that is, about the time of school entry. It was found that teachers identify these differences earlier than parents. Again, it seems that like intellectual and school achievement, social class differences in rates of deviance gradually increase over the pre-school and early school periods.

The longitudinal results of the study show a strong relationship between behaviour problems at age three and later behavioural deviance at age eight. An important finding to emerge from this research was the association between the language structure of the three-year-old child and later behavioural deviance. In three-year-olds without behaviour problems a poor language structure is associated with later excess of neurotic deviance, indicating a specific association between early language and later behaviour. The authors suggest that since language structure is closely related to the child's ability to formulate ideas and thoughts into words, difficulties in this area are perhaps more likely to give rise to problems in interpersonal relationships.

Although it may be tempting to think that the associations found in this study between early behaviour problems, early language problems and later behavioural deviance at age eight indicate the efficacy of early screening in identifying children at risk for later behavioural disturbance, the authors warn that the 'false alarm' rate in their data was also very high: for example, in this research, if a child was thought to be at risk either because he or she showed a behaviour problem at three years of age or had a poor language structure score, such an 'at risk' designation would have identified 56 per cent of the children who were to show behavioural deviance at age eight. However, of the children thus defined as 'at risk', 61 per cent did not show behavioural deviance at age eight years. In short, the results suggest that although one could identify at an early age half of the children who were later to show behavioural deviance at school, any intervention programme based on such an 'at risk' designation would be wasteful of professional time because nearly two-thirds of the children so identified would not show deviance at age eight (p. 228).

## Reading 9

# ON ASKING
# CHILDREN BIZARRE QUESTIONS

## *M. Hughes and R. Grieve*

## INTRODUCTION

In the study of cognitive and linguistic development it is a commonplace procedure to ask children questions. Yet it is remarkable how little we understand of this interrogative process.

What happens when we ask a child a question? While a full answer to this question is not available, the present paper reports novel information on one aspect of the process. Namely, when presented by an adult with a question, children will locate an answer for the adult's question *even if that question is conceptually ill-formed.*

Usually, of course, when adults ask children questions, these questions are intended to be perspicuous. Their meaning, at least to an adult, is intended to be clear, and the child's answer is frequently used to gauge his cognitive/linguistic understanding. However, it is becoming increasingly clear that the gap between questions as adults present them (intended questions), and questions as children respond to them (received questions), is wider than is often supposed.

But how wide is this gap? One way of considering this problem is to present to children questions intended to be bizarre, i.e. unanswerable as they stand. If children demur at attempting to answer such questions, this will indicate that children consider the conceptual well-formedness of what they are asked. But if children do not demur, and attempt to answer bizarre questions, then we will need to reconsider what we think is happening when we present children with questions in studies of their cognitive/linguistic development.

In what follows, we first describe what happens when bizarre questions were presented, in an informal way, to a number of children of different ages. We then describe a study where several bizarre questions were presented in a more systematic way to groups of children, aged five and seven years.

Hughes, M. and Grieve, R. (1980) 'On asking children bizarre questions'. *First Language,* **1,** 149–60.

## Informal observations

If young children are presented with bizarre questions, such as: 'One day there were two flies crawling up a wall. Which one got to the top first?', it might be expected that they will be bamboozled, or amused. But when five-year-old children were presented with this question, they replied. And their replies, for example '*The big one*', were deadpan. (We owe this observation to G.P.T. Finn.) When we presented a different bizarre question to another child, Sally (six years, eight months), we asked 'Is red wider than yellow?' '*Yes*', she replied. 'Why?' '*Because yellow's thinner than red.*' We then presented these two questions to Jenny (five years, eight months). To the 'flies' question she replied: '*The one on the left.*' That bamboozled us, and we had to ask: 'Why?' '*Because he's the biggest.*' For the 'red wider than yellow' question, she repeated it: '*Is red whiter than yellow?*' 'No, not whiter, *wider*. Which is widest, red or yellow?' '*Red*' 'Why?' '*Because it's got more colour.*' 'What about yellow and blue – which is the widest one?' '*Blue.*' 'Why?' '*It's darker.*'

To the 'colour' questions, Jenny's responses seem based on saturation – the more highly saturated member of the pair is judged to be 'wider' because it has 'more colour', or is 'darker', than the other. (And note that the responses do not seem a function of Jenny's initial mishearing of 'wider' and 'whiter', for then we would expect her choices to have been the opposite.) However responses to bizarre questions involving colour do not invariably involve appeal to their relative saturation. When Alison (six years, nine months) was asked a different bizarre question: 'Which is bigger, red or yellow?' she initially looked baffled, then looked around the room and said: '*Yellow*'. When asked why, she pointed to two objects in the room and said: '*Cos that red cushion there is smaller than that yellow curtain there.*' A similar response was given by Sarah (five years, four months), who was asked the 'red bigger than yellow' question out of doors, near a colourful boating pond. Again the child searched for and compared two differently sized objects of the specified colours.

When such bizarre questions were presented to Andrew (four years, eleven months) he replied to the 'flies' question, ' . . . Which one got to the top first?' '*The first one.*' 'Why did he get to the top first?' '*Because he started first, silly.*' To the 'red wider than yellow' question he replied: '*Red*', but would give no justification other than '*Just because.*'

Fiona (seven years, two months) gave a different response to the 'red wider than yellow' question (the 'flies' question was not presented). First she did the same as Jenny, mishearing 'wider' as 'whiter': '*Which is the whitest?*' 'No, not whiter, *wider*. Which is the widest one?' (These 'wider' questions were presented to Jenny and Fiona by the same adult, whose pronunciation of 'wider' was probably indistinct. Note that both children spontaneously reiterated the question, presumably to provide an opportunity for the adult to confirm that they had got the question right. It is of course not clear that they misheard the question. Possibly they did hear 'wider', but supposed that 'whiter' must have been intended, especially in a question involving colours, and where 'wider' taken as 'wider' is bizarre.) *'Oh, is red "wider" than yellow? What do you mean?'* 'Which is the widest, red or yellow?' *'I don't know what you mean. Do you mean when they are written down, is red or yellow longer on the page?'*

These informal observations suggest that children do tend to provide answers to bizarre questions. However they justify or implicitly justify their responses in various ways. Sometimes they use linguistic knowledge (e.g. Sally utilizes her knowledge that 'thinner' is opposite to 'wider'); sometimes they utilize extralinguistic knowledge or knowledge of objects in the environment (big flies travel faster than flies that are not so big; or colours can be distinguished on the basis of their relative saturation; or a yellow object in the immediate environment is identified as being bigger than a red object); and sometimes an aspect of the language leads into an extralinguistic justification (e.g. Andrew's reply to 'Which fly got to the top *first*' was 'The *first* one' which '. . . started *first*'). Thus these children provide answers to these bizarre questions by importing various sorts of knowledge to the situation. While the oldest child does not conform to this pattern in one sense – she is the only child to make explicit that the meaning of the question is not immediately clear – in another sense she does, for having made explicit the obscurity in the meaning of the question, note how she immediately tries to establish one: 'I don't know what you mean. Do you mean . . . '

To consider this phenomenon further, the following study was undertaken, where larger numbers of children were asked several bizarre questions in less informal circumstances.

# EXPERIMENT

Different types of bizarre questions were presented to groups of five- and seven-year-old children, in their usual school setting.

## Subjects

A group of eight five-year-olds (four male, four female; mean age five years, four months; range four years, eleven months to five years, ten months), and a group of eight seven-year-olds (four male, four female; mean age seven years, seven months; range seven years, three months to seven years, eleven months) were studied. These children knew the adult experimenter, having worked with him on a different, unrelated experiment a week to ten days previously.

## Materials

Four questions, each intended to be bizarre, were prepared: (1) *Is milk bigger than water?* (2) *Is red heavier than yellow?* (3) *One day there were two flies crawling up a wall. Which fly got to the top first?* (4) *One day there were two people standing at a bus-stop. When the bus came along, who got on first?*

These questions are intended to be bizarre in the sense that they do not permit direct answers. This is so for different reasons. (1) and (2) are intended to involve 'category mistakes', and a reasonable response might be to say: 'I don't know what you mean', and request further clarification. The meaning of (3) and (4) on the other hand is perfectly clear, but a reasonable response might be to say: 'I don't know', and request further information.

It is of course difficult to be certain that a question intended to be bizarre is received as such. For example, linguistic philosophers suggest it would be a category mistake to predicate time or place of number. But we have all heard both, not only predicated, but bellowed, of number – for example at boating lakes where small craft are rented by the hour: 'Come in, Number Four, your time is up.' Or, home decorators' manuals may describe certain combinations of colours as being 'too heavy'; and we are familiar with red, orange and yellow being described as 'warm colours', compared with 'cold colours' such as blue and green. Further, (3) and (4) perhaps become more acceptable with slight modifications – e.g. 'If several people were standing at a bus stop, when the bus came along which one would we expect to get on first?' The present questions are intended to be bizarre in the sense that they cannot be answered directly. As they stand, they require clarification of their meaning ((1) and (2)), or the provision of additional information ((3) and (4)), before they can be answered.

## Procedure

Children were tested individually by the same experimenter. Adult and child sat at a table on which lay some papers, including a sheet on which the adult noted the child's responses, but there were no toys or pictures to be looked at. The adult simply said: 'Listen, is milk bigger than water?' or whatever. The questions were always presented in the order: (1), (3), (2), (4). If the child failed to give a response, or said 'Don't know', the question was repeated once. If the child gave a response without justifying it (e.g. 'Is red heavier than yellow?' '*Yes*'), he was asked 'Why?'

## RESULTS

We wish to know whether children answered these bizarre questions; how they answered them; whether there were any differences between different types of question; and whether there were any differences between children of different ages. Before summarizing on these points, we first describe the responses given.

## (1) Is milk bigger than water?

Of the eight younger children, only one child failed to respond (he was the youngest, aged four years, eleven months). Instead he grinned at this, and every other question, saying '*I don't know*', or '*No idea*', or '*Don't know, never tried it before*'. (This calls to mind Brendan Behan's story (Behan, 1963) about the new assistant in a Dublin bookshop who was asked if she liked Kipling. 'How could I know,' she replied, 'when I never kippilled.') Of the remaining seven, one said they were the same, and the other six said: '*Yes*'. When asked why, most responses were either in terms of the origins of the liquids (e.g. water comes out of taps, and milk comes out of either cows or bottles), or in terms of their extension (e.g. there is more milk than water when you pour them into bottles). Only one child said that milk was bigger because it was 'heavy'.

All the older children gave a response. However there were two immediately apparent differences in the responses given. First, the older children were more likely to respond in terms of the characteristics of the liquids themselves – e.g. milk is bigger '*because it's got a colour*', or '*'cos it's more creamier*', or because '*milk is heavier*', or '*because it's more thicker*'.

We will refer to this distinction in terms of the extent to which the children *import context* into their replies. While five of the younger children import context into their replies, talking about where the liquids originate, or what happens when they are poured into containers, only two of the older children do so. Rather than importing additional context, the older children are more likely to remain with the objects referred to in the question, commenting on inherent characteristics such as their colour, texture or weight.

But the more obvious difference between the younger and older children is that the latter tend to qualify their responses in some way, using phrases such as 'I think' (e.g. '*I think milk's bigger than water*') or, more frequently, by replying with questions, which range from: '*Eh?*' to '*Milk is heavier, isn't it?*' or '*Is it because it's more thicker?*' or '*Milk, I think. "Bigger" did you say?*' Six of the older children gave what we will call 'qualified responses' of this sort, but none of the younger children did so.

## (2) Is red heavier than yellow?

Seven five-year-olds gave replies as did all of the seven-year-olds. An interesting response in the younger group was initially obscure: 'Is red heavier than yellow?' '*Yes.*' 'Why?' '*Because there's much more red than yellow.*' 'Why?' '*Because there's water in it.*' 'There's water in what?' '*The paint.*' The explanation becomes clear from another child: '*Yellow is a little. Yellow's got a little plastic box and the red paint's got a big plastic box.*' In school, the children use powdered paint which is mixed with water in plastic containers. So if there is more red than yellow, red *is* heavier! (So much for intentions; and so much for category mistakes.)

Only one of the younger children responded in terms of the characteristics of the colours themselves, rather than the characteristics of the paints which may be mixed using these colours: '*Red's heavier than yellow.*' (Why?) '*Yellow's not bright and red is.*' This sort of response was quite common in the older children: red is heavier '*Because it's darker*'(twice), or '*Cos it's more darker*', or because '*Red's a darker colour than yellow*' (twice).

So there is again a difference between the groups in the extent to which they import context: the older children tend not to, confining their justifications to a difference between the colours themselves (such as saturation), while the younger children do tend to import additional context, concerned with a situation such as mixing paints from such colours, and referring to attributes such as the size, weight and water content of the containers.

The consistency with which the children responded to this presented colour question in terms of saturation merits further inquiry. Possibly, saturation is a more important characteristic of colours than brightness or hue with young children (R.N. Campbell, personal communication). In the present study, the children's recourse to saturation in response to the presented colour question is certainly very consistent.

There is also a difference in the extent to which the groups qualify their responses, but the distinction is not so marked as in (1). One of the older children says: '*I think red's just as heavy as yellow*', one says: '*Yes, I think so*', and one is explicit in his question-as-answer: '*Red . . . Was it "heavier"?*'

The reduction in the extent to which the older children qualify their responses may be due to an order effect – recall that question (2) was in fact the third question, presented, and the children may be learning that when their replies, initially given in a tentative manner, are accepted by the adult, there is no need to continue to qualify them.

## (3) Which fly got to the top first?

All children answered this question, save the youngest child. Four of the five-year-olds initially said they did not know, but then replied when the question was repeated.

Differences between the groups, in terms of imported context and qualification of response, are not now apparent. One of the younger children imported context, saying that the fly who reached the top first was: *The first one. 'Cos that was the one leading the other one, taking the other one up.'* One of the older children did likewise, saying: *'The left one.'* (Why?) *'He flew up.'* (And the other one?) *'He crawled up.'*

Otherwise children from both groups replied in terms of the situation described in the question, and responses concerned characteristics of the fly who arrived first: *'The biggest one. Because he got the longest legs'*, or because *'He went more faster'*, or because he was the one who *'thought of it first'*, or because *'He started first'*, or because he was *'the one that had been drinking milk . . . Milk makes you stronger.'* (Note that (3) was presented just after (1).) Alternatively, responses concerned the relative location of the two flies; the one who got to the top first was: *'The one nearest the top'*, or the one who was *'nearly at the top'*. Thus appeal was mostly made to the fly's size, length of legs, or strength; to his speed; to his time of departure; or to his place of departure. Importing other factors into the situation was rare.

There was also no qualification of responses, in either group. The 'I think it was the big one', or 'Was it the big one?' types of response were not observed.

## (4) Who got on (the bus) first?

The youngest child remained amused. All other children gave a response. As with (3), there was no qualification of responses.

Two of the younger children imported context, saying that the person who got on first was *'The one who was taking the other one'*, or *'The mummy (taking the child)'*, as did one of the older children, saying that the stronger person got on first because he had been drinking milk, and was stronger than the other one who had been drinking water. (Note this child's use of elements from a previous question, (1). Here, with question (4), the elements do not work well, for we have to conjure up a primaeval struggle at the bus-stop. But they do work well in her answer to the 'flies' question (3), where the stronger one got to the top first. This phenomenon – importing as context elements from previous questions – may have occurred elsewhere, though not so clearly. For example, to what extent do the judgements that red is heavier than yellow because of relative water content in the paints arise from the fact that the children have previously been dealing with water in question (1): where it comes from, how it is used (poured into containers), and so on?)

However there was a difference between the two groups, related to their appeal to a rule which might be expected to hold in the circumstances of the question – namely, rules of queuing. For example, the person who got on first was '*The one there first*', or '*The one who got there first. The one at the front of the line*', or this rule was overridden by another concerning good manners: '*The lady*' (Why?) '*Because ladies should go first before men*'. This sort of response was utilized by only two of the younger children, but by five of the older ones. The remainder replied in terms of the person who was '*Nearest the bus*', or who '*Saw the bus come first*'.

These observations are summarized in Table 9.1, which shows the number of responses given to the four questions, whether these responses were qualified, and whether context was imported to the situation in the ways indicated above (the maximum entry in any cell is 8).

Table 9.1   Responses to bizarre questions

| | Five-year-olds | | | Seven-year-olds | | |
|---|---|---|---|---|---|---|
| *Question* | Responses given | Responses qualified | Context imported | Responses given | Responses qualified | Context imported |
| (1) Milk | 7 | 0 | 5 | 8 | 6 | 2 |
| (2) Red | 7 | 0 | 4 | 8 | 3 | 1 |
| Total | 14 | 0 | 9 | 16 | 9 | 3 |
| (3) Flies | 7 | 0 | 1 | 8 | 0 | 1 |
| (4) Bus-stop | 7 | 0 | 2 | 8 | 0 | 1 |
| Total | 14 | 0 | 3 | 16 | 0 | 2 |
| Totals | 28 | 0 | 12 | 32 | 9 | 5 |

# DISCUSSION

The results are reasonably clear. When presented with questions intended to be bizarre – questions which cannot be answered directly without clarification of meaning (CM questions) or provision of further information (PI questions) – young children almost invariably provide replies. Younger five-year-old children frequently do so by importing additional context to the situation, especially with CM questions, but older seven-year-old children are less likely to do this, tending instead to remain with characteristics of the elements referred to in the questions, or appealing to rules which might be expected to apply in the situation to which the question refers. The other major difference between the groups is that while the older children frequently qualify their responses in some way, indicating uncertainty, the younger children never do so. The result of this paper, that young children answer questions even if these questions are bizarre, confirms the previously mentioned finding of G.P.T. Finn. It is also akin to results detectable in the data of other studies.

For example, in a study of three- and four-year-olds' understanding of prepositions, Wales (1974) presented children with a toy doll and a toy house, and instructed them to: 'Put the doll *in/on/at* the house'. To estimate whether the children had any response bias, Wales also presented this instruction without any preposition, namely: 'Put the doll the house'. The great majority of children made a response to this anomalous instruction, failures to respond being very infrequent (4 per cent). It can also be noted that this result is not restricted to children from but one culture, speaking but one language – Wales's study was conducted with Scottish children speaking English, Indian children speaking Tamil, and Bornean children speaking Lun-Bawang. Children also respond to sentences made anomalous, not through deletion of an element as in Wales's study, but through substitution of a nonsense term for a term in the language. Carey (1978b) asked three- and four-year-old children to play a game where they had to give a puppet *more*, or *less*, tea to drink. When she asked the children to give the puppet *tiv* tea to drink, over half the children responded to this anomalous request without comment – some children gave additional tea, some reduced the amount of tea, some stirred the tea, some pretended to drink the tea themselves, and so forth. Children will also respond to questions where the meaning of terms may be to them obscure. In a study of young children's understanding of homonyms (words with the same sound, but different meanings, as in *key* and *quay*), Campbell and Bowe (1977) found that three- and four-year-olds would attempt to interpret such homonyms, even though their interpretations might be grotesque in relation to the rest of the context. For example, if the children knew the *key*, but not the *quay*, sense of the homonym, the term might be grotesque in relation to the rest of the context. Thus the child might envisage someone visiting the seaside, going for a walk along a *key*, seeing a rubber *boy* floating in the water, and so on.

These observations on the data of other studies extend the present result. Young children not only provide answers to questions that are bizarre: they do the same for questions whose terms' intended meaning may be obscure (Campbell and Bowe, 1977), and for questions which are anomalous in various ways (Wales, 1974; Carey, 1978b).

Why young children do this is not clear. It may be a characteristic of the exchange of discourse that, other things being equal (e.g. where conversational maxims such as those considered by Grice (1975) may be supposed to apply), the participants at least try to afford each other's utterances meaning, or at least suppose that each other's utterances are intended to have meaning. The task in discourse is thus not so much to *decide whether* the other's utterances have meaning, but to *identify what* his meanings are. This characteristic of human discourse may be fundamental, and can be observed in mothers 'communicating' with their infants long before the child is capable of understanding language, far less producing it.

But if we do not know why children provide answers for bizarre questions, the present paper indicates that this is what children usually do. That they do so, for the sort of bizarre questions presented here, either in terms of the information presented in the question, or by importing additional context into the situation, suggests that the child does assume that the questions are intended to have meaning, and that his task is to identify meaning in what has been said to him.

The observation that children seek to interpret questions that are bizarre, seems at first sight an extraordinary finding. Yet we wonder whether it is as extraordinary as it appears. Perhaps making something of whatever information is presented to him, or that information supplemented by imported information, is what the child has to do most, if not all, of the time. Recall that he must be well used to such a task, for when he is younger and still acquiring the language, the meaning of much of what is said to him cannot be immediately transparent. We know that when language is still being acquired, the young child derives meaning not simply from aspects of the language itself, but also from his knowledge of the extralinguistic contexts to which the language refers – his knowledge of objects in the environment, how these customarily are, or should be, related, and so on. We have suggested elsewhere that the young child's early comprehension of language should be viewed as a process concerned with how, from the child's point of view, such elements of linguistic and extralinguistic context interact. What the present paper suggests is that later cognitive and linguistic development might well be viewed in a similar light. Thus presenting five- and seven-year-olds with bizarre questions may simply simulate what he has been used to at an earlier age; and his interpretation of these bizarre questions may simply represent the child's practice of a familiar, well-established skill.

Thus the child's propensity to answer questions, even if they are intended to be unanswerable, may not be as startling as might at first be supposed. Nevertheless, the fact that the child will attempt to locate an answer to whatever question he is presented with has significant implications for what we think is happening when we attempt to gauge the young child's cognitive/linguistic abilities by means of the question and answer process.

Psychologists and linguists – and all others who rely on questioning young children – can no longer treat the child as merely a passive recipient of questions and instructions, but must instead start to view the child as someone who is actively trying to make sense of the situation he is in – however bizarre it may seem.

## TOPICS FOR DISCUSSION

1. Discuss the authors' contention that 'presenting five- and seven-year-olds with bizarre questions may simply stimulate what the child has been used to at an earlier age, and so his response to and interpretation of these bizarre questions may be, in fact, simply the child's practice of a well-known and well-established skill'.
2. 'Perhaps making something of whatever information is presented to him, or that information supplemented by imported information, is what the child has to do most, if not all, of the time.' What are some of the most important implications of this statement for teachers (and parents) of young children?
3. 'The task in discourse is thus not so much to *decide whether* the other's utterances have meaning, but to *identify what* his meanings are.' How far does this answer the question of why young children will usually provide answers to bizarre questions?

## SUGGESTIONS FOR FURTHER READING

1. Campbell, R.N. and Macdonald, T.B. (1983) 'Text and context in early language comprehension', in Donaldson, M., Grieve, R. and Pratt, C. (eds) *Early Childhood Development and Education: Readings in Psychology*. Oxford, Basil Blackwell, pp. 115–26.

The authors describe a study concerned with words that have two distinct meanings but sound the same (for example, 'branch' – branch of a tree or branch of a bank, or 'hair' and 'hare'). Young children were told stories which related to the *less familiar* members of such pairs of terms (e.g. 'hare') with the result that one-third of the children's interpretations were based on the *more familiar* meanings (e.g. 'hair') producing grotesque results which did not appear to bother them. In contrast to the study by Hughes and Grieve (Reading 9) where the subjects displayed a strong desire to make sense of things, Campbell and Macdonald demonstrate that young children also share a capacity to accept and tolerate the nonsensical, and explain their findings in terms of the relation between text and context.

2. McGarrigle, J., Grieve, R. and Hughes, M. (1978) 'Interpreting inclusion: a

contribution to the study of the child's cognitive and linguistic development'. *Journal of Experimental Child Psychology*, **26**, 528, 50.

The authors demonstrate that when adults ask questions, these questions are intended to be perspicuous. Their meaning, at least to an adult, is intended to be clear, and the way in which the child responds is most often taken as a measure of his or her cognitive/linguistic understanding. However, there is increasing research evidence to suggest that the gap between questions as adults present them (intended questions) and questions as children respond to them (received questions) is very much wider than is usually supposed.

3. Carey, S. (1978) 'Less never means more', in Campbell, R.N. and Smith, P.T. (1978) *Recent Advances in the Psychology of Language, Vol.1. Language Development and Mother Child Interaction*. London, Plenum Press.

Carey shows that young children not only readily offer answers to questions that are bizarre, but they do the same for questions whose intended meaning may be obscure, and for questions which are anomalous in various ways. In this study of relational terms, Carey considers a number of instances of misunderstanding in pre-school children which are best explained, he suggests, *not* by supposing that the child has assigned wrong values to these terms in analysing the texts containing them, but by supposing that the results of such analyses are insufficient to determine a message and, hence, a response. As a result, the child is forced to rely on the resources of contextual projection or, failing that, of various standby procedures and response biases in order to reproduce a response (Campbell and Macdonald, 1983).

# Reading 10

# TEACHING ARITHMETIC TO PRE-SCHOOL CHILDREN

## M. Hughes

This paper describes the development and evaluation of a method for introducing simple arithmetical symbolism to pre-school children. The symbols used were commercially available magnetic numerals (1, 2, 3 . . .) and operator signs ( +, − ). The children played games in which they learned, for example, that the numeral '2' on the lid of a box meant there were two bricks in the box. Later they might learn that '2+1' on the lid meant that a further brick had been added to the box, making three bricks altogether.

The idea that pre-school children should be learning to use arithmetical

Hughes, M. (1983) 'Teaching arithmetic to preschool children'. *Educational Review*, **35**, 2, 163–73.

symbols in this way runs directly counter to much current theory and practice in early mathematics education. For example, in their introduction to the Schools Council *Early Mathematical Experiences* booklets (1978), Matthews and Matthews state that: 'There is so much to learn before even the simplest calculations have any meaning that the idea of "sums for the very young child" is ludicrous.' A similar assumption underlies two of the most popular infant school mathematic schemes, Fletcher Maths and Nuffield Maths (Howell et al., 1979; Moore, 1979). Neither scheme introduces addition or subtraction until the children have experienced a range of activities, such as matching and sorting concrete objects, designed to develop their general concept of number. Even then, addition and subtraction are first introduced using concrete objects well before the children are taught the appropriate formal symbolism.

The main theoretical justification for these practices comes from the work of Piaget. In *The Child's Conception of Number*, Piaget (1952) argues that children are unlikely to understand addition and subtraction until they achieve concrete operational thought, at around seven years. More recent research, however, casts doubt on Piaget's claim, and emphasizes instead the numerical competence of very young children. In particular, Gelman and Gallistel (1978) and Hughes (1981) have demonstrated that pre-school children can carry out a range of simple additions and subtractions, particularly if the numbers involved are small and if the task is embedded in a meaningful concrete situation. Thus Hughes (1981) showed that most children aged between three and five years know that, if two bricks are added to a box which already contains one brick, then there will be three bricks altogether in the box. However the same children were unable to answer questions expressed in the formal code of arithmetic, such as 'What does one and two make?'

These findings suggest that providing young children with further concrete experiences of addition and subtraction may not be the most appropriate educational activity, for they are already relatively competent at the concrete level. Rather the educational problem is one of finding ways to help children free their thinking from the concrete, so that they can express the concepts they already possess in formal arithmetical symbolism. This process of disembedding – as Donaldson (1978) has argued – is not likely to be easy, as it goes against the fundamental nature of the young child's mind. However, it may be facilitated if we can convince the child that there is a clear and useful purpose to be served by using formal symbolism. This principle underlies the method described here.

In the first part of the method, the child uses magnetic numerals to represent the contents of a set of identical boxes. The child is not, however, simply instructed to place the appropriate numerals on the boxes. Instead a game is developed in which the child has to guess which box contains a particular number of bricks. When the game is played without the numerals, the child has no means of distinguishing the boxes, and guesses at random. The numerals are then introduced, and it is suggested that they might help the child play the game. In other words, the context of the game makes it clear that the child will benefit from placing numerals on the appropriate boxes.

A similar rationale underlies the introduction of the operator signs '+' and '−'. This time a teddy is employed who adds bricks to the boxes (or takes them out) while the child's eyes are closed. The game involves guessing what the teddy has done. Clearly this is impossible without some help, and the operator signs are then introduced as a way in which the teddy can help the child discover what he has done. If the teddy adds a brick, then he puts the signs '+1' on the box; if he takes a brick out, he puts on the signs '−1'. Again the context of the game means that the child will benefit from the introduction of the operator signs.

Pilot work with the games raised the question of children who were not familiar with the numerals '1', '2', '3' . . . etc. Several of these children, however, made the interesting response of using the magnetic numerals in one-to-one correspondence with the bricks. That is, they would place one numeral on the box containing one brick, two numerals on the box containing two bricks, and so on. Such children were called *iconic* responders. In contrast, those who placed the appropriate numeral on each tin were called *symbolic* responders (see Hughes and Jones, 1983, for further discussion of these terms).

Operator signs were introduced in a slightly different way for iconic responders. When a brick was added, this was represented by a single plus sign '+'; when two bricks were added, this was represented as '++', and so on. A similar convention was adopted for bricks which were subtracted ('−', '−−', etc. . . .).

Once the method had been developed it was used in a systematic manner with a representative sample of middle-class and working-class four-year-olds. The aim was to discover whether the children would be able to learn arithmetical symbolism in this way; what they would find easy and what they would find difficult; and whether there would be any spontaneous generalization to other contexts.

# METHOD AND FINDINGS
## Subjects

Subjects were 20 four-year-old children attending nursery school in Edinburgh. Ten children (seven boys, three girls; mean age 4 years 7 months; range 4 years 1 month to 4 years 11 months) attended a school in a working-class area severely deprived of resources and amenities: their fathers were either absent, unemployed or had unskilled occupations. Ten children (five boys, five girls; mean age 4 years 7 months; range 4 years 1 month to 4 years 11 months) attended a school in a comfortable middle-class suburb: their fathers were all employed in professional or managerial occupations. The children were chosen at random from the available four-year-olds in the school. The mean IQ (British Ability Scales) of the working-class children was 98.3 (range 80–112), and that of the middle-class children was 112 (range 104–121). These means differed significantly.*

## Materials

The materials consisted of four small identical tin boxes (4″×3″×1″), a small teddy, a large number of bricks (1″ side) and a collection of magnetic numerals (1, 2, 3, 4, 5, 6, 7 and 0) and operator signs (+ and −). These magnetic numerals and operator signs are commercially available in the UK, and are plastic symbols, about 1½″ high, with small magnets hidden underneath them. They were usually arranged at random on a metal board. The teddy had previously appeared in studies of conservation (McGarrigle and Donaldson, 1974) and class inclusion (McGarrigle et al., 1978).

## Procedure

All children were seen individually by the same male experimenter on eight separate sessions over a period of six weeks. The sessions took place in a small room off the main nursery area. Each session lasted about 15–20 minutes and usually started with a game or puzzle unconnected with the study. The contents of each session were as follows:

Session 1:     Pre-test.
Session 2:     Introduction of numerals.
Sessions 3–6: Introduction of operator signs.
Session 7:     Standard evaluation.
Session 8.     Generalization.

All sessions were video-taped for subsequent analysis.

---

* The term 'significant' refers to *statistical significance* throughout the extract.

## Session 1: Pre-test

The pre-test established that all 20 children fulfilled the criteria for the study. That is, they could all say how many bricks were present when 1, 2, 3 or 0 bricks were placed in front of them (overall score 100 per cent); they could all carry out simple additions and subtractions involving small quantities of bricks (overall score 94 per cent); and they all had difficulty when the same additions and subtractions were presented in the formal code ('How many is one and two?' etc.: overall score 18 per cent). There were no social class differences on any of these measures.

The pre-test also investigated the children's ability to identify magnetic numerals and operator signs. The middle-class children identified significantly more of the numerals '1'–'7' than did the working-class children. Only four middle-class children and one working-class child identified zero as 'nothing' or 'zero' although three middle-class and two working-class children said it was an 'oh'. Other replies were that it was an 'eight' or a 'round'. Only one child (middle-class) identified the plus sign as 'plus', and no child correctly identified the 'minus' sign. Other children described the plus sign as a 'cross', a 'star', a 'kiss' or an 'x', while minus was usually called a 'one' or a 'line'.

## Session 2: Introduction of numerals

Four identical boxes were placed on the table, and the child established that they contained one, two, three and zero bricks respectively. The lids were replaced, and the experimenter suggested they play a game in which the child had to guess which box was which. The experimenter shuffled the boxes, asked for a particular box, then shuffled the boxes again. After four trials the experimenter got out the magnetic numerals and suggested the child should stick them on the lids of the boxes so she[1] would know how many bricks were in each box. The boxes were shuffled again, and the child asked, as before, to guess which box was which. If a child was unable to use the numerals to identify the boxes the experimenter suggested she use them in a particular (iconic) fashion: that is, he suggested she place two numerals on the box with two bricks in, and so on.

Seventeen children spontaneously used the numerals to identify all the boxes correctly, and only three children required help. Many children made spontaneous comments to show they appreciated that the numerals would help them (e.g. 'It's easy now, 'cos we got the numbers on') and most showed signs of pleasure at being able to use the numerals. Fourteen children spontaneously used the numerals in a symbolic fashion to represent the quantities 1, 2 and 3: that is, they fixed a '1' on the box with one brick in, a '2' on the box with two bricks in, and so on. Three working-class children spontaneously used the iconic method of fixing one numeral on the box containing one brick, two numerals on the box containing two bricks, and so on; the other three children (two working-class, one middle-class) used this method when it was suggested to them. There was, not surprisingly, a close correlation between the method of representation used and whether or not a child had correctly identified the numerals '1', '2' and '3' in the pre-test. Thirteen out of 14 symbolic responders correctly identified two or more of these numerals in the pre-test, while only one out of six iconic responders had done so. For the working-class children only, iconic and symbolic responders were compared for age and IQ, but there were no significant differences on either measure.

All 10 middle-class children, but only three working-class children, used '0' to represent the contents of the empty box. Six working-class children left the lid blank, and their comments indicated this was deliberate (e.g. 'There's none in there, so I'll no put any on'). One working-class child placed the numeral '7' on the empty box then proceeded to identify it correctly. Of the 13 children who used '0', only five had identified it as 'zero' or 'nothing' in the pre-test: of the others, five had called it an 'oh', and the remaining three had said they didn't know what it was.

## Session 3: Introduction of '+1'

The experimenter got out the three boxes containing 1, 2, and 3 bricks. On the lids were the numerals which the child had placed on the boxes in Session 2. The experimenter got out the teddy, and explained that they would play a game in which the teddy would put another brick in one of the boxes while the child's eyes were shut. When the child opened her eyes again she was asked to guess which box the teddy had added a brick to. Whichever box she chose was opened, and the contents compared with the numeral(s) on the lid. If the child could not work out whether the teddy had added a brick, the experimenter helped her with questions like 'How many bricks were in the box before?', 'How many are in now?' etc. The game was repeated until the child seemed to have grasped the idea.

The experimenter then introduced the '+' sign. He explained that this sign (which was always called 'plus') was one of the teddy's 'special signs' which he would use to help the child. For symbolic responders, Teddy added '+1' to the right of the numeral showing the contents (e.g. '2+1'). For iconic responders Teddy added '+' to the right of the numeral(s) showing the contents (e.g. '35+'). The experimenter demonstrated this to the child, and then played the game using these signs. When the child had correctly identified the box, the experimenter asked her to work out how many bricks were inside now. In between each trial the added brick was removed from the box and the 'special signs' removed from the lid.

After three trials in which the experimenter had manipulated the teddy, the game was reversed. The experimenter gave the teddy, the numerals and operator signs, and the extra brick to the child, and shut his eyes. If the child put the symbols on in the wrong order, or in the wrong place, the experimenter explicitly pointed out where they should be placed. The experimenter also explicitly verbalized his thinking when working out what the teddy had done: e.g. 'There's a "plus" on that box, so he must have done something to it', 'It says "two plus one" so that means there were two to begin with and then the teddy added one more'. This part of the procedure gave the child direct experience in handling the teddy, the symbols and the bricks, and was particularly enjoyable for the children. It was usually continued for as long as the children wanted to play.

## Sessions 4, 5 and 6:
### Introduction of '−1', '+2' and '−2'

These sessions followed the same general procedures as Session 3. Each session started with a review of what had been learned in the previous session. The new symbols were then introduced (one operation per session) and the session ended with the game being reversed.

## Session 7: Standardized evaluation

This session consisted of a standardized evaluation of the child's understanding of the symbols. The experimenter first asked the child to identify the three boxes containing 1, 2 and 3 bricks on the basis of the numerals on their lids. He then examined the child's understanding of the symbols used to represent the operations 1+1, 2−1, 1+2, 3−2 and 1−1. Thus for the operation 1+2 the experimenter first asked the child to shut her eyes. He then took the box with one brick in and added two more bricks. Finally he shut the lid and placed either '+2' on the lid (symbolic responders), or '++' (iconic responders). For each operation the child was asked to identify, from the symbols on the boxes:

1. which box the teddy had done something to;
2. what the teddy had done to the box;
3. how many bricks were now in the box.

All 20 children correctly identified the boxes on the basis of the numerals on the lids. Similarly, all 20 children could work out from the signs which box had been added to or subtracted from. However, not all the children could say what the teddy had done to the box, or how many bricks were now in the box. Those who did so with no help from the experimenter were given a score of two points for each trial; those who did so with a certain amount of

Table 10.1   Performance on standardized evaluation (Session 7)

| | 'What Teddy did to the box' | | | 'How many bricks in the box now?' | | |
|---|---|---|---|---|---|---|
| | Poor 0–3 | Fair 4–6 | Good 7–10 | Poor 0–3 | Fair 4–6 | Good 7–10 |
| Working-class | 3 | 1 | 6 | 5 | 4 | 1 |
| Middle-class | 0 | 1 | 9 | 0 | 1 | 9 |
| All | 3 | 2 | 15 | 5 | 5 | 10 |

help were given a score of one point, while those who were unable to do so despite help from the experimenter scored 0 points. The 'help' usually consisted of breaking the problem down into smaller units. For example, if a child (C) could not say outright how many bricks had been added when the box showed '1+2', the experimenter (E) might proceed as follows. E: 'Did the teddy put something in, or take something out?' C: 'Put something in'. E: 'How many bricks did he put in?' C: 'Two'. E: 'OK, he put two bricks in' (etc.).

Overall, the middle-class children (MC) were more successful than the working-class children (WC), both at working out what the teddy had done (MC mean 9.0 out of 10; WC mean 5.4) and at working out how many bricks were now in the box (MC mean 8.6 out of 10; WC mean 3.6). The working-class children, but not the middle-class children, were significantly better at working out what the teddy had done than at working out how many bricks were now in the box.

For the working-class children, there were no significant differences between the symbolic and iconic responders, either in calculating what the teddy had done (symbolic mean 5.8, iconic mean 5.0) or in working out the final number of bricks in the box (symbolic mean 3.4, iconic mean 3.8). It was impossible to do a similar analysis for the middle-class children, since all but one of them used the symbolic mode. However, the single middle-class child who used the iconic mode was one of the three children who scored maximum points on every measure.

In order to obtain a more detailed picture of the children's learning in each social class group, the children we classed as 'poor', 'fair' or 'good' according to their scores (out of 10) on the two main measures. As Table 10.1 shows, the performance of the middle-class children was identical on the two measures, with nine out of ten children in the 'good' category and the remaining child in the 'fair' category. In contrast, the working-class children performed somewhat differently on the two measures, with six children in the 'good' category for 'What Teddy did' and five children in the 'poor' category for 'How many in the box?'

## Session 8: Generalization

The aim of this session was to evaluate how far the children's understanding of the symbols would generalize to contexts outside the game. Three separate tasks were used:

1. *Symbols on boxes – not in game.* When the child entered the room there were four boxes already on the table with the following signs and numerals attached to the lids: '2−1', '2+1', '3−1' and '3−3' (or the iconic equivalent). The experimenter explained that the boxes had been left at the end of a game with another child, and asked the child to work out how many bricks were in each box.

2. *Tambourine game.* The experimenter put away the bricks and boxes but left a single lid, the symbols and the teddy on the table. He brought out a tambourine and explained that the teddy would tell the child how many times to bang the tambourine. When the child's eyes were shut, the teddy would put symbols on the lid, and the child would bang the tambourine the appropriate number of times. After a practice trial, the teddy placed the following symbols on the lid: '2', '3', '3−1', '2+1' (or the iconic equivalent).

3. *Formal code questions.* No materials were present. The experimenter presented the following formal code questions exactly as in Session 1: 1+1, 2−1, 1+2, 3−2 and 1−1. The addition questions were phrased (e.g.) 'How many is one and two?' and the subtractions (e.g.) 'How many is two take away one?'

Overall, the amount of generalization was low, particularly when the operator signs were involved. Performance on the first generalization task was 54 per cent for the middle-class children, and 27 per cent for the working-class children. The predominant response to this task was to ignore the operator signs and respond to the numeral(s) indicating the initial contents of the tin. Some children, however, particularly amongst the middle-class group, were able to work out the final contents when reminded that the teddy had done something to the tins.

The same inability to interpret the operator signs outside the game context emerged in the tambourine task. All the children were able to bang the tambourine the appropriate number of times if the lid showed a numeral or numerals only, but few could do so when the lid showed operator signs as well as numerals. Indeed many children expressed a considerable amount of surprise at seeing the operator signs at all.

Finally, there was a somewhat unexpected increase in the performance of
the middle-class children on the formal code tasks between Sessions 1 and 8.
This increase, although statistically significant, was small, and performance
on Session 8 was only 36 per cent. There was no comparable change in the
performance of the working-class children on the formal code questions.

## *Correlations with IQ, mental age and physical age*

A combined 'learning score' was constructed by summing the child's score
on the three measures with the most individual variation – that is, interpreting operator signs (What Teddy did), and calculating the contents of the box
both inside the game situation (Session 7) and outside it (Session 8). The
findings are discussed below.

# DISCUSSION

These findings make clear that most four-year-old children are capable of
understanding and using a simple form of arithmetical symbolism. All the
children in the study were able to use numerals – either symbolically or
iconically – to represent the initial contents of the boxes, and all of them
grasped the idea that operator signs could be used to indicate which box had
been added to or subtracted from. Seventeen of the 20 children also
achieved 'good' or 'fair' understanding of the use of operator signs to
represent particular additions and subtractions (e.g. that '+1' meant 'Teddy
put one in'), and 15 children were 'good' or 'fair' at calculating the final
contents of the box on the basis of the numerals and operator signs on the
box. In addition, children's ability to use the symbols themselves – when the
game was reversed – matched their ability to understand the symbols,
although this could not be evaluated systematically. For the majority of the
children, then, the method was to a large extent successful.

Some possible reasons for this success can be suggested. First, the method
was embodied in a game which the children found enjoyable and interesting.
By the final session the children were just as keen – if not keener – to come
out for a game as they were at the beginning. At the same time, some aspects
of the method were undoubtedly difficult, and many of the children recognized this: 'That's a hard one' or 'I don't know, I'll have to think' were
typical comments. It is worth noting that many pre-school children appear to
appreciate and enjoy intellectual problems which are pitched at the limits of
their understanding.

A second important factor was that the symbols were introduced in a way
that provided a clear rationale as to why they were being used. The numerals

were introduced so that the child 'would know how many bricks were in each box', while the operator signs were introduced 'so that teddy can let you know what he's done to the box'. This was a fundamental feature of the method which had been built into it from the start.

While the method was generally successful with most children, it was significantly more successful with the middle-class group. At first sight one might suppose this social class difference simply reflects the higher IQ, or mental age, of the middle class children. This explanation, however, is not supported by the data. There was indeed a significant positive correlation between IQ and the extent of the children's learning when both groups of children were taken together. However, there was no significant correlation when either group was looked at separately, suggesting that the overall correlation may be a reflection of social class differences rather than an explanation for them. Nor was there any significant positive correlation between mental age and the children's learning, either for both groups together or for the groups by themselves: indeed, there was a significant *negative* correlation for the middle-class children between mental age and the extent of their learning. Inspection of individual scores suggested that this negative correlation was mainly due to two separate clusters of children: a group of three girls whose mental ages were relatively high but whose performance on the games was less than optimum, and a group of three boys who did very well on the games but whose mental age was lower. The IQ measure used (British Ability Scales) has a strong verbal component and this clustering may represent an early separation of verbal and mathematical skills. However it is wrong to read too much into this finding, in view of the small size of the sample and the relative lack of variation in the middle-class children's learning scores.

A more fruitful perspective on the social class differences comes from a session-by-session analysis of the children's learning progress. The first signs that some of the working-class children were having difficulty came in Session 3, when the teddy added a brick to one of the numbered boxes. Several of the working-class children had difficulty understanding that they could work out which box had been added to by looking for a *mismatch* between the contents and the numeral(s) on the tins. In other words, they had difficulty in carrying out the logical argument:
1. this box has 3 bricks in;
2. this box has the number '2' on it;
3. ∴ the teddy put a brick in here.

Further difficulties arose when the operator signs were introduced to represent what teddy had done. There was a strong tendency among some of the children to represent the current contents of a box rather than what the teddy had done to it. Thus one working-class child when shown that '1+1' meant that teddy had added one brick to the one already in the box, wanted to know, quite understandably, why he did not just put a '2' on the box. Other children showed a tendency to confuse the numerals involved in the addition with the contents of the box, so that '1+2' might be read as showing that there were now two bricks in the box. Those children using an iconic system did not have this confusion on addition trials, where the one-to-one correspondence between symbols and contents was retained. Not surprisingly, these children did better on addition than on subtraction, where the one-to-one correspondence was lost.

While the representation of addition and subtraction by operator signs proved altogether too difficult for some of the working-class children, it was fairly easily grasped by all the middle-class children. Even for the middle-class children, however, this understanding was still restricted to the game situation. Performance dropped for all children when they were asked to identify the contents of boxes bearing numerals and operator signs outside the game, and dropped even further when they were asked to bang the tambourine, for example '2+1' times. On the one hand, this lack of generalization at least shows that their good performance *within* the game was a genuine interpretation of the symbols and not a rote association of '2+1' with 'three' – for if this were the case, generalization would have been much higher. On the other hand, the lack of generalization reveals there is still a gap between learning to use arithmetical symbols in one situation and knowing that the symbols have a timeless meaning which is independent of the situation in which they are acquired.

Does this mean that pre-school children are incapable of acquiring this timeless meaning? The present study does not allow a definite answer to this question. The most we can say is that children can be taught arithmetical symbols in one context but do not spontaneously generalize to new contexts. We do not know whether they are incapable of such generalization, or whether they could do so with some help. In the present study the experimenter did not attempt to make links between the use of symbols in the tambourine game and their use in the teddy game: it is possible that a small amount of help is all that would have been required to achieve generalization.

There was, however, a certain amount of generalization from the teddy game to the formal code questions. Within the middle-class group only, there was a small but significant increase in performance on the formal code questions between Sessions 1 and 8. This should not be interpreted as showing that some children had learned, for example, that 'one and two makes three' through playing the games. Rather it seems likely that some children were now able to translate the formal code questions into the game context. This was done explicitly by one child, who answered the question 'How many is two take away one?' with the response 'One in the box': it may also have been done implicitly by others.

What, in conclusion, are the implications for early mathematical education? First, this study provides further evidence of the considerable numerical competence which children possess before they even start school. While other studies (e.g. Gelman and Gallistel, 1978; Hughes, 1981) have demonstrated pre-school children's ability to carry out concrete numerical calculations, the present study shows they can also grasp a rudimentary form of arithmetical symbolism in which numerals and operator signs are used to represent concrete quantities and events. Indeed, the picture which is emerging suggests that, from a cognitive point of view, pre-school children may well possess many of the prerequisite skills required for learning arithmetic. What skills they do lack appear to be primarily linguistic in nature – such as understanding how symbols can be used to record a message of what has been done, or learning how to read a set of symbols in a particular order, or in realizing that symbols learned in one context can be used in a variety of other contexts.

This analysis, if correct, points to a shift in emphasis within early mathematics education. The current preoccupation with providing a range of concrete activities designed to develop numerical concepts could perhaps be reduced, with correspondingly more emphasis placed on the introduction and use of arithmetical symbols in a variety of communicative situations. From this point of view, the games described here perform an important illustrative function. First, they demonstrate an approach which could easily be extended to other aspects of arithmetical symbolism. For example, games like the ones used here could be developed to introduce the equals sign ('='), or to demonstrate arithmetical laws such as commutativity ('1+2'= '2+1'). More importantly, perhaps, is the general principle embodied in the games. By introducing symbols in meaningful communicative situations the games show young children that there are situations where arithmetical symbols can be used to make life easier, and where there is a purpose for making translations betweeen formal symbols and concrete objects and events. If this idea can be communicated effectively to young children, it may have a profound effect on their subsequent mathematical education.

# NOTE

1. Because the experimenter was male the child was referred to as 'she' throughout.

## TOPICS FOR DISCUSSION

1. 'There is so much to learn before even the simplest calculations have any meaning that the idea of "sums for the very young child" is ludicrous.' Discuss this statement in the light of Hughes' paper.
2. What are the implications of the author's assertion that 'these findings suggest that providing young children with further concrete experiences of addition and subtraction may not be the most appropriate educational activity . . . rather the educational problem is one of finding ways to help children free their thinking from the concrete so that they can express the concepts *they already possess* in formal arithmetical symbolism' (p. 154).
3. The author claims that his experimental technique demonstrates 'an approach which could easily be extended to other aspects of arithmetical symbolism'. Try to design a game (or games) which would demonstrate the arithmetical law of commutativity ('1+2' = '2+1').

## SUGGESTIONS FOR FURTHER READING

1. Donaldson, M. (1978) 'What the school can do', chap. 9, pp. 96–109, and 'The desire to learn', chap. 10, pp. 110–120, in *Children's Minds*. London, Fontana.
   A theme that underpins much of Donaldson's research and writing is that 'the *process* of becoming literate can have marked – but commonly unsuspected – effects on the growth of the mind' (p. 97). In the same way that there is a very large gulf between the language we speak and the language we write, with the consequence that young children will learn best to grapple with possibilities of meaning if they are weaned on the familiar cadences of the spoken tongue, so too, Donaldson argues, 'if the child is taught to operate with the decimal system without coming to understand that it is one system among other possible ones then, to quote Vygotsky, "he has not mastered the system but is, on the contrary, bound by it" ' (p. 99). Thus, although we cannot commence teaching arithmetic by introducing the concept of a numerical base, the author argues that from the beginning we *can* be conscious of working towards such an end. This, in effect, means that we can try from the very beginning to help the child to acquire some degree of understanding of the general nature of the learning activity in which he or she is engaged, so that 'before he gets down to the confusion of the detail, he has at least a rudimentary sense of the kind of thing he is attempting' (p.100). Becoming 'literate' – in a broad sense of the word – is a theme echoed by Hughes in Reading 10 when he argues that 'the picture which is emerging suggests that, from a cognitive point of view, pre-school children may well possess many of the prerequisite skills required for learning arithmetic. What skills they do lack appear to be primarily *linguistic* in nature – such as understanding how symbols can be used to *record* a message of what has been done, or learning how to *read* a set of symbols in a particular order, or in realizing that symbols learned in one context can be used in a variety of other contexts' (p. 165). Donaldson comments on the ease with which teachers can help the young child to achieve *new learning*, reminding readers of Jerome Bruner's comment that to be 'ready' to learn a given skill is precisely to be already equipped with other prerequisite skills.
   In Chapter 10 Donaldson examines the question of what makes us want to learn, arguing that although babies – and other creatures – certainly learn to do things

because certain responses lead to 'rewards', babies will also learn to behave in ways that produce results in the world with no reward except the successful outcome. In short, the author claims, there exists a fundamental human urge to make sense of the world and to bring it under deliberate control. As the young child grows, Donaldson writes, 'there is a fundamental human urge to be effective, competent and independent, to understand the world and to act with skill' (p. 113). As well as this basic urge to 'manage' there is added very strong social approval of various kinds of competence which the young child must also master. It is Donaldson's contention that in all kinds of ways we do *not* encourage competence – we very often tend to keep our children too dependent for too long, which denies them the opportunity to exercise their very considerable capacity for initiative and responsible action (p. 113). This is exactly the point which Hughes makes regarding young children's arithmetical potential, and why he writes, 'by introducing symbols in meaningful communicative situations the games show young children that there are situations where arithmetical symbols can be used to make life easier, and where there is a purpose for making translations between formal symbols and concrete objects and events. If this idea can be communicated effectively to young children, it may have a profound effect on their subsequent mathematical education' (p. 165).

2. Wells, G. (1985) 'Language, learning and the curriculum', in *Language, Learning and Education*. Windsor, NFER-Nelson, chap. 9, pp.152–75.

Wells argues that by the time that children come to school at the age of five, they have learned a very great deal and have done so as active *meaning-makers*. He contrasts children's learning at home, which, because of its almost complete spontaneity, has been sporadic, unsystematic and, to a considerable extent, idiosyncratic, with the opportunities presented by school, which, because of its more systematic approach to learning, would help them:

–  to go beyond the immediate event and the response it arouses, to set it in a wider context;
–  to construct a broader and more coherent inner model, integrating new with old experience;
–  to communicate through speech, and later through writing, with those who have had different experiences;
–  to begin to reflect upon events, thoughts and feelings, and to use language to construct and explore imaginary and hypothetical 'possible worlds' – to engage in 'disembedded thinking'. (p.157)

Of paramount importance for the teacher is the task of sharing interests and enthusiasms and helping young children to *think* and *talk* about what they are doing, helping them:

–  to articulate their aims and to formulate plans of action;
–  to recognize problems and to consider alternative means of resolving them;
–  to use available resources to the best effect, e.g. books, equipment and material;
–  to evaluate the outcomes of their activities, both functionally and aesthetically. (p. 157)

It is precisely the argument of Hughes in Reading 10, specifically concerned with 'arithmetic', and of writers like Bruner, Donaldson, Tizard and her collaborators, concerned with wider aspects of learning, that a very important part of the job of the teacher of young children is 'to guide the child towards tasks where he will be able objectively to do well, but not too easily, not without putting forth some effort, not without difficulties to be mastered, errors to be overcome, creative solutions to be found' (Donaldson, 1978, p. 114).

3. Donaldson, M. (1978) 'What *is* and what *must* be', in *Children's Minds*. London, Fontana, chap. 5, pp. 51–9.

Donaldson contrasts the kind of reasoning of which young children seem to be capable if one observes their spontaneous behaviour with that of their behaviour in 'test' or laboratory-type situations. She shows, for example, that children's difficulty lies not in the inferential processes which the task demands, but often in certain perplexing features of the apparatus and the procedure adopted by the experimenter. When these are changed in ways which do not at all affect the inferential nature of the problem, young children often successfully solve the problem (p. 54). See, for example, Donaldson's account of the work of Hewson, on pages 54–5. The author concludes from the evidence she presents that young children are not at any stage as egocentric as Piaget has claimed, and that the gap between children and adults is not so great in this respect as has recently been widely believed. Furthermore, children are not so limited in their ability to reason deductively as Piaget – and others – have claimed.

## Reading 11

# QUESTIONING THE PRE-SCHOOL CHILD

## *H. Wood and D. Wood*

In this paper, we present an account of a recent study of conversations between a teacher and some of her children in a nursery school. While our emphasis is on the importance of conversations for young children and on the nature of conversation between adults and children, this should not be taken to imply that we feel this type of activity is the only or indeed the primary goal of pre-school education. We fully share the view that play, for example, and spontaneous interactions between children also form an important part of pre-school provision. Recent work provides convincing evidence, for example, that teacher–child and child–child interactions help achieve different goals in the service of the pre-school child. So, our work on conversation should be viewed simply as an exploration of one aspect of the tasks facing teachers and other pre-school workers. But why study conversation at all?

There are several answers to this question [. . .]. Let us briefly outline

Wood, H. and Wood, D. (1983) 'Questioning the pre-school child'. *Educational Review*, **35**, 2, 149–62.

some of our own reasons for an emphasis on dialogue. First, conversation is one of the activities which teachers and playgroup workers themselves see as an important facet of their job. One of our tasks, as researchers, is, we believe, to provide feedback to people about the nature and effects of their strategies or styles for achieving their own objectives. Secondly, we believe that through talk with an interested and responsive adult, children find an avenue to discover things about other people and, through their reactions to them, to find out things about their own, social selves. Thirdly, we know from several recent studies, that children in the pre-school years are still developing their own linguistic and communicative competence. On several different levels – vocabulary, syntax, pragmatics and powers of self-expression – the young child is still discovering what language and communication are and how to become a competent and independent communicator. Indeed, though this is not the place to argue our point in detail, we believe that it is only through conversation and through listening to other people involved in conversation, that the child can come to master several different features of the linguistic system.

On another level, the child must discover the social practices which govern responsive and socially acceptable participation in 'group talk'. In the playgroup or nursery school, where the child must begin to function as a relatively independent agent free of his parents and family, he or she meets many new demands for social interaction and interpersonal communication. Finally (though not, necessarily, exhaustively), it is largely through language that the child begins to learn about the world outside his own personal experiences. Competence in the understanding of 'disembedded' or 'decontextualized' language is fundamental to effective participation in formal schooling.

Those, then, are the primary reasons why we believe conversation to be an important activity in the pre-school years (and beyond). Now to our study and its origins.

## THE STUDY

In a previous study, as part of the Oxford Pre-School Research Group, we worked with 24 nursery teachers and playgroup workers to try to articulate with them their objectives in working with young children and the different techniques or strategies they used in attempting to achieve these. We looked at play, instruction, management and conversation. In our studies of conversation, we found, as other researchers have, that most linguistic exchanges between adult and child were characterized by a high frequency of questioning by the adult. Although different teachers and playgroup workers varied in their reliance on questions, most used them freely. In fact, they comprised, on average, 50 per cent of all 'moves' in a teacher's conversations with children. It can be argued, of course, that questions are fundamental both to group management and teaching. At best, questions might stimulate children into cognitive effort and towards new realms of understanding. However, many 'pre-school' questions are not challenging. They tend to be neither stimulating nor particularly interesting (e.g. 'What colour are your shoes?'; 'Did mummy buy you that dress?'). It is still possible to argue, however, that only through demanding questions can a teacher meet with high-level responses from her children. Consequently, we have included in this study an exploratory investigation of the relationships between teacher demand and the cognitive level of children's responses. Basically, we ask if one needs always to ask questions in order to receive back high-level responses from children.

The second aspect of questioning which motivated the present study centres on the effect they have on children's initiative and involvement in conversation. Basically, we found in the Oxford study that those teachers who used 'high control' in conversation, i.e. those who asked most questions were: (a) the least likely to receive questions back from children; (b) least likely to engender not only answers to questions but also get back elaborations on those answers from children; and (c) least likely to encourage children to make spontaneous comments or contributions overall. In general, we found that the linguistic initiative shown by young children went down as a function of how often they were questioned.

Given such correlations between styles of teacher talk and children's initiative it is tempting to conclude that some teachers are more successful than others in encouraging children to talk. However, it is possible that teacher style reflects differences between children. In other words, one may ask questions more often of a child who is linguistically less forthcoming. One weakness of the Oxford study was that we had no information about the children which might help us to see whether some factors to do with children were responsible for any such effects. One way to tackle this question is offered in this paper. Here, as we have done in other studies, we ask a teacher systematically to change her style of conversation with the same pairs of children. Our prediction is that as the teacher changes her style, so too will her children – in predictable ways. If children do respond in such predictable ways, then this reinforces the view that the locus of control over what a child does in conversation lies at least in part in her own hands.

We have already undertaken parallel studies to the one discussed here with teachers of hearing-impaired and deaf children. These showed that as teachers changed their style their children did indeed show predictable patterns of response (about which, more later). Thus, even with children facing formidable linguistic problems, teachers can influence how much they say and how readily they will talk. These studies also showed that not only did children's initiative in asking questions, making comments, etc. change systematically as a function of teaching style, but also the actual numbers of words they used in any conversational 'turn' also varied systematically. Thus teaching style influenced both how much initiative children showed and how talkative they were.

Two final points need to be made before we outline the design of the study. The first concerns our choice of teacher and children for the study. The teacher involved is a very experienced and self-confident one. Both are important ingredients of our work. The ability to adopt deliberately different styles of talking to children in a fashion which is not too artificial for the children is not a trivial one – thus the need for experience. Having research workers looking over one's shoulder and, potentially, dissecting one's style, is also very threatening and demands a good deal of self-confidence. The children involved – six in number – were also selected with a number of criteria in mind. Basically, we did not want only children who were linguistically very able. Our work with the deaf showed that changes in style were most likely to achieve dramatic results with the linguistically more able children. Consequently, we wanted to include in the present study children who were less linguistically developed. We therefore selected some children for whom English was not their native tongue. Another reason for including this group was that we wanted to see how far the principles of conversation we shall be discussing are truly general ones likely to be of interest not only to pre-school workers in general but also to those who are responsible for 'E2L' (English as a second language) children.

The second point about the study concerns the small sample used. We shall be talking about one teacher and six children. The sample is small partly because of the immense amount of work involved. Each child is involved in some 50 minutes of conversation. Every conversation has to be transcribed word for word, categorized and analysed. Three hundred minutes of talk involves a massive investment of time in analysis. But there is another reason for the sample size. We believe that the principles of conversational structure we are discussing are extremely powerful and general in school-type settings. If we are right, then statistically significant differences should emerge even from small groups. This, plus the fact that parallel studies by ourselves and others have all produced results consistent with our Oxford study, leads us to expect reliable results from a small sample.

# THE CHILDREN

Children took part in the study in pairs. They were chosen by their teacher on the basis of age and level of proficiency in English. The first pair of children were to be four-year-old English children who were as 'average' as possible, neither very chatty nor very reticent. The second pair were to be of a similar age and come from non-English-speaking backgrounds such that they would be having difficulties with English, but be in no other way 'disadvantaged'. Pair 3 was, in fact, added to the study by their teacher when she found that the pair 2 children were more forthcoming than she had anticipated. The major characteristics of the children are listed in Table 11.1.

Table 11.1

| i | Age | Sex | Nationality |
|---|-----|-----|-------------|
| Pair 1 | 4:1 | F | English |
| | 4:2 | F | English |
| Pair 2 | 4:0 | M | Egyptian |
| | 3:6 | M | Egyptian |
| Pair 3 | 3:5 | F | Iraqi |
| | 3:0 | M | Egyptian |

# METHOD

Each teacher and child pair took part in at least five different ten-minute sessions. We had envisaged that it would be necessary to familiarize the children to chatting in front of the camera by means of an initial 'normal' chat session in which the teacher, using a picture book as an initial 'prop' to initiate conversation, would talk to the children adopting a style that she considered representative of her usual style. However, after only a few minutes she considered pairs 1 and 2 to be relaxed enough to go on with the study proper. There followed four 'experimental' sessions in which the teacher attempted to bias her conversation towards giving priority conversation time to four different conversational 'moves' in turn (categories 2, 3, 4 and 5 in Table 11.2). Each session was recorded on a different occasion and sessions were usually one week apart. Finally, the teacher returned to her normal style. This last session was introduced to control for any familiarity effects due to repeated filming of children, and, in the case of pairs 1 and 2

Table 11.2  Levels of control in conversation

*Five main levels*

(four of which form the focus for the four strategies in this study)

| | | |
|---|---|---|
| 1 | Enforced repetition | 'Say – I went to the park' |
| 2 | Two-choice questions | 'Did you have a good time?' |
| | (require only yes/no | 'Did you go on the swings or the |
| | or one of two) | roundabout?' |
| 3 | Wh-type questions: | 'Where did you go over the weekend?' |
| | (all 'Wh' questions plus | 'What happened?' |
| | how, 'Tell me about') | 'What colour is your dress?' |
| 4 | Personal contributions: | 'I like going to the park too' |
| | (comments and statements) | 'That must have been awful!' |
| 5 | Phatics: | 'Oh the park, lovely/super/good!' |
| | ('Conversational oil') | 'I see', 'Hmm' (nodding) |
| | | (or repeating what child just said) |

*Mixtures of the five levels commonly found*

| | | |
|---|---|---|
| 5.1 | Requests for repetition: | 'Pardon?', 'What?' |
| 5.2 | Tag phatics: | 'Did you?', 'It was green, was it?' |
| 4.2 | Tag contributions: | 'That's green, isn't it?' |

*Responsive moves*

| | |
|---|---|
| √ | Appropriate answer to a question (even if factually wrong) |
| √4 | Appropriate answer plus elaborating contribution |
| X | Clear misunderstanding of what required in question |
| X4 | Clear misunderstanding but child goes on to add a contribution |
| nr | No response |
| ? | Unintelligible and/or not codable |
| Other: | any move not covered above, e.g. teacher pointing to picture. |
| | For larger groups of children categories for 'management' |
| | ('sit still and listen') and 'chairing' ('Sharon?', or 'You |
| | can have a turn after John') have been added |

this also included a short repeat of the two-choice question session to check on the effects of holding such sessions on the first day of filming.

# MATERIALS

Filming was carried out in a small quiet 'reading' room within the nursery school and the teacher chose a Ladybird book, *In the Park*, as a focus for all the conversations. She was also given a pamphlet outlining the project and she prepared roughly the things she might say in each session. It was stressed that each session should be as similar in interest and scope as possible – as far as her efforts were concerned – although the children were to be allowed to develop the conversation as far as they were willing and able.

## CODING CATEGORIES
### Levels of conversation

Each turn in a conversation by both teacher and children was classified into a number of distinct 'move types'. A move is classified as an utterance or, in some cases, a failure to respond within a 'turn' in the dialogue. [...]. Where participants made more than one move in a turn this was noted (e.g. where a child not only answered a question but went on to add more information). Where the teacher made more than one move (for example, if she first made a statement and then immediately asked a question) the child was deemed to have responded to her 'last' move. The major categories of move types are given in Table 11.2.

### Cognitive demands and responses

The second analysis of our data examines the level of 'cognitive demand' displayed by the teacher in different sessions and the level of 'cognitive response' displayed by children. The system used is a very simple categorization which is based on that developed by Tizard et al. (1982) [. . .]. The aim of this analysis is to explore the extent to which a child's level of cognitive performance is related to teacher demand.

What we did, then, was to code as a 'high' demand, any occurrence of a request which Tizard includes under the heading 'explanations and generalizations' (including interpretations, hypotheses, etc.). All of her other cognitive demands were coded as 'medium'. This category includes requests for labels, descriptions and recall. This left a variety of 'low' cognitive demands which were not included in Tizard et al.'s system, e.g. two choice questions, tags, comments and phatics. In order to categorize the children's responses, we merely took the mirror-image of Tizard's classifications – i.e. we substituted 'child gives . . .' (recall, reason, label, etc.) for 'adult demands . . .'. These responses were then coded high/medium/low as for teacher demand with 'low responses' consisting of 'no response', inadequate answers, simple 'yes – no' replies and repetitions of what had just been said. As children's questions proved to be difficult to classify they will not be considered here.

The next step was to combine the two coding systems outlined above in such a way that we could tabulate the level of child response after each move/demand type (this involved a subdivision of wh-type questions into low/medium/high and comments into informational/speculative).

# MEASURES USED

## Power and initiative *(from Wood et al., 1982)*

### Teacher power

The proportion of questions, enforced repetitions and requests for repetitions in teacher speech (excludes tags).

### Child initiative

The proportion of moves which contain contributions or questions not directly solicited by the teacher. Initiative is measured in four ways:

(a) All contributions and questions from a child as a proportion of all his or her moves in a session.

(b) The proportion of answers to a teacher's two-choice questions or tags which are followed by an elaborating contribution or question from the child.

(c) The proportion of responses to teacher contributions and phatics which include contributions or questions from the child.

(d) The proportion of all appropriate answers to all teacher questions and tags which are followed by elaborating contributions from the child.

### Child loquacity

The mean number of words spoken by a child in response to teacher moves (MLT, or mean length of turn).

## Cognitive demand and response

### Teacher demand

This is expressed as the proportion of all teacher moves which fall into the high/medium/low categories.

### Child response

Likewise this is expressed as the proportion of all child moves which fall into high/medium/low categories.

# MAJOR PREDICTIONS

On the basis of our earlier studies we can make a number of predictions about the outcome of the present experiment. These are:

1. Teacher power over all sessions will be significantly* and negatively correlated with measures A, B and D of child initiative and child MLT. We have no firm predictions about measure C since, in the past, this has

---

\* The term 'significant' refers to *statistical significance* throughout the paper.

Table 11.3   Changes in teacher moves

| | Percentage moves in four main levels of control | | | |
| Session | 2 | 3 | 4 | 5 |
| --- | --- | --- | --- | --- |
| Two-choice | 52 | 10 | 9 | 13 |
| Wh-type | 20 | 48 | 6 | 12 |
| Contribution | 2 | 5 | 42 | 25 |
| Phatic | 4 | 5 | 6 | 46 |
| Final (normal) | 15 | 32 | 17 | 16 |

always been negatively correlated with teacher power but not always significantly so.

2. Children will display different MLTs to different move types in teacher speech. They will say most after teacher contributions and phatics and least after wh-type and two-choice questions.

3. The analysis should also reveal a significant interaction between move type, MLT and session. When teachers ask large numbers of questions, MLT to most move types should be depressed. So, for example, MLT following phatics should be higher in the low control than in the high control sessions.

## MAJOR RESULTS

### Could the teacher change her style?

It is quite possible that teachers become so fixed in their styles of talking to young children that they are unable to change as demanded by the present experiment. If so, further analysis would obviously be fruitless. However, as Table 11.3 shows, the teacher in the present study (in company with those who participated in earlier studies) was able to change as and when requested. Although the pattern shown is summed over all three groups of children, the pattern in each group is very similar.

### Did the children respond systematically?

In Table 11.4, we list the teacher's power measures for each session with each pair of children. It also lists the initiative measures (as a percentage of all possible occasions on which initiative could have been shown) and MLT averaged over the two children in each pair for each session. An inspection of this table shows, as predicted, that children show most initiative in the low control sessions and least in the questioning sessions. Mean length of turn shows a similar pattern.

The degree of teacher power over each pair in each sesssion was used

Table 11.4  Teacher and child measures

| Pair | Session | Teacher power | A | B | C | D | MLT |
|------|---------|---------------|---|---|---|---|-----|
| | | | Child initiative | | | | |
| | [2] | 72 | 28 | 22 | 76 | 16 | 2.7 |
| | [3] | 68 | 32 | 46 | 68 | 18 | 3.4 |
| 1 | [4] | 16 | 69 | 56 | 81 | 42 | 5.5 |
| | [5] | 23 | 57 | 26 | 84 | 10 | 4.6 |
| | [F] | 51 | 37 | 41 | 76 | 15 | 3.2 |
| | [2] | 59 | 33 | 18 | 84 | 16 | 2.3 |
| | [3] | 69 | 28 | 32 | 75 | 8 | 2.6 |
| 2 | [4] | 12 | 67 | 62 | 75 | 32 | 3.5 |
| | [5] | 19 | 66 | 60 | 88 | 28 | 3.9 |
| | [F] | 56 | 29 | 26 | 64 | 10 | 3.1 |
| | [In] | 71 | 14 | 19 | 34 | 4 | 1.2 |
| | [2] | 61 | 20 | 15 | 39 | 13 | 1.5 |
| | [3] | 77 | 17 | 22 | 58 | 11 | 2.1 |
| 3 | [4] | 6 | 52 | 43 | 57 | 39 | 2.5 |
| | [5] | 13 | 64 | 35 | 87 | 17 | 2.9 |
| | [F] | 42 | 26 | 21 | 44 | 8 | 1.8 |

together with each pair's corresponding initiative and loquacity measures to derive correlations both for each pair and for the group of six children. The results show that the more questions a teacher asks, the less likely children are: (a) to take up any opportunity to show initiative; (b) to follow her two-choice questions or tags with additional, unrequested information; (c) to elaborate on their answers to all questions – including wh-type questions; and (d) give long utterances overall. The only correlation which did not generally reach significance (although it did with pair 1 – the most fluent in English) was measure C. In other words, while children showed a general tendency to take up a greater proportion of opportunities to make a contribution following a teacher's contribution or phatic in the low control sessions, the results were not always significant.

Children did, then, respond systematically in the ways we had predicted.
[. . .]

## EFFECTS OF SESSION

We have, then, correlational evidence that children gave longer utterances in low control sessions than in questioning ones. [. . .].

We can, however, find no evidence that the young children in this study made progressively better use of their opportunities to be expansive after low control moves when they were frequent in teacher talk. Differences between sessions seem to be entirely due to the fact that low control sessions contain more of those moves which engender relatively long responses.

## EFFECTS OF MOVE TYPES

[. . .] Given that children only rarely elaborate on their answers to teacher questions, it follows that the two-choice questions usually met with single word responses. Not surprisingly, MLTs after these were significantly shorter than those following any other moves. Wh-type questions met with shorter responses than either contributions or phatics. Thus as we had predicted, children say less after the more controlling moves.

In summary, then, low control moves engender longer responses than do questions – which has predictable effects on sessions containing many such moves. However, although children were more likely to elaborate on their answers to questions when there were relatively few put to them, this did not produce the interaction between session and move type which we had predicted.

## Child–child moves

There are, however, a group of moves made by children which we have never analysed in detail before but which are worthy of mention here. These are moves where a second child speaks after the first not to give a second response to the teacher's move but to follow on from the other child or interrupt with a new comment. We had noticed in previous studies that such utterances were often very long and sometimes prevalent with teachers who were low in control. This pattern was very variable over different teachers and classrooms, however, but here, where we have one teacher varying degrees of control with three pairs of children, it is possible to look at these moves in a systematic way.

The first finding is that for this group of children child–child (or C–C) moves were on average quite long, longer even than moves following phatics. Furthermore, these moves were far more frequent in low control sessions (constituting 15 per cent of all their moves) than they were in questioning ones (2 per cent of moves), and correlations between power and frequency of C–C moves proved to be consistently negative for all three groups, and significant for pairs 1 and 2 and over the three groups combined.

It would seem, then, that the simple ploy of requesting a teacher to vary the amount of questioning in different sessions led, not only to varying levels of initiative and loquacity, but also to sessions which were qualitatively different in terms of the relationships established between teacher and children. But does a change in the relationship necessarily entail a change in the quality of cognitive functioning within those sessions?

## Cognitive demand and response

If young children can only be led to speculate, reason and offer interpretations of events through direct questioning by teacher, then we would expect two findings to emerge from our data. First, we should find that a teacher's high-level wh-type questions are the only moves to be associated with a high frequency of such responses from children. Secondly, since the wh-type question session contained a far higher proportion of such demands from the teacher (e.g. 19 per cent with pair 1), this should emerge as the most 'stimulating' session for the children.

Neither prediction is unequivocally borne out by the data, however. When we look at the children's responses to high-level demands over all sessions, we find that they did usually provoke high-level responses. For example, pair 1 gave high-level responses 64 per cent of the time. However, speculations, reasons and so on put forward by the teacher also received such responses – 55 per cent of the time. All other move types lagged far behind, including ordinary comments and wh-type questions (which received only 15 and 4 per cent respectively).

When we look at the children's behaviour in the different sessions a somewhat different picture emerges. Although the 'wh-session' contained more high-level demands, children did not produce more high responses here than they did in the less controlled contribution and phatic sessions (20, 17 and 22 per cent respectively). When we look at children's medium-level responses – giving information, etc. – we find a similar pattern (43, 50 and 47 per cent respectively).

We thus have the situation where demanding questions will produce 'the goods' they require, but the attempt to simply pack more of them into a session does not bring about any perceptible increase in the amount of reasoning, hypothesizing, remembering or describing which goes on. There is in fact a significant correlation between the proportion of questions asked in sessions overall (power) and the amount of time children spend in giving low-level replies. One of the factors involved in this is the fact that the two-choice question sessions yielded worst results of all. Another factor lies in children's willingness to contribute information and reasons when not specifically asked to do so. A third factor, however, concerns the fate of individual questions in different sessions. Just as the results of this study and our previous work have pointed to a decrease in elaborations after questions when they are frequent in teacher talk (see Table 11.4, columns B and D), the rough analysis we have been able to carry out here also indicates that questions are least effective in getting the required answer in sessions where there are many of them. Too many questions therefore not only make children passive and terse, they also tend to depress their level of performance. Thus, if we see a child apparently failing to meet the demands of his teacher's questions, we must not ask simply if the child is relatively incompetent or 'unready' for them. We must look at the place such questions occupy in the overall structure of the discourse in which they are embedded.

What is at stake here, then, is not the value of questions per se, but the effects of stringing many of them together. As we did not ask the teacher involved here to maximize her children's cognitive effort in each session, we cannot draw any firm conclusions as to how this might be done effectively using different strategies. What is of interest, however, is the fact that children did respond to their teacher's attempts to reason and speculate in their presence. There may be more than one way, therefore, of raising the level of discourse should this be the main aim of teachers dealing with young children (though Tizard et al. found only 2 per cent of teacher moves requested high-level cognitive effort).

If more extensive studies were to produce confirming evidence on this point, then it would follow that teachers might, as it were, have their conversational cake and eat it too. For it would follow that they are able to stimulate children to think and reason in discourse without paying the price in terms of children's relatively low initiative and loquacity which a lot of questions entail.

## DISCUSSION

We began this small-scale study of conversations with pre-school children with two main, explicit aims in mind. First, we wanted to see whether the correlations discovered in earlier work between the conversational styles of teachers and children's patterns of responding simply reflected differences between the children involved or were causally related to teaching approach. We certainly would not deny that a child's stage of language development or powers of understanding place considerable constraints on what teachers can achieve with them. However, the present study, in company with previous work, shows that, within these constraints, there is considerable latitude for variation in terms of how readily children will talk and how much they will say. The way in which a teacher talks to young children helps to determine how active, forthcoming and competent they may appear. Whether the children involved are pre-schoolers or older pupils; deaf, hearing or perhaps coming to English as a second language, the same basic 'rules' of conversation hold. If a teacher seeks to get children talking and thinking through question after question, then she is unlikely to hear children spontaneously elaborate on the theme of conversation, or go beyond her questions to add more information. Their talk will tend to be elliptical and terse. Without a systematic study of language exchanges between teachers and children, however, we could never be fully confident that the differences found in our transcripts could be attributable to teaching style – and not to factors such as the inherent talkativeness of a child, the quality of the relationship he has with the teacher or the specific topic at hand. Our research to date has convinced us that, whilst such factors as these may not be irrelevant, the style of teacher talk itself helps to determine how talkative and competent a child appears.

But why take so much trouble to look in such detail at such a specific and relatively banal aspect of teaching activities? We suspect that the type of response any teacher makes to the line of work just outlined will be symptomatic of some fundamental aspects of their educational philosophy. Certainly, in our personal encounters with teachers, we have felt both support and hostility which seems to correlate with their views on early child education. One frequent reaction, for example, is that such work as that just outlined is merely an elaborate and time-consuming demonstration of the obvious. Of course one should not question children all the time and ask those silly questions to which the teacher knows the answer and which the child knows they know. But at the same time there are other commonsense views which are in contradiction with what has just been said but which the same teachers may well believe: only through questions can one get some children thinking and talking; the child has to learn how to participate in such activities because they are fundamental to later classroom learning and so forth. Furthermore, although a teacher might seem to 'know' what we are trying to explore already, it may not be the case that he or she actually acts on that knowledge in the classroom. [ . . . ]

Another reaction is much more difficult to evaluate, however. Some teachers argue that simply getting children 'chatting' is not a profitable use of their time or their children's. [ . . . ] For them, systematic questioning by the teacher and relatively quiet and attentive responding from the child are ingredients of successful teaching–learning encounters. We do not, of course, deny the importance of skilled and sensitive questioning. At best, a good question (and the definition of 'good' is a problem of the first order) helps a child to 'decentre' himself from his own immediate perspective; to 'disembed' or to 'decontextualize' his thinking; to explore his own thoughts, to discover ambiguities, inconsistencies and gaps in his knowledge and so forth. But questions are also an exercise in power. He who questions, controls, and he who answers runs the risk of appearing ignorant or silly, perhaps in the company of his peers in whose eyes he wants and needs to appear competent. All too often, questions seem to promote not competence and extended thinking but apathy and withdrawal. Although our study of cognitive demands and response is in no measure definitive or conclusive, it does suggest another course of action which might achieve both the goal of encouraging children to play an active and, sometimes, leading role in an interaction with the teacher, whilst, at the same time, displaying evidence of reasoning, hypothesizing and so forth. It can (and no doubt will) still be argued that the teacher needs to control not only the level of children's responding but also its direction. If people work with an image of young children which holds that they are likely to avoid demanding, constrained thinking in new and difficult task situations, then they are likely to persist in the belief that control and questioning are primary to the effective pursuance of their role. We have no evidence to gainsay such views and have no desire to suggest that this point of view is not a legitimate and interesting one.

Of those who share this image of the learner, however, we ask that they consider the other side of questioning and controlling which we have been discussing in this paper; to question themselves as to whether their questions really do have the effects they desire and do not have the side-effects we have been discussing.

More generally, however, we hope to stimulate more debate and thought about the nature not only of questions but also other types of conversational moves towards young children. We hope that our discussion of questions and control provides a convincing case for treating both as important topics for educational enquiry; that such an enquiry brings together discussions of the linguistic, cognitive, personal and social aspects of young children's development in school. Elsewhere we have started to consider the issue of what constitutes a good and timely question, although only in a very preliminary way. We hope that the present study will inspire others involved in early education to question the role of questions along with us.

## TOPICS FOR DISCUSSION

1. 'Competence in the understanding of "disembedded" or "decontextualized" language is fundamental to effective participation in formal schooling.' Discuss the concept of 'disembedded' language and its implications for teachers working with young children.
2. 'The way in which a teacher talks to young children helps to determine how

active, forthcoming and competent they may appear.' Discuss.
3. What kinds of 'styles' do teachers adopt in their conversations with young children, and what happens when they change their 'styles'?

## SUGGESTIONS FOR FURTHER READING

1. Robson, B. (1983) 'Encouraging dialogue in pre-school units: the role of the pink pamfer'. *Educational Review*, **35**, 2, 141–8.

A substantial part of the research into early language development has concentrated on adult–child interactions, mainly between the pre-school teacher and the child and more recently between children and their parents. As a consequence, studies of communication between children have received less attention. This paper is based on a study which investigated language in pre-school units by means of radio microphone recordings. The research examined two aspects of the study of dialogue in the nursery. The importance of peer stimulation is considered in terms of the influence of older, more able children over younger children and those with communication problems. The author suggests that language development is enhanced by learning through imitation, by direct teaching and by opportunities to practise and experiment. Second, Robson emphasizes that teachers can improve their own dialogue with children by having greater understanding of the *processes* of dialogue between children.

2. Donaldson, M. (1978) 'What is said and what is meant', in *Children's Minds*. London, Fontana, chap. 6, pp. 60–75.

Donaldson writes that 'one way to describe the difference between child and adult would be to say that it lies in the amount of weight that is given to *sheer linguistic form*. The question seems to be whether the meaning of the language carries enough weight to over-ride the meaning of the situation.' For this reason, she asserts, we have to take into account that what children expect to hear is liable to be influenced not only by things which give them clues about the speaker's intentions but also by more impersonal features of the situation they are considering. Donaldson reasons that children's interpretation of what the teacher says to them is influenced by at least three things (and the ways in which these interact with each other) – their knowledge of the language, their assessment of what the teacher intends (as indicated by the teacher's non-linguistic behaviour), and the manner in which they would represent the physical situation to themselves if the teacher were not there at all (p. 69).

3. Tizard, B. and Hughes, M. (1984) 'How the children fared at nursery school', in *Young Children Learning: Talking and Thinking at Home and at School*. London, Fontana, chap. 8, pp. 180–213.

Tizard and Hughes set out to describe the ways in which young children learn from their mothers at home. They questioned the assumption that 'professionals' have a good deal to teach parents about how to educate and bring up children, arguing instead that professionals might learn a great deal from observing children talking to their parents at home. They wondered also whether the claims made about the value of nursery schools as a source of linguistic and intellectual stimulation were justified, and found, when observing typical nursery sessions, that individual children's conversations with nursery staff were surprisingly infrequent, often restricted to very brief exchanges. It seemed, therefore, unlikely that the language environment of the nursery was richer than that of the home. The authors found that conversations in working-class homes were just as prolific as those in middle-class homes, and whilst there were social class differences in the mothers' conversation and style of interaction, the working-class children were clearly growing up in a rich linguistic environment. Conversely, however, when Tizard and Hughes analysed the conversations with adults at home and nursery school, pronounced differences were found, especially for working-class children. In this chapter they discuss how the children observed at home fared at nursery school, describing the differences between educational methods, curriculum and discipline of the nursery school and the home, and especially how children's conversation with teachers is often in sharp contrast to their talk with mothers at home. Of particular relevance to Reading 11 are the numerous examples which the authors offer (and analyse) of why young children very frequently *fail* to respond to their teachers' cognitive demands.

## Reading 12

# THE RELEVANCE OF FANTASY PLAY FOR DEVELOPMENT IN YOUNG CHILDREN

## *P.K. Smith*

It is a morning late in March, and some 20 children, three to four years old, are nearing the end of the morning session of their pre-school playgroup. There has been a lot of fantasy play, recorded by an observer watching unobtrusively. Two girls have been playing 'mother and baby', one wheeling the other around in a pram. Several of the older boys have been chasing each other, being 'monsters', and pretending to shoot each other with outstretched arms and fingers. At one point they besiege the Wendy house which the girls are in. Later, Simon pretends to be a captain on a boat (a long chair at the end of the room). To attract attention, he yells 'I'm a dead captain – I've got an arrow in there', pulling up his vest and poking his tummy. 'Let's take the arrow out', says Christopher; 'Let's leave him – till he gets better', says Mark. However, Simon does not like being left alone, and announces he is a shark. More chasing play, but then they set up some stools in a row and turn it into a 'chair-train', pushing the chairs backwards along the floor (until stopped by the playgroup supervisor) and making train noises.

Jane has joined in some of the monster play and is on a chair making monster noises. Kate runs up to join her: 'I know you're a monster, Jane, but

Smith, P.K. (1984) 'The relevance of fantasy play for development in young children', in Cowie, H. (ed.) *The Development of Children's Imaginative Writing*. London, Croom Helm, chap. 1, pp. 12–31.

I'm a monster. Those two boys and those two girls, we'll make them scream and they'll run away from us, we'll be monsters.' They run and chase some other children, then crawl under a table together. 'I know what, I'll be a witch', says Jane. 'Yes', says Kate, 'put my hat on.' She pretends to put a hat on her head. 'I'll get my stick', says Jane. 'Oh yes, my stick', says Kate. They pretend to get on imaginary broomsticks and ride off on them, developing into a chase with both girls yelling 'We are witches, we are witches! We will spell you!' (Another girl, Emma, watches and runs off by herself, muttering 'We are witches.') Jane runs up to Mary and clasps her with her arms: 'We've got you, we are witches!' Mary says 'No!', but Kate pretends to wind string round her, 'I've tied her up'. They run off to a book corner. Kate says, 'These are special witch books, you know! Set them out like this', putting half a dozen books in a row. Jane fetches more books. 'We are witches, we are witches, we will turn you into a monster', Jane shouts to Mary. 'We are turning, we are turning you into a nasty monster', Kate shouts to Stephen, adding. 'No, you're not having these books', as he grabs at them. The play is ended by the arrival of parents at the end of the morning.

These examples of fantasy and sociodramatic play are fairly characteristic of young children in our society. They are characterized by pretence, imagination and drama. It is pretend play, as the girls are not really witches, they do not have real hats or spells. The term *imaginative play*, often used synonymously with pretend, fantasy or symbolic play, refers to the imaginative use to which children can put ordinary objects such as chairs and books, and to how they can imagine absent objects as well. And clearly, there is drama in the action. At an age before they have learnt to read or write, these children are making up and acting out little adventures, many of them prosaic imitations of home life, some more removed from domestic reality. When children are acting out roles together, this is referred to as *sociodramatic play*.

In some important respects the fantasy and sociodramatic play of children can be thought of as the precursors of later imaginative story-writing or telling. There are structural similarities, and some psychologists have suggested more direct links. In this chapter I shall review what we know about these forms of play, highlighting links to language, creativity and writing skills where appropriate.

## THE DEVELOPMENTAL SEQUENCE OF FANTASY AND SOCIODRAMATIC PLAY

Fantasy play seems to develop in a fairly regular way as children get older. Piaget (1951) was one of the first psychologists to describe this in detail, and since then several other investigators have described the changes which occur up to two and a half or three years of age.

The earliest pretence behaviours are generally seen around 15 months of age. These are typically self-directed behaviours – for example, Piaget observed his daughter Jacqueline at this age lie down with her head on a cloth, suck her thumb and blink her eyes (as if going to sleep) – and smile. By two years of age other-directed actions are more common, such as putting a doll or teddy bear to sleep.

Another clear developmental trend is the lessening dependence on realistic objects for fantasy. Up to two or three years, children most easily fantasize with the aid of miniature items such as toy cups, combs, dolls, etc. As they get older, they are more able to make fantasy use of unstructured materials such as boxes, sticks and so on, transforming them in play into such things as boats or guns. The more such transformations are simultaneously involved, the more difficult for the child. One experimental study showed that at 20 to 26 months of age, 93 per cent of children would imitate making a detailed horse model 'drink' from a plastic cup. Only 33 per cent would imitate making a horsey shape 'drink' from a clam shell. If the horse alone or the cup alone was realistic, the figures were 79 per cent and 61 per cent respectively.

Pretence sometimes involves imagining an object when no substitute object is present (for example, the witch's hat, and the string, in the opening example). This is possible for three- and four-year-olds, but is easier still in middle childhood. For example, when asked to pretend to brush their teeth or comb their hair, most three- or four-year-olds use a substitute body part such as a finger; whereas most six- or eight-year-olds imagine the toothbrush or comb in their hand.

Pretence-play episodes also involve more combinations as children get older – combining a number of objects in play, or different actions on the same object (for example, bathing, dressing and feeding a doll). As such combinations and sequences develop, we can talk of role play, with a child acting out a role such as 'mother'. When two or more children role play together – either similar roles, such as the 'witches' example, or different roles such as 'mother' and 'baby' – then sociodramatic play develops.

There has not been such intensive study of developmental changes in fantasy play after three years, but it is fairly clear that sociodramatic play increases in occurrence at least up to five years of age. Older children engage in more role play than object fantasy play, and in more socially interactive pretend play. However, after the age of six or seven years, symbolic play generally becomes less frequent as children engage more in rule-governed games such as hopscotch, tag and football.

# SYMBOLIC PLAY AND
# THE ACQUISITION OF LANGUAGE

Both early words and early pretence substitutions in play are thought by many cognitive psychologists such as Piaget to be reflections of a general capacity for symbolic representation. The ability to pretend that a doll is a baby may be linked to the ability to 'pretend' that the word 'baby' refers to a baby; both seem to imply a symbolic concept of what a baby is, going beyond just a sensorimotor response to an actual baby, such as smiling or touching.

Several psychologists have attempted to draw closer parallels between the development of pretend play and the development of early language. One of these is McCune-Nicolich (1981), who suggests there are parallels between the two domains first in presymbolic behaviours; then in initial pretending and first referential words; then in the emergence of combinatorial behaviours in both domains; and finally in the hierarchical organization of symbolic play and language.

For example, the sorts of combinations in symbolic play which were mentioned earlier have been found to occur at about the same time as two-word language combinations, such as 'baby bath'. However, as McCune-Nicolich states, additional research is needed to confirm how close and how invariant these parallels are.

Further evidence for such a link between symbolic play and language has been reported by Corrigan (1982). She showed two-year-old children certain play behaviours, such as making a doll walk across the floor saying, 'I'm dirty. Now I'm going to take a bath.' They were then asked to imitate the same actions. Corrigan also got the children to imitate sentences such as 'The mummy is giving the baby a bath'. In their imitations the children seemed to go through a similar developmental sequence of increasing complexity in imitating the play actions and the spoken sentences.

Several other studies have found parallels between the development of symbolic play and the development of language. For example, Ungerer and Sigman (1981) found that autistic children showed similar impairments in both their symbolic use of play objects and in language comprehension. However, it is important to remember that these parallels do not necessarily mean that symbolic play and language influence each other *directly*; it could be that they are both aspects of a general symbolic or cognitive development. Also, one longitudinal study of Canadian infants found that symbolic play measures did not correlate with language (although measures of the latter were restricted to utterance length and vocabulary).

# STRUCTURE AND CONVENTIONS IN SYMBOLIC PLAY EPISODES

Whatever the link between symbolic play and language production or comprehension, there is another parallel with written, narrative language. Fantasy and sociodramatic play episodes are themselves acted-out narratives or stories. Several psychologists and linguists have discussed the narrative-like features of fantasy play, the conventions governing sociodramatic play, and the fantasy/reality distinction. These analyses have usually been based on audio-taped or video-taped interactions in nursery or laboratory playroom settings.

The simple forms of symbolic play seen up to two years of age do not often tell any sustained story, or have a plot. Wolf and Grollman (1982), working with the Harvard 'Project Zero' research on the development of children's symbolic abilities, have constructed a developmental scale for levels of narrative organization in play. At the *scheme level*, a child just performs a simple action or brief series of actions; for example, feeding a doll with a spoon. At the *event script level*, a child performs at least two schemes which are part of the same process or part of achieving the same goal; for example, pouring a 'drink' into a cup, adding 'sugar', and offering it to drink. At the *episode level*, a child performs at least two script events aimed at achieving a particular goal; for example, first stirring some 'food' and 'cooking' it; then serving out the 'meal' on plates at a table. Wolf and Grollman looked in very great detail at a small sample of only four children, who reached episode-level play at round about two years of age. In this and previous work, these researchers also distinguish between *styles* of play. They hypothesize that *patterners* primarily explore the uses and properties of objects, whereas *dramatists* more often imagine non-present objects, events or persons, and use objects as props in social interaction.

While solitary fantasy play may have quite a complex narrative structure, the latter becomes particularly obvious when one child plays with another, or with an adult; the play episode needs first to be initiated, and then continued along a plan, often with the participants adopting certain roles in sociodramatic play.

Some of the ways in which four-year-old children initiate fantasy play have been described by Matthews (1977). She observed six main ways of introducing a transformation from reality to fantasy:

> *Substitution.* A child directly gives a new identity to an object; for example, picking up a stick and saying 'This is my space gun'.
>
> *Attribution of function.* A child ascribes a pretend function to an object;

for example saying 'Don't shoot me' when another child picks up a stick.
*Animation*. A child attributes animate characteristics to an object; for
example tucking a teddy under a cushion saying 'Go to sleep, baby'.
*Insubstantial material attribution*. A child refers to non-existent objects;
for example picking up an empty box saying 'I've got some presents in
here for you'.
*Insubstantial situation attribution*. A child refers to a non-existent situation; for example announcing 'Come on, let's go to the party!'
*Character attribution*. A child directly adopts (or gives to another child) a
role; for example saying 'I'll be mummy, okay? You be daddy.'

The first three modes of initiation Matthews calls *material*, and the latter
three *ideational*. Matthews found more ideational initiations amongst girls
than boys (though her sample of 16 subjects is really rather small for such
comparisons). She also found that they became more common with increasing familiarity between play partners.

When a fantasy episode is initiated, how do the participants know what to
do next? If it is to continue, some theme, plan or narrative must be followed.
This has been most thoroughly discussed by Garvey (1977). She suggests
that fantasy themes are generally built around certain plans, the popular
ones being 'averted threat', 'telephoning', 'packing', 'taking a trip', 'shopping', 'cooking', 'dining', 'treating/healing' and 'building/repairing'.

Garvey suggests that each of these plans has a basic structure; for
example, 'averting threat' has the three-sequenced components: identification of threat or danger/defence/outcome. The threat might be another child
running up saying 'I am a witch', the defence might be running away, and the
outcome that the first child is caught and 'tied up' (see episode at beginning
of this chapter). As another example, 'telephoning' involves initiating a
call/greeting/body of call/closing. Within a plan, one or more components
might be omitted; not all pretend telephone calls have a greeting, for
example – or some might *just* be a greeting! Also, there are many possible
transformations within a component; a threat might be a snake, a fire, a
bomb, etc.

The most common roles adopted, according to both Garvey and Matthews, are *relational* ones, such as parent–child, or wife–husband. These can
of course be fitted into a number of plans, such as 'shopping' or 'dining'.
Garvey also distinguishes *functional* roles, defined around actions such as
driver/passenger; and *character* roles, stereotyped or fictional, such as
cowboys or Santa Claus. Finally, *peripheral* roles are just referred to by the
child; imaginary friends, for example.

These roles can be enacted using knowledge the child has, either directly in the family (relational roles), through wider experience (functional roles), or TV or stories (character roles). Garvey found that the youngest children were confined to relational roles; and even in older children, it is these relational roles which often have the most detailed repertoire of narrative plans.

Roles may be exchanged between children; for example, two children might exchange the role of 'mummy' and 'baby' after a while. Most roles remain sex-appropriate, with a girl being 'mummy'. According to Matthews (Brooks-Gunn and Matthews, 1979), girls more often adopt relational roles in domestic-type plans such as 'cooking' and 'dining'; almost three-quarters of the time in her observations. Boys engaged more in a wider variety of plans, such as 'taking a trip', or 'averting threat', or in more unusual plans such as 'firework displays' or 'marching bands'.

Watching role adoptions and portrayals in three- and four-year-olds reveals their sex-role perceptions in a very clear way. For example, in one episode observed by Matthews, 'mummy' doesn't mend a broken ironing board because 'when daddy comes home, he'll fix it'. Sometimes there are disagreements though; later on when 'daddy' arrives and mends the ironing board, he grasps the toy iron and starts to do some 'ironing'. 'Mummy' quickly grabs the iron, saying 'No, no, daddies don't iron.' 'Daddy' thinks for a bit, then says 'But when mommies are gone, they iron.' 'When, when mommies are gone, daddies iron?' stutters 'mummy' incredulously. 'Yeah', says 'daddy'. 'Oh', says 'mummy' and goes back to the 'cooking'.

During negotiations of roles, and disagreements over action, the 'fantasy' nature of an episode may be momentarily suspended. In her study, Matthews (1978) found that 21 per cent of interactive fantasy play was taken up with interruptions; these were caused by wandering attention, disagreements, distraction by other objects, exchanging real-life information, intervention by others, or 'real' discussion of how to continue or elaborate the fantasy.

Such breaks and resumptions of the fantasy show that the children are fully aware of the fantasy/reality distinction, and are able to negotiate their way in and out of it without great difficulty. Indeed, fantasy episodes can sometimes call upon or reveal a great deal of social skill. The example below, adapted from Garvey's (1977) work, shows how a three-year-old girl is both acting out the 'baby' role, and directing the 'care-taker' role, coming in and out of the fantasy as necessary.

The girl (aged three years three months) initiates a baby/care-taker sequence with a boy (aged two years nine months) and carries it through 12 exchanges before a 'real-life' query ends it.

| Girl | Boy |
|------|-----|
| Say 'Go to sleep now' | |
| | Go to sleep now |
| Why? (whining) | |
| | Baby . . . |
| Why? | |
| | Because |
| No, say 'Because' (emphatically) | |
| | Because! (emphatically) |
| Why? Because why? | |
| | Not good. You bad |
| Why? | |
| | 'Cause you spill your milk |
| No, 'cause I bit somebody | |
| | Yes, you did |
| Say 'Go to sleep. Put your head down' (sternly) | |
| | Put your head down (sternly) |
| No | |
| | Yes |
| No | |
| | Yes. Okay I will spank you. Bad boy (spanks her) |
| My head's up (giggles). I want my teddy bear (petulant voice) | |
| | No, your teddy bear go away (sternly) |
| Why? | |
| | 'Cause he does (walks off with teddy bear) |
| Are you going to pack your teddy bear? | |

## THE ROLE OF THE ADULT IN NARRATIVE STRUCTURE

On the one hand some aspects of children's fantasy episodes can seem remarkably sophisticated. On the other hand many episodes are mundane or even dull; a high proportion of actions are simple imitations of domestic tasks – tucking in baby, washing dishes, eating food.

Potentially, an adult can do much to enrich a child's fantasy. This is true both for the early episodes of one and a half- to two-year-olds, the socio-dramatic play of three- and four-year-olds, and the thematic fantasy play and sociodrama of older children.

The role the adult can have in extending the fantasy play of younger children is described by Sachs (1980), enlivened by transcriptions of play between her, or her husband, and their daughter Naomi when she was aged between 21 and 25 months. In the earlier episodes the adult is mainly suggesting actions to the child, for example, 'Get the baby and bring him to bed', or 'Can you feed Georgie with the spoon?' The separate components or building blocks for later narratives or plans are being suggested, but as yet Naomi does not provide this integration. A few months later, however, Naomi begins to be able to establish a storyline in her play when helped by an adult. Now, the adults' comments help Naomi move from one action to the next, for example Naomi (putting dolls in sitting position): 'Baby sit there'; adult: 'Do they want something to eat?' Quite possibly, the prompts provided by an adult (or older sibling, perhaps) when a child is only two years old help the child to create his or her own plans in sociodramatic play a year or so later (see later section on individual differences).

In the three- to five-year age range it is by now well established that adults can encourage sociodramatic play in children who do not engage in it spontaneously to a very great extent. This *play tutoring* was pioneered by Smilansky (1968) in Israel. She was concerned at the low levels of socio-dramatic play which she observed in immigrant children in Israeli kindergar-tens, and examined a number of ways of facilitating it. Taking the children on visits (e.g. to zoos, hospitals) and providing appropriate props helped, but most effective was if an adult suggested themes to the children and/or helped sustain the narrative. This technique has since been employed widely in the USA, UK and elsewhere. Follow-ups show that play tutoring does facilitate the subsequent spontaneous sociodramatic play of the children. What other benefits it may have will be reviewed in a later section.

With older pre-school children, another possibility for adult involvement is via *thematic fantasy play*. Here, children are helped to act a story whose plot is already sketched out; for example, folk tales or fairy tales such as The Three Billy Goats Gruff, Hansel and Gretel, Little Red Riding Hood. It is argued that thematic fantasy play demands more of the children than much sociodramatic play, since the roles and behaviours acted out are further removed from ordinary experience.

With older children still, forms of dramatic play or role-playing can be employed in the curriculum. For example, Iannotti (1978) asked six- and nine-year-old boys to act out short stories or skits, sometimes switching roles, in an attempt to encourage altruism and empathy. Hartshorn and Brantley (1973) organized eight- and nine-year-olds in dramatic play in a child-size city they constructed, as a way of increasing problem-solving skills and social responsibility. Chandler (1973) asked delinquent and non-delinquent eleven- to thirteen-year-old boys to participate in film/drama workshops to improve role-taking ability and decrease antisocial behaviour. These latter researches are closer to work on role-playing in adults, and it is outside the scope of this chapter to consider them more fully.

## INDIVIDUAL DIFFERENCES IN FANTASY PLAY

Children differ very greatly in the amount and complexity of fantasy play in which they spontaneously engage. For example, in two pre-school play-groups in which I made observations, I recorded incidents of fantasy play over a total period of 6 hours; a couple of children were seen in fantasy play for a total of only 2 or 3 minutes; whereas another, in the same environment, spent over 2½ of the 6 hours in fantasy activities.

Social class and cultural differences have both been implicated in the causation of such differences. Observations in nursery schools, and interviews with parents, suggest that children from lower socioeconomic backgrounds engage in less fantasy and sociodramatic play, and receive less encouragement from parents to do so. For example, Newson and Newson (1968) found that in their sample of four-year-olds there was a large social-class difference in the extent to which children talked about fantasies or imaginary companions to their mothers, and also the extent to which mothers participated in the children's play. Smilansky (1968) and others have reported subcultural differences too. Such conclusions have been criticized on a number of methodological criteria; for example, social-class differences found in nursery schools might not be observed in streets or playgrounds.

Rather than simply stating that social class is an important variable, it is necessary to try and find out exactly what environmental factors are important. We have seen that the kinds of toys young children are provided with may or may not facilitate fantasy. Also the encouragement of parents may or may not serve to both scaffold early fantasy narratives, and allow, or forbid, the expression of the child's imagination. Two quotes from mothers in the Newsons' (1968) study – both from working-class backgrounds – express these different parental attitudes. Encouragement: 'Oh yes, I always play house – he plays house, and he's the mummy and I'm the auntie and come to visit him.' Discouragement: 'I've said to him, you know, "That's never happened, you're imagining things!" I've told him, I've said,

"Now that's *wrong* – you've got a vivid imagination".'

The role of adults is also important in considering the effects of different pre-school or infant school curricula. Adult tutoring of fantasy play in the pre-school can have considerable impact. Such adult tutoring seems to have more direct impact than either simple or mediated use of television films. The effects of the mass media on fantasy are complex; many of the role adoptions in sociodramatic play are taken from TV serials, but most studies find that watching a great deal of television correlates with less imaginative or fantasy play.

Singer (1973) has written about 'high-fantasy' (HF) and 'low-fantasy' (LF) disposition in children. He assessed this by asking children about the kinds of games they liked, whether they ever had pictures in their head, and whether they had make-believe friends or imaginary companions. He found that six- to nine-year-olds of HF disposition, when asked to tell stories to a suggested topic (e.g. a mother and son; they look worried), produced stories which were rated as more creative or imaginative. Pulaski (1973) confirmed that in a sample of five- to seven-year-olds, HF predicted to a much higher level of observed fantasy play with objects than did LF disposition. In this study the experimenter asked the child to make up a fantasy story with the materials available. HF children produced more imaginary details in their stories, which were better organized, less anchored to everyday reality, and showed a greater variety of themes.

Similarly, Lieberman (1977) has argued that children vary on a general playfulness factor. She, and others, have found some evidence that playfulness, and a disposition for pretend play, correlate with creativity. However, there are problems with concluding too directly from their work that playfulness or fantasy disposition, and creativity or narrative skill, are directly related. First, much of the evidence on children's playfulness is based on teachers' ratings, and teachers might tend to think that playfulness and creativity go together and let this influence their ratings, irrespective of whether it was actually so; direct observations of the children would be better. Also, a correlation may be due to some third factor which is the important causal influence; for example, some or all of the link between playfulness and creativity may be due to general intelligence influencing both.

This raises an important point about the significance of fantasy play. Children with HF disposition or who do a lot of fantasy play may tend to be those who are creative, intelligent, as well as cooperative, popular and less egocentric, and with higher levels of reading readiness. Does this mean that encouraging fantasy play would encourage these other attributes? We cannot infer this from correlational studies; the intelligence might cause the fantasy, not the other way round. Experimental studies can potentially answer this question, though as we shall see, they have their own problems of methodology and interpretation.

## DIRECT TRAINING OF FANTASY AND SOCIODRAMATIC PLAY

The work of Smilansky (1968), and others since, has shown the possibility of enhancing the fantasy and sociodramatic play of children in nursery schools, playgrounds and kindergartens, by means of adult tutoring in which an adult (usually a teacher) actively interacts with the children. This can involve either *outside intervention* or *inside intervention*. With outside intervention the teacher remains outside the play episode but provides comments or encouragement; for example, saying 'What are you going to cook for supper?' to two children in the Wendy house. With inside intervention the teacher actually takes a role and joins in the play; for example, saying 'Let's pretend that we are washing dishes', miming the actions, and perhaps assigning roles to the children.

Christie (1982) provides a readable account of how to carry out and assess intervention in sociodramatic play. He suggests that the six essential elements for a teacher to work on are (1) imitative role play; (2) make-believe in regard to objects; (3) make-believe in regard to actions and situations; (4) interaction with play partners; (5) verbal communication related to the play episode and (6) persistence in the play episode. When the child has been observed participating in play that contains all these essential elements, Christie suggests that play intervention should be phased out. As he also points out, this sort of direct intervention is not appropriate for children who are already engaged in high-quality sociodramatic play, where indirect stimulation via vocabulary, props and theme ideas, is more relevant.

Since Smilansky's work, numerous researchers have confirmed that play tutoring does work; sociodramatic play can indeed be encouraged and developed in this way. This may be valuable in its own right, but will boosting sociodramatic play help a child in other ways? Some lines of evidence would suggest so. We have seen that the structure of such play episodes and the interpersonal cooperation and role-taking involved may make considerable demands on a child's social and perspective-taking skills. Correlational evidence links fantasy play disposition with creativity and symbolic skills such as language, which may develop in step with it. If in fact there is a real causal influence here – if the experience of pretend play directly helps language and perspective-taking skills, for example – then boosting pretend play should develop these other areas of competence too.

| *Subjects* | Usually children aged three to five years from lower socioeconomic backgrounds, attending nursery or kindergarten |
|---|---|
| *Pre-test Assessments* | Levels of spontaneous pretend play, and measures of social, linguistic, or cognitive development, creativity, etc. |

↓

Children then divided into

*Experimental Group*

Receive period of extra play tutoring; outside or inside intervention by adult to encourage fantasy or sociodramatic play, or role-playing activities

*Control Group(s)*

Receive period of (1) no treatment control – no extra tutoring; or (2) extra tutoring in some non-fantasy activities, e.g. arts and crafts, dimensionality training

↓                            ↓

*Post-test Assessments*    Usually same as at pre-test assessment

Figure 12.1    Typical design of research projects on the effects of play tutoring.

In the 1970s a large number of studies were carried out, using what became virtually a research paradigm, employing play-tutoring and comparing its effects with a control condition. The basic research plan is outlined in Figure 12.1. These studies were mostly done in the USA, on kindergarten children from lower socioeconomic groups. The findings of some dozen research projects were generally positive: play-tutored children increased in social, cognitive and language skills, and creativity, more than control children.

One example of research in this paradigm is that of Lovinger (1974). Eighteen four-year-olds in a pre-school nursery were assigned to an experimental group, and 20 to a control group. All the children were first observed, to record verbalizations in play, and were tested on the Verbal Expression scale of the Illinois Test of Psycholinguistic Abilities. There were no significant differences between the two groups at this stage. The experimental group then received extra play-tutoring intervention during the free play period of one hour a day, over 25 weeks; the control group experienced the regular nursery programme. The children's language abilities were then reassessed. It was found that the play-tutored children, but not the control children, had improved on both spoken language and tested Verbal Expression.

Saltz and Johnson (1974) used thematic fantasy-play training, and compared it to dimensionality training and no-treatment controls. The play-trained children were found, amongst other things, to have a better memory for stories, and when asked to tell stories from pictures they provided longer and better organized narratives. Similarly, Yawkey (1979) used a *social relations curriculum* with five-year-olds, which involved setting up role-play experiences. Children in the control group had art and craft activities. The role-play group improved more on the Gates MacGinitie Reading Readiness Skills Test, and also on the Singer Imaginativeness Inventory.

However, despite these and other positive findings, there are difficulties in the methodology and interpretation of findings of most or all of the play-training studies to date.

There are two common methodological problems. First, the testers have often been aware of the training condition of the children, so that scoring bias cannot be ruled out. Secondly, the control conditions have usually either involved no extra stimulation, or an unspecified amount of interaction. The point of the latter criticism is that play tutoring involves both boosting pretend play, and a good deal of individual or small-group adult–child interaction and verbal communication. It may be the latter, and not the pretend play per se which has benefits for language and other skills. Unless the control group is equated with the play-training group for verbal stimulation and adult–child interaction, this possibility cannot be excluded. In one study in which such a control group was carefully equated on these measures, the differential improvement of the play-trained children was largely restricted to pretend play, and peer social participation.

There are also problems in interpreting the pattern of results from different studies. In some areas, notably perspective-taking skills, some studies have obtained positive results and others have not. The size of positive effects is sometimes quite small, even when statistically significant. The permanency of any improvements is also open to question, as very few of the studies have used a delayed post-test some time after the play intervention has ceased. Finally, it should be borne in mind that play training may have some results that could be negatively evaluated in the classroom; for example, increases in noisy physical activity, and, in the case of severely emotionally disturbed children, increases in overt aggression and poor concentration.

Having made these qualifications, we see that play training is clearly an enjoyable activity, and even if it should prove the case that some or many of the gains made by the children are due to the adult contact in training rather than the play per se, nevertheless the gains are made. Play training is clearly one effective way of bringing about sensitive adult–child involvement, and (unlike many forms of adult involvement in children's activities) it seems to increase peer interaction as well.

## THEORETICAL PERSPECTIVES ON FANTASY PLAY

The review of experimental training studies shows that we are still uncertain about the exact importance of fantasy and sociodramatic play in development. This is paralleled by the range of viable theoretical perspectives on these forms of play.

One school of thought, although at present times a minority one, is that in fantasy play a child loses touch with reality to an undesirable extent, failing to get to grips with real difficulties in his or her environment. Pretending that a block is a cake does not help the child learn anything real about wooden blocks, or cakes, according to this line of thought. This was the argument of Montessori; the positive side of this view is the emphasis on even quite young children helping with real-life tasks, washing real dishes and baking real cakes rather than pretend ones. This different emphasis may help to explain any lesser encouragement of pretend play in working-class families (Newson and Newson, 1968) and its possibly lower incidence in UK families of Asian origin.

Piaget was influenced by the Montessori tradition, and he also puts emphasis on the child's adaptation to external reality. Fantasy play (called 'symbolic play' by Piaget) is seen as a necessary stage of development, but one which in general is a reflection of the child's existing skills; assimilation rather than accommodation. Such play does consolidate existing skills, and it can give a child confidence in this; but it does not especially cause the growth of new skills.

On the other hand many theorists have seen fantasy play as having a more direct and positive importance. Freud and other psychoanalytic thinkers saw play as a means of wish fulfilment, and of working through anxious or traumatic events. This latter aspect, of the child gaining mastery over anxieties and conflicts, was continued by Erikson, and has lain behind the development of play-therapy techniques. Empirical evidence for the cathartic or mastery theories of play is rather sparse.

Psychological theorists have, however, more often emphasized the cognitive or creative aspects of fantasy play. Vygotsky (1967) emphasized the distinction between literal, and non-literal, thought and language in pretend play, arguing that it therefore fostered symbolic and creative thinking. Mead (1932) discussed how sociodramatic play called on children to act out other roles and coordinate with each other, and thus developed perspective and role-taking abilities.

These hypothesized benefits of fantasy and sociodramatic play for symbolic thought, creativity and social cognition have been echoed by later writers such as Berlyne, Bateson, Bruner, Singer and Sutton-Smith. They also encouraged the play-training studies discussed earlier, which, as we have seen, give some support, strongly qualified by methodological reservations, to these positions.

Another theoretical position is that fantasy play may have direct or indirect benefits, but that these can be realized by other means as well. For example, I have argued (Smith, 1982) that fantasy makes play more complex, and therefore more useful as a developmental experience for the child; but other experiences, such as non-fantasy training, might be as or more effective in various domains – hence the varied results of the play-training studies. Rubin (1980) considers that the primary benefit of fantasy play may be via the increased peer interaction which it can bring about, resulting in social-cognitive growth; but peer interaction does not necessarily take the form of sociodramatic play.

## SUMMARY: THE RELEVANCE OF FANTASY PLAY FOR THE STUDY OF LANGUAGE, IMAGINATION AND WRITING SKILLS

The ability to fantasize or pretend is, like early language and like the recognition of self, a basic component of the symbolic ability of the child on which everything which is distinctively human will develop. The parallels between the structural development of early pretend play, and the structural development of early spoken language, are close; it may be the case that the two are very directly linked, although whether this is so and quite what such a linkage would imply in terms of developmental processes, changes and effects, has yet to be firmly established.

From two years of age onwards, a child's fantasy play has a non-literal narrative action structure which has obvious parallels with the later production of spoken or written stories. Relevant aspects of this correspondence are: the creation of imaginary roles, actions and events; the coordination of a sequential plan or story structure, including the initiation and termination of episodes; the reflection of stereotyped knowledge, including sex-role stereotypes, and exposure to the mass media, on the content of the narratives; and the potential role of an adult in encouraging and scaffolding narrative development. Relevant differences are: the appreciably earlier appearance of acted to written narratives, and the fact that in sociodramatic play at least the narrative is jointly constructed with one or more other play partners.

Children who have a high-fantasy disposition or engage in much pretend play, have generally been found to be more creative, socially skilled, and better at perspective-taking tasks. There are several ways of interpreting such findings. It may or may not be the case that the parallels of pretend-play narratives to written stories also imply a causative developmental link between the two. Such a link, if it is found, could be due to indirect factors; for example, pretend play might encourage perspective-taking skills, which could later be reflected in more mature story construction.

Whether pretend play has certain causes, or consequences, can only be ascertained with reasonable certainty by careful investigations. Similarly, it could be all too easy to jump to conclusions about the causes or consequences of later imaginative writing. The research on pretend play has been extensive, and has uncovered a number of methodological problems and difficulties in interpretation. Such considerations too may have implications for the future study of how children's imaginative writing develops.

## TOPICS FOR DISCUSSION

1. Discuss the assertion that the fantasy and sociodramatic play of the young child can be thought of as the precursor of later imaginative story-writing or storytelling.
2. Trace the developmental sequence of fantasy and sociodramatic play and its relationship to the acquisition of language.
3. Discuss the ways in which young children *initiate* fantasy play and their reasons for doing so.

## SUGGESTIONS FOR FURTHER READING

1. Barnett, L.A. (1984) 'Research note: young children's resolution of distress through play'. *Journal of Child Psychology and Psychiatry*, **25**, 3, 477–83.

Barnett suggests that it has often been speculated that play is important to the child in coping with distress in the environment. This study is an attempt to replicate and expand the research of Barnett and Storm (1981) in which pre-school children were introduced to a conflict situation following which some were allowed the opportunity for free play. Various measures of anxiety confirmed expectations that play served to alleviate distress engendered by the conflict. In this study, the 'conflict' situation chosen focused on the departure of the mother on the child's first day of school. Children designated either high or low in anxiety were allowed the opportunity of free play or were placed in a control condition. Comparison of changes in anxiety level as a function of initial anxiety level and of play versus control experience tested the hypothesis that play serves to neutralize distress created by the mother's departure. A second hypothesis concentrated on the manner in which distress may be alleviated through play. Freud reasoned that the crucial element to this resolution is a type of transference process whereby peers are used as a substitute agent on whom the disturbing experience is expressed. In contrast to this view is the argument that it is the imaginative, sociodramatic type of play in which the child actively *re-creates* the experience which leads to resolution. Barnett's paper is particularly relevant to Reading 12, for example to the discussion by Garvey (1977) of children's fantasy themes being generally built around certain plans, whose structures define the relational, functional and peripheral roles of the participants.

2. Davenport, E. (1983) 'The play of Sikh children in a nursery class and at home'. *Educational Review*, **35**, 2, 127–40.

In this study, Sikh children were observed in a multi-ethnic nursery class. A time-sampling method was used to record the numbers of children involved in different activities during free play. Staff involvement was also recorded. Sikh children were compared with indigenous white children and some significant differences were found between the results of the two groups. In the second part of the research, Sikh children were observed as individuals and their interactions, activity and location were recorded on a structured precoded observation schedule. It was found that the highest proportion of time was spent in fine perceptual motor activity, that there were few extended complex play bouts and that parallel play was observed most frequently.

3. Camaioni, L. and Laicardi, C. (1985) 'Early social games and the acquisition of language'. *British Journal of Developmental Psychology*, **3**, 31–9.

The aim of this study was twofold: (a) to analyse developmental changes in the social games played by mothers and children during normal home activities; (b) to examine how mother's linguistic production during games episodes could be related to the child's pattern of language acquisition. Three mother–child dyads were studied longitudinally for 12 months, beginning when the children were six months old. Thirty-minute observation sessions once every 20 days were carried out during a free-play situation in the family environment, using video-tapes later segmented into interaction episodes defined as games. Games were categorized as conventional and non-conventional. The results were analysed in terms of both developmental changes and individual differences in characteristics of play behaviour. The authors suggest that the importance afforded to the study of the nature and development of social games played by mother and child during infancy can be explained by three different considerations: (a) games occur regularly in the everyday activities of mothers and infants; (b) they can serve as a convenient 'index' of developmental changes in the social and cognitive capabilities of infants; and (c) playing games with a repetitive and rule-governed structure may be an early way of acquiring the conventions of human social interaction and in particular may help the infant to master the rules of language.

Recent studies have shown that mothers with four- to six-month-old babies tend to initiate games that stimulate the children's attention and excite them, and at eight months old, mothers mainly produce games structured according to conventional roles, which can easily be assumed by the children themselves. This development is accompanied by a gradual change in the child's role during the game from mainly *passive* to mainly *active*. Other research studies have demonstrated that 'play has the effect of drawing the child's attention to communication itself, and to the structure of the acts in which communication is taking place' (Bruner, 1975, p. 10). Thus, the rules of play themselves become the object of attention and the mother and child are seen to be working out a *restricted* and *shared* set of 'meanings' which could be acting as referents for more advanced communication. In studies of this sort, the fact that the mother repeatedly produces certain standard formats enables the child (a) to interpret the actions and signals of the mother starting from the positions they occupy in the routine sequence, and (b) subsequently to reproduce the same actions and signals in the sequence, usually moving from the use of non-standard signals to the use of standard lexical items (Ratner and Bruner, 1978, p. 31).

The authors conclude that their results emphasize the importance of the first 6 to 12 months of life for the growth of social games, in terms of both the quality and variety of the games played and of the child's capacity for actively participating in them. Developmental changes tend to remain fairly constant from 13 to 18 months of age, a time in which the emerging novelty is that of the child's capacity to mark linguistically his or her participation in the game. They suggest also that the 'contingency' between mother's linguistic production and child's active participation in *conventional* games episodes enables the child to relate specific actions to specific interactive contexts (games) as well as to relate sounds to action objects shared within the game. It may well be, therefore, that some of the contextual variables which affect the course of early language acquisition are concerned with the extent to which the mother's speech is matched to the type of ongoing interaction (conventional versus non-conventional game) and to the type of child participation (active versus passive).

*Note*: Non-conventional games: 1. Tactile and or motoric stimulation. 2. Perceptual stimulation (visual and/or acoustic). 3. Vocal imitation. 4. Gestural imitation.

Conventional games: 5. Give and take. 6. Peekaboo. 7. Horsie. 8. Pat-a-cake. 9. Bye-bye. 10. Ball. 11. No. 12. Build–knock down. 13. Point and name. 14. Put on–take off, slip on–off, open–shut. 15. Joint book-reading. 16. Question–answer. 17. Linguistic imitation. 18. Other.

# TEACHERS,
# PARENTS AND CHILDREN

# INTRODUCTION

Section Four of the sourcebook consists of two readings concerned with parents, teachers and children. In Reading 13 the authors write that 'While parents can choose the type and extent of play activities in which they wish the child to engage and how much or how little they participate with the child in these activities, some childcare requirements are essential and involve every child and his parents' (p. 205). The reading deals with these aspects of childcare and includes the related affective areas of child-rearing practices encountered by the researchers in their study. The authors collected their data from two sources: assessment from direct observation, which accounted for the majority of the items, and parental replies to questions during interviews. These comprehensive data included: the use of dummies and thumb sucking, carrying objects and comfort objects, toilet training, washing and bathing, food and concern over eating, the social aspects of meal times, sleep, bedtime and associated problems, parental supervision (outside the confines of the home), discipline, control and misbehaviour and indices of affection and dependency. Interesting findings are reported concerning differences in child-rearing practices between working-class and middle-class parents.

Reading 14 explores how the sexual inequalities inherent in our education system are introduced at a very early age, in fact during the pre-school years. The crux of Thomas' argument is that sex-typed roles restrict personal fulfilment for *both* males and females by severely limiting the options that each is allowed to pursue. The 'message' is that sexual equality is dependent on the elimination of sex bias in the earliest years of education and that primary school teachers must be committed to this goal. Recent research adds support to earlier evidence that education in the early years is unduly geared towards boys' interests, that boys receive more time and attention from their teachers than do girls, and that in the early years of schooling teachers classify children according to their sex and expect sex-stereotyped behaviour from them. Thomas provides illuminating evidence to suggest that this state of affairs continues.

# Reading 13
## ESSENTIAL CHILD-REARING PRACTICES
### *C.E. Davie, S.J. Hutt, E. Vincent and M. Mason*

Every child has to eat, sleep and be kept clean. Every parent is going to control and guide their child to behave in a way the parent finds socially acceptable. Children cry, laugh and have temper tantrums. They need affection and physical contact. While parents can choose the type and extent of play activities in which they wish the child to engage and how much or how little they participate with the child in these activities, some childcare requirements are essential and involve every child and his parents. This chapter deals with these aspects of childcare and includes the related affective areas of child-rearing practices encountered in the study.

The data come from two sources: assessment from direct observation and parental replies to questions in the interview. The majority of items are observational; some of these were recorded in the 30-second time interval in which they occurred. Other items were assessed by the observer at the termination of all the observation sessions. Details of which type of observational assessment was used will be given when a particular item is discussed. We wished to avoid directing parents' attention to specific aspects of the child's behaviour and so possibly cause them to alter their own behaviour. Therefore direct questions to parents on child-rearing practices were kept to a minimum and only asked where the information, for instance the length of the child's waking day, was essential to the planning of the observation sessions.

Davie, C.E., Hutt, S.J., Vincent, E. and Mason, M. (1984) 'Essential childrearing practices', in *The Young Child at Home*. Windsor, NFER-Nelson, chap. 4, pp. 36–58.

# DUMMIES AND THUMB SUCKING

Parents' replies to the question whether their child used a dummy might have been affected by their feeling that dummy use is socially undesirable. Consequently, the observer assessed, after the final observation, whether the subject had used a dummy at all. There is a modern trend in favour of dummy use. For instance, Spock (1955) advises: 'If you feel that your baby needs a dummy and are worried only about what the neighbours or relations will say, tell the neighbours that this is a very modern practice (or tell them that this is your baby)'. Similarly, Leach (1975), more recently, writes ' . . . slipping a dummy into the mouth of a crying baby who is *not* hungry is often very effective', although she does go on to suggest that dummy use should be restricted to rest periods and sleep times to prevent it getting in the way of oral exploration. However, dummies or comforters are still a source of social embarrassment to some parents and several mothers felt the need to justify their child's use of a dummy to the observer. One teacher's wife explained how she tried to restrict her three-month-old daughter's dummy use when in the home to times when there were no visitors. She described her embarrassment on meeting her GP in the street when her child was sucking a dummy. In her confusion, she drew the doctor's attention to the dummy and was laughingly assured that the doctor had used a dummy for all her own children. In the first observation session with a plumber's little girl, the grandmother was babysitting and the child asked for her dummy. Her grandmother replied that she could not have it, whereupon the subject said to her grandmother's embarrassment 'Can I have it when the lady's gone?'

The number of dummy users dropped significantly* with age. Twenty-four per cent of the three to three and a half-year-olds were using dummies, 11 per cent of the three and a half- to four-year-olds were doing so and none of the four-year-olds. Dummy use did not vary with social class.

As it is argued that giving a child a dummy can prevent thumb sucking, we examined the data to see if the children using dummies were less likely to suck their thumbs. Thumb sucking (in which we included any finger sucking) was recorded as a checklist behaviour category. We found that children who used dummies were as likely to suck their thumbs as those children who did not use dummies. They were also likely to spend as much time sucking their thumbs as the non-users. The 38 per cent of the children who sucked their thumbs did this for a mean time of 3 per cent of their waking day. While the incidence declined steadily across the three age-groups, the decline was not significant.

---

*The term 'significant' refers to *statistical significance* throughout the extract.

# CARRYING OBJECTS AND COMFORT OBJECTS

Children were assessed as using a comfort object if an object was held or carried around on more than one occasion and not used in any other play activity. It was impossible to make this assessment except in 'post hoc' terms. Therefore a behaviour category 'Auto-manipulate minus look' defined as 'not looking at object while holding, manipulating, mouthing' was recorded on the checklist and the object in question was also recorded. Subsequently, all objects held in this way were listed out and those recurring on two separate observation sessions were categorized as comfort objects. Children, in our sample, spent 13 per cent of their day clutching a wide range of items, such as scraps of paper, matchboxes, teaspoons and small toys, which they were not currently using in their activities. There was a tendency for this 'general clutching' behaviour to decline with age, but this is not a significant drop.

Ten per cent of the sample were observed to use a comfort object according to our criteria. The majority were items of pram or cot bedding such as blankets or eiderdowns but they also included a few soft toys, and idiosyncratic objects such as 'big thing', which was an adult pillow covered with ticking and in another case a plastic hammer.

It is possible that dummies and comfort objects fulfil the same function. If this were the case, children who had dummies would be less likely to have comfort objects. The numbers of children who used either one or both objects were compared, but the data did not vary from the expected frequencies. Therefore, children who used a dummy were not less likely to use a comfort object or vice versa.

# TOILET TRAINING

All the children were toilet trained during the day, but some were not dry throughout the night. Rather than ask the parents directly if their child was dry in the night, observers recorded if the child was still put to bed in a nappy. This assessment assumes that nappy wearing reflects lack of bladder or bowel control. Ten per cent of the children were still wearing a nappy at night, most of them in the three to three and a half age band and more of them middle-class than working-class. Significantly more of them were boys, 13 boys to 3 girls.

Only casual and anecdotal evidence is available on the mothers' attitudes to their children still wearing nappies at night. It seemed to be generally one of unconcern. The only mother who did show concern about the topic had a child who suffered from chronic constipation and her concern was with the

Table 13.1   Percentages of children using lavatories as opposed to potties by age

| | Pot only (%) | Both pot and lavatory (%) | Lavatory only (%) |
|---|---|---|---|
| 3–3½ yrs | 3 | 9 | 26 |
| 3½–4 yrs | 1 | 8 | 26 |
| 4–4½ yrs | 0 | 1 | 28 |

physical condition which was causing the child to dirty his nappy at night.

Usually, training the child to use the lavatory is seen as the next step after potty training. A few children in the sample were using a potty only; some were using both the lavatory and a potty, but the majority were using the lavatory all the time. Observers noted which was used during the observations. Almost all the four to four and a half-year-olds had stopped using a potty (see Table 13.1).

## WASHING AND BATHING

Over half the children were not observed taking a bath, 22 per cent of these were middle-class, 34 per cent working class. We distinguished bathing from washing by stipulating that bathing had to include body immersion at some point in the proceedings. Eleven per cent of the parents chose not to use the bath for this purpose and this included only one child whose family did not have a fixed bath. Most of these children were bathed in the kitchen sink, but people also used a zinc bath, baby baths and washing-up bowls.

## FOOD AND CONCERN OVER EATING

The majority of families ate their main meal in the evening. It was usually (except in hot weather) a cooked meal including meat or fish and vegetables. Often the vegetables were tinned or frozen and potato chips were very popular. This was frequently followed by a simple sweet course, such as jelly, blancmange, rice pudding or a shop-bought cake. Breakfast generally consisted of cereal followed by toast or the latter on its own. In exceptional cases, a cooked breakfast was eaten, such as boiled egg or bacon sandwich. Fruit juice, milk, milk shakes, coffee and tea were drunk during the day and with meals. A midday meal often consisted of sandwiches, beans on toast or a local speciality, grilled oatcakes with bacon and cheese.

Table 13.2 gives a typical example. It is the diet of a joiner's son aged three

Table 13.2　Example of one subject's diet sheet

| *Time child commenced eating or drinking* | *Items* |
|---|---|
| 8-06 | Weetabix, sugar & milk |
| 8-29.5 | Drink of milk (1) |
| 9-44.5 | Biscuit (1) |
| 9-49 | Biscuit (2) |
| 9-52.5 | Drink of milk (2) |
| 10-24.5 | Biscuit (3) |
| 11-12.5 | Sweet (1) |
| 11-39.5 | Sweet (2) |
| 12-07 | Sweet (3) |
| 13-00 | Banana sandwich |
| | Drink of milk (3) |
| 14-31 | Stick of celery |
| 14-40.5 | Drink of milk (4) |
| 15-02 | Drink of water |
| 17-15 | Shepherd's pie, peas |
| 17-57.5 | Drink of orange squash |
| 18-46.5 | Drink of milk (5) |
| 19-55 | Drink of milk (6) |

years, three months. His diet sheet is from a total of 12 hours' observation, in six two-hour sessions, covering the subject's entire waking day. Each session was on a different day and therefore one whole day is pieced together with information from six separate days.

Eleven per cent of the mothers considered that their child had problems with eating. This was assessed by the observers as being the case if the mother frequently raised the matter with the observer, asking the latter's advice or opinion or mentioned that they had taken the child to the doctor because of their concern with his eating. In one case the mother's anxiety was that the child was overweight and ate too much while in the others it was because they feared that the children were not eating enough. The latter cases included a child who suffered from chronic constipation. This mother had been advised to persuade him to eat foods high in roughage but, in his mother's opinion, he refused to eat a sufficient amount if she attempted this because he had strong food preferences. In all cases except this last one, the children were observed to eat an adequate diet in the observer's estimation. A sub-sample of the main sample participated in a research project examining calorific intake, conducted by Mary Griffiths of the London School of Hygiene and Tropical Medicine. These mothers kept diaries of their children's food intake over a week. They also kept a duplicate portion of food actually consumed by their children and this was later assessed for calorific value. This sub-sample included a number of children whose mothers had felt they were eating inadequately. Mary Griffiths considered that all the children were eating sufficient for their needs. A common reaction of the mothers after completing their diaries was amazement at the amount of food their children were in fact eating. Frequently, for instance, they had been unaware of the amount of milk that their children were drinking.

Eating problems, perceived by mothers, did show a tendency to decline with age. Of the 11 per cent of the children who were considered to have eating problems, 7 per cent were in the three to three and a half age band, 4 per cent in the three and a half to four year group and only 1 per cent in the oldest group. There was also a tendency for working-class mothers (9 per cent of the children were working class, 2 per cent middle class), rather than middle-class mothers, to perceive their children as having this problem.

In only one exceptional case did an observer consider a child was receiving an inadequate diet. This was not one of the children whose parents had expressed concern. This was again a child who had been observed for 12 hours and the observer felt that she had recorded a valid sample day's diet for the child. She was woken for breakfast with a packet of potato crisps and went through the day having a series of snacks: a jam sandwich; a packet of sweet cigarettes; a fancy cake; tea with lots of sugar lumps; more sugar lumps on their own; a rusk crushed and moistened with Ostermilk; and occasional sips of milk out of the milk bottle which she sneaked from the pantry to her mother's displeasure.

Snacks of biscuits, sweets, ice-pops, ice-creams and lollies were eaten frequently between meals by the majority of children. A few parents had a policy of offering raw vegetables and fruit as snacks and a few provided the child with his day's sweet ration during the morning leaving it to the child to eat them all immediately or save some for later in the day. The majority of children were given snacks when they asked the parents for them and were always bought sweets when they accompanied their parents out shopping or passed a sweet shop on the way, for instance to collect an older sibling from school. There was a tendency for the working-class children to spend more time eating snacks than the middle-class children.

## THE SOCIAL ASPECTS OF MEAL TIMES

Meal times can provide an opportunity for a child to talk and interact with his parents. We thought it would be interesting to assess how many children in the sample were offered this opportunity. Initially, we considered the simple category of 'sitting round a table while eating' would suffice. It became evident during the pilot study that the majority of families were likely to assemble informally for meals, sitting in armchairs with a tray on their laps, or using television tables pulled up to their chairs or standing round a breakfast bar. All these gatherings might still provide the social situation in which we were interested and we therefore defined a checklist category, 'Dining'. 'Dining' may be defined by actual eating or by the individuals concerned assembling in a specific situation before eating, or remaining there during or after eating. Further rules governed precisely whether another individual was dining with the child.

The majority of the sample had a specific place to sit for some or all of their meals. This is more a middle-class tendency than a working-class one. Less than half the subjects took part in this activity when it constituted a family gathering. Sometimes a child sat at the kitchen table along or with his brothers and sisters while the parents or mother, if it was a midday meal, took theirs into the sitting room (see Table 13.3). In a few families the father came home later in the evening and ate his meal separately. In several cases where this was the arrangement, the mother ate neither with the children nor with her husband and appeared only to eat pickings while she was cooking and scraps when she cleared up after the meals. Frequently the children who did not sit down at a set place were eating sandwiches or food from plastic bowls. They wandered about the living room or kitchen, or sat on the floor to eat while watching television.

Table 13.3    Percentage of children dining with or without adult company

| Class | Dining observed | No dining observed |
|-------|-----------------|--------------------|
| Middle | 83 | 17 |
| Working | 67 | 33 |

| Class | Dining observed with adult | No dining observed with adult |
|-------|----------------------------|-------------------------------|
| Middle | 58 | 42 |
| Working | 35 | 65 |

## SLEEP, BEDTIME AND ASSOCIATED PROBLEMS

Parents reported that their children slept a 12-hour night. There were no differences between groups. Parents also reported that no child in the sample still had a regular nap during the day, although some of the children did drop off to sleep occasionally in the course of the day. A number of the children slept during part of an observation period. In some cases they woke up in the morning later than their mothers had predicted, in others they needed to go to bed earlier than usual and some dropped off for a nap during the day. There was no variation in this between groups.

Primarily to help plan observation times, parents were asked when the children got up in the morning and when they went to bed. Getting up included actually coming downstairs as opposed to being awake in their own beds or possibly snuggling in with their parents. The times show quite a wide variation, peaking at 8.30 in the morning, but there were no consistent group variations. Similar variation was shown with bedtimes, with a peak at 20.20 hours; again there was no group difference (see Table 13.4).

Table 13.4   Children's rising and bedtimes

|         | Times (to nearest 0.5 hr) | % of children |
|---------|---------------------------|---------------|
| Rising  | 6-30                      | 1             |
|         | 7-30                      | 15            |
|         | 8-00                      | 13            |
|         | 8-30                      | 40            |
|         | 9-00                      | 13            |
|         | 9-30                      | 13            |
|         | 10-00                     | 4             |
|         | 10-30                     | 1             |
| Bedtime | 18-30                     | 2             |
|         | 19-00                     | 2             |
|         | 19-30                     | 16            |
|         | 20-00                     | 15            |
|         | 20-30                     | 35            |
|         | 21-00                     | 12            |
|         | 21-30                     | 11            |
|         | 22-00                     | 4             |
|         | 23-00                     | 1             |
|         | 23-30                     | 1             |

When asking parents when their children went to bed, we found this was not always a clear-cut issue. Most, but not all, children were put to bed and left to go off to sleep on their own. Other children often dropped off to sleep in the living room and then were carried to bed, asleep, by their parents. A number of these children were not carried up until their parents went to bed, which accounts for most of the later bedtimes. The reverse occurred with one child, a four-year-old, who required very little sleep. His mother reported his bedtime as 11.30pm in the initial interview. Frequently, he was left by his parents to potter about downstairs on his own, playing and watching television, after they had gone to bed. He would come up by himself, usually when the television closed down, and pat them to wake up so that they could tuck him into bed. A few children needed parents to stay with them until they went to sleep, for what, in some cases, the parents felt to be an excessively long time. In one extreme case, the child insisted that the mother actually went to bed at the same time as she did. The father was a policeman. He was out on shiftwork for a fair proportion of the evenings. The mother actually had to get undressed and into the twin bed in her daughter's room and pretend to go to sleep. When the father was out, she ended up going to bed at 8.30pm with her daughter, and spending the night in the twin bed. In another household, there were no beds for the children and so they spent the entire night on the settees in the living room. Another sleep problem which beset a few parents was when the child refused to stay in his own bed throughout the night and persisted in coming into their bed.

Observers assessed whether parents perceived either of these two areas as a problem. If parents discussed the matter with the observer and were seeking ways of changing the child's behaviour or if they described the situation as seriously interfering with their own domestic lives, it was scored as a problem. More children gave difficulty going off to sleep than in getting out of their beds in the night. A very small number of children presented their parents with both of these problems (see Table 13.5). Seventy-nine per cent of the children who gave rise to the first problem were working class; the social class difference is not significant.

Table 13.5 Percentage of children considered by parents to have sleep problems

|  | *Stays in own bed* (%) | *Will not stay in own bed* (%) |
| --- | --- | --- |
| Goes off to sleep easily | 86 | 2 |
| Will not go off to sleep easily | 8 | 4 |

# PARENTAL SUPERVISION

We thought it would be interesting to assess whether children were allowed beyond the curtilage of the parental home, using curtilage in the legal sense. In other words, was the child allowed to go unaccompanied into public areas beyond the garden, yard or drive of his own home, or step out of the front door into the pavement or street where, for example, a terraced house was concerned? This was assessed by the observer both in terms of the child's observed behaviour and also from anecdotes reported by parents or references arising in the course of conversation between the parent and the child. Given that the vast majority of children did have access to some outdoor play space, this seemed an interesting point for comparison across the children. This limitation showed no change with age: 54 per cent of the children were allowed out and 46 per cent were not. Neither did this tie in with the busyness of the immediate street, nor show any class or sex differences. A large number of those who were allowed out had closely circumscribed points beyond which they were not allowed to pass: for example, as far as a particular lamp post on one side of the home and the letter box on the other, while parents frequently monitored the child's whereabouts and tapped on the window or shouted if he over-stepped the prescribed limits.

Often parents were in a dilemma because they would have preferred their child not to play outside their home boundaries but other children in the neighbourhood were doing so. Either they had to enforce a rule to the effect that their child remained in their garden or yard, which meant that neighbouring children who were playing outside were unavailable to him, or they had to overcome their anxiety and let him play beyond their boundaries. Sometimes the neighbouring children were slightly older than their child and so, in order that he could play with them, the parents had allowed the child his freedom when he was younger than they would have wished. This could operate in reverse. For example, one child in the pilot study who lived in a terraced house was allowed on the 'front' but the immediately neighbouring children were not. Consequently his sole contact with other children was through the crack under their yard gate and a great deal of time was spent pushing objects of mutual interest through the crack. The observer never saw the other children at all in the entire course of observation.

In some terraced streets there seemed to be an excellent mutual monitoring service. A little boy played on his 'front' and then crossed over the street and was wandering up and down the opposite side. A passing woman peered at the observer and said 'Is he with you?' The observer was concentrating on her recording and was slow in answering. The woman turned back to the child, told him off for being across the street and saw him back across the road to his 'home' side.

One child did give an observer concern and reflected the occasional overestimation of young children's understanding shown by a few parents. The family lived in a quiet terraced street but their home was only 50 yards from a very busy main road at the bottom of the street. The child was three years, two months old and was allowed the use of the street but frequently went into the main road. The observer wished to let the mother know that the child was doing this. However, when she managed to introduce the subject the mother showed that she was fully aware by saying that the child's best friend had been killed there a couple of months earlier, which she would have thought would have stopped him going down to the main road.

The open nature of new housing estates can give rise to problems when parents know that their child is unwelcome in a neighbour's house or garden where he is continually attracted by the neighbour's children. One mother found this situation with an adjacent neighbour acutely embarrassing, and resorted to taking her daughter for long walks to avoid bother with her about going round to the neighbour's. On the other hand, a few parents seemed insensitive to their neighbour's attitudes to the visits of their children. One little girl in a new small private housing estate persistently called at various houses and was frequently rejected in very firm tones. On several occasions she was allowed in briefly and the observer (after a brief explanation of the study, neighbours were very accommodating in allowing the observer in as well) was amazed at the acerbity of the neighbours and that the child still wished to visit. For example, her remarks were either ignored or answered sharply, as in: Child (noticing Wimbledon on the television) conversationally, 'I don't like tennis'. Neighbour, shortly, 'Well that's too bad, isn't it; it's not your TV'.

Similarly, a few parents found a persistent small visitor a nuisance. By and large, most parents seemed tolerant of their own and other people's children's visits and excursions. A few families lived in small cul-de-sacs where all the families seemed to have children. This appeared to work very well with a wide range of children mixing and playing at times together. No family objected to balls and missiles being thrown about and the occasional father who appeared in the evenings to play with his own children ended up organizing games involving all the children.

While the formal rule of whether the child was permitted to go beyond his home boundaries did not show a variation with the child's age, another measure that we took did. This was a detailed observed recording on the checklist of what proportion of the working day was spent by the child not 'under the eye' of his mother or other care-taker figure; we defined this as when the child was 'Out of the same room and out of sight of parents or care-taker'. Thus, this was not scored if both the child and his mother were, for instance, in the living room and he was hidden behind the sofa, or if he moved into the hall but was still visible to his mother. It was scored if he moved out of sight into another room. Similarly, if he was playing outside, this would not be recorded while the care-taker was watching from the window, but would be scored when no one was watching or the child was out of view from a window. The three to three and a half-year-olds spent 74 per cent of their time under a care-taker's eye; this decreased with age to 67 per cent. Youngest children spend the least time, 65 per cent, the only children most, 74 per cent. Neither the difference across age groups or family positions is significant.

# DISCIPLINE, CONTROL AND MISBEHAVIOUR

Parents differed widely in what they considered to be socially acceptable behaviour from their children. Some parents were prepared to tolerate aspects of their children's behaviour which other parents would find totally unacceptable. This tolerance varied both with events leading to damage and disruption in the home and to concern with behaviour likely to cause injury to the child himself or to another child. For example, one mother walked into her bedroom to find her three and a half-year-old daughter, five-year-old son and two other children leaping from the top of the wardrobe on to their parents' double bed, having pulled all the bedclothes off to clear the way. The mother smiled and commented: 'I'll have to see to the bed when you've all finished'. In contrast, another mother insisted that her small son pack up and return to the toy cupboard any toy with which he had been playing before he fetched another. Some children were not allowed access to any potentially harmful objects such as knives, scissors and electric points, while another child regularly leant into the stove and stirred the embers with a poker, without the mother commenting. However, both the child permitted to lay waste the parents' bedroom and the one who was allowed to stir the fire, were smacked and severely told off for swearing, which their parents obviously considered was intolerable behaviour in a young child.

On a few occasions children were seen to behave differently when they were or were not 'under the parental eye'. One girl discreetly departed into the best 'front' sitting room while her mother was busy in the kitchen, climbed on to the back of an armchair and from there on to the mantelpiece, and spent some time examining the fragile glass ornaments kept there. At a later date the observer learnt from the mother that these ornaments were strictly 'out of bounds' to the child. Similarly, a four-year-old boy, who was looked after everyday by his grandmother, was playing on the kitchen floor with some marbles. The grandmother finished washing up the breakfast things, announced that she was going upstairs to make the beds and left. The child immediately opened a cupboard door, inside which were gold-stemmed champagne glasses; he dropped his marbles into the glasses and whirled them around inside. Eventually, footsteps were heard coming downstairs and before his grandmother came into the kitchen every glass was back in the cupboard and the child was again innocently rolling his marbles in front of the cupboard.

More serious incidents also occurred occasionally. One little girl, when her mother was not watching, repeatedly teased, mauled and pinched a large, boisterous puppy which the family had recently acquired. Eventually, the dog would snap at the child's fingers and she would burst into tears, then run to her mother, crying that the dog had bitten her. The dog was then severely punished. A four-year-old boy repeatedly taunted his two-year-old brother who would become enraged and finally, if he managed to catch his older brother, bite him. The older child would rush to his mother and display the wound. This mother was very concerned about the younger child's habit of biting and did punish him when it happened, but had her suspicions as to why it was happening. In another case, the reverse seemed to occur. A four-year-old girl was extremely jealous of her new baby brother; in her mother's presence she attempted to slap pieces of plasticine on the baby's head, pull and pinch his cheeks and grab at his hands and feet. While the mother was concerned not to exacerbate the situation by betraying her lack of trust in the older child, she was frightened of leaving the girl alone with the baby. However, when the mother was out of the room, the child stopped molesting the baby and behaved affectionately towards him.

While parents had been told that the observer was not going to interfere with the child's behaviour unless the child was going to hurt himself or someone else, there were a few occasions when this posed a dilemma. One instance was when a brother, the subject and some neighbourhood friends assembled in the parents' bedroom and were pouring water and talcum powder into the parents' bed and generally creating havoc. The parents were extremely house-proud and the observer felt that she would be unwelcome for another observation if they were not informed of what was going on upstairs. However, the observer had to be careful that her own standards did not intrude. For example, in the pilot study, a little girl was taking rides on the back of her friend's chopper bike. They were hurtling down a very steep cobbled bank and she was holding on precariously to the other child's jersey while both of them were screaming with laughter and a nasty accident seemed imminent. The observer drew the mother's attention to what was happening and the mother came out, saw what her daughter was doing, and half-heartedly told her to stop. The children continued and the mother laughed and turned to the observer, saying 'I've told her about it before', leaving the observer with the impression that it was a frequent occurrence and she should not have interfered.

Most children were well behaved and successfully controlled by their parents. Occasional flare-ups were precipitated by property disputes between sibling and friends, refusals to eat at meal times and summons from a parent to come into the house for a meal or bedtime when the child was out playing with his friends. Particularly if the child was hungry or tired, a temper tantrum would result. Parents, in general conversation with the observers, suggested that the frequency of temper tantrums was declining with the children's ages. Whereas parents ruefully described times when

Table 13.6    Percentage of children observed to have temper tantrums

| Age | Temper tantrum (%) | No temper tantrum (%) |
|---|---|---|
| 3–3½yrs | 13 | 24 |
| 3½–4 yrs | 13 | 21 |
| 4–4½ yrs | 3 | 26 |

their children had caused them acute embarrassment by throwing a temper tantrum in public, out shopping for instance, these incidents were now a thing of the past. We recorded the behaviour as a temper tantrum if at least one or some of the following occurred: muscular rigidity; breath held; repeated violent limb movements; body hurled on to the floor; head banging; shouting and screaming; objects hurled. Twenty-nine per cent of the children were observed to have at least one temper tantrum in the course of observation. The incidence of temper tantrums declined significantly with age (see Table 13.6).

Physical punishment from parents to attempt to stop a temper tantrum was not seen, although frequently being smacked and told off was the precipitating event. Parents used both verbal and physical punishment to control their children. [ . . . ] Thirty-eight per cent of the children were smacked by their parents in the course of observation; in the majority of cases the mother did the smacking. In all cases the parents used their hands and a single smack was involved. One child was threatened with a cane in a way which implied that he was beaten with it on some occasions. A small number of children were physically restrained by their parents as a punishment. In one case a child was thrown with considerable force by the mother onto the settee, in a way which caused the observer severe concern. This followed a series of episodes when the child had been smacked and then finally tried to hide from her mother behind the observer, when she was dragged out and thrown on to the settee. The child had virtually no toys and was confined the whole time to the sitting room where she spent most of her time running wildly around the room hurling the chairs over and screaming. Her family made no attempt to provide her with any activity apart from television watching. Her behaviour, as a result, was obviously causing considerable strain in the mother and there were also three younger brothers and sisters, all of whom, except for the baby, behaved in the same way. A few of the subjects were punished by being made to go to their bedrooms.

Most parents attempted to distract their children from events which were likely to lead to a confrontation and so divert them before a temper tantrum occurred. 'Options' were used in this way. The parents would suggest that

Table 13.7   Percentage of children who hit another child

| Family position | Hit another child (%) | Did not hit another child (%) |
|---|---|---|
| Eldest | 31 | 10 |
| Only | 8 | 20 |
| Youngest | 16 | 16 |

the child took part in some activity and so prevent him from committing a misdemeanour.

Disputes between children usually centred round property, one child wanting an object which another child had. For example, two little girls were dressing up and the younger sister, the subject, wanted the only available piece of net curtain which her sister was already wearing as a bridal veil. The dispute was eventually resolved when their grandmother found another piece of net for the younger child. Fifty-four per cent of the children hit another child in the course of a dispute, and 34 per cent received a blow. While being hit by other children did not vary with any of the four independent variables, there was a significant effect according to family position, for hitting another child. Eldest children did most hitting, only children least.

Weeping, regardless of cause was recorded in one category. This declined significantly with age. Laughter, on the other hand, varied with family position, eldest children laughing least.

Table 13.8   Mean number of intervals in which children wept

| Age | Mean number of intervals |
|---|---|
| 3–3½ yrs | 7 |
| 3½–4 yrs | 4 |
| 4–4½ yrs | 2 |

Table 13.9   Mean number of intervals in which children laughed

| Age | Mean number of intervals |
|---|---|
| Eldest | 36 |
| Only | 45 |
| Youngest | 46 |

## AFFECTION AND DEPENDENCY

Without exception, the parents delighted in their children. The overwhelming impression was that the parents were immensely proud of their children and considered their accomplishments as 'special' and remarkable. This is not to say that all the parents were perfect. In a few cases parents spent very little time with their children, but all parents gave the impression of the intention of doing their best for their children. For example, one child, the youngest of three, received very little attention from her parents as did her older brother and sister. The mother considered, however, that expensive toys and clothes were of paramount importance to her children. Until immediately before the study started the mother had been working full time in a pottery factory. She had not intended to go back to work until the last child went off to school, but the previous Christmas she had got heavily into debt over the children's presents. Each child had had to have as much spent on him as the others. The boy received a new bicycle and the girls a doll's pram apiece, the most luxurious the observer had ever seen. To pay off the debt the mother had got a job and paid the nextdoor neighbour (who was not a registered childminder) to look after the youngest. She described the neighbour as 'as thick as a plank' and the observer's incidental observations of the neighbour suggested that the woman was not an ideal childminder. Yet the mother intended to return again to what she herself saw as inadequate care for her child, in order to provide the children with expensive presents the following Christmas.

Affectionate physical contact ranged widely between families. Eight per cent of the children were never observed being cuddled, hugged or sitting on a parent's lap. Kissing seemed to be mainly reserved for formal, symbolic occasions or farewell. Fathers would often ask for a kiss on return from work or children were expected to give and receive a kiss on the way to bed. Forty-one per cent of the children gave kisses and 53 per cent received a kiss. Neither cuddling nor kissing showed variation with the independent variables. [ . . ] 'Functional' physical contact was also recorded, i.e. when a child was held to have his face washed, shoes put on or to cross a busy road. Similarly, this did not vary between groups.

Partings from parents or other members of the family were still an occasion for distress with some of the children. A few fathers would slip discreetly off to work without the child seeing in order to preclude tears. With some parents, this aspect affected their attitudes towards playgroup or nursery school attendance.

# DISCUSSION AND CONCLUSIONS

Interest in thumb and finger sucking and dummy use has been inspired by both psychoanalytic theory and the potential relationship between persistent sucking habits and malocclusion, for example buck teeth. Data on sucking in older children have mainly been gathered from parental interviews. Klackenberg (1949) found that thumb sucking decreased gradually from 47 per cent at two years to 21 per cent at age six. Traisman and Traisman (1958) report that the average age at which thumb sucking ceased in a large sample of children was three to eight years. Our data agree with these findings, in that the decline in thumb sucking is gradual between the ages of three to four and a half years. While diverse findings have been reported on the relationship between early infant feeding styles and later thumb sucking, Traisman and Traisman considered that thumb sucking took over from dummy sucking when the dummy was withdrawn. The Newsons (1968) also thought this accounted for the class difference in thumb sucking which they found in their study of four-year-olds. They concluded that social pressure encouraged middle-class parents to remove dummies from their children earlier than they were removed from working-class children and as a result there was more persistent thumb sucking among the middle-class subjects in their sample. Probably, changes in social outlook account for the lack of class difference in dummy use in the present study. Our finding, that children who use a dummy sucked their thumbs as much as children who did not use a dummy, may be explained by partial dummy removal, in that many children were restricted to particular times when they were allowed their dummies and compensated by increased thumb sucking in the intervening periods. Our measurement of total time spent thumb sucking is probably an underestimate, as this behaviour is most likely to occur immediately the child wakes and before he finally drops off to sleep, the periods most likely to be under-represented by the observation schedules.

Far fewer children in this study were observed to use a comfort object than the number reported to the Newsons, 10 per cent as opposed to 31 per cent. We suspect this may be a function of misreporting on the part of the parents despite the Newsons' prompt: 'Would he make a fuss if you couldn't find it one night?' Several parents volunteered the information that their child was very dependent on a particular object and gave accounts of family hunts at bedtime to find the beloved object. When it had not been seen throughout the course of observation, the observer commented that the particular object had not been in evidence and in these cases it was eventually located. Usually it had been stuffed into the bottom of the toy box or a cupboard, where it had obviously lain for a while, suggesting that the parents had not noticed that a habit they took for granted had now ceased.

The Newsons found that more working- than middle-class children were still wetting their beds, at least occasionally, at four years of age. The measure we used to indicate bladder or bowel control, that the child wore a nappy at night, may not be directly comparable to their data. Anecdotal evidence suggested that several children, although out of nappies, still had occasional accidents at night. Our measure was chosen as a reliable observational measure, but is an underestimation of the total number of children who were still not totally toilet trained at night. Perhaps again, the fact that more middle-class children are still wearing nappies at night and that the prevailing attitude was one of unconcern about toilet training is a reflection of changing attitudes.

Similarly, mothers were tolerant in allowing children to continue to use a potty rather than a lavatory. Potties have the advantage, to the child, of being potentially available in a warm place, such as in front of the sitting room fire or in the kitchen. Their use also means that the child does not have to isolate himself from the general social situation by trudging up the stairs or 'out the back'. The prevailing attitude seemed to be that it was important to get the child used to using a lavatory before he went to nursery or infant school – where he would have to use one.

The variation according to the social class of children observed to take a bath suggests that a daily bath is still largely a middle-class practice. However, an appreciable number of both classes chose not to use the family bath for bathing their children. One obvious disadvantage to a full bath is that it takes more hot water than a baby bath or washing-up bowl. However, other considerations were also important. A child can be bathed in a receptacle in a warm kitchen or in front of the living room fire. Often bath time coincided with the time when the mother was busy cooking the evening meal and the child was under her eye, playing happily in the water, whilst she alternated between washing him and tending the cooker.

A major cause of parental anxiety seems to be unnecessary concern that the child is eating an insufficient amount of food. Given the experience of parents' relief when they keep records of the child's actual intake and that a wide social range of mothers were capable of doing this, it might well be helpful for family doctors or health visitors, when parents seek their advice, to suggest that the latter keep a simple diary.

A small number of working-class parents considered that an important function of nursery school was to teach their children manners, in particular table manners. Given that so many families do not have meals in a traditional, formal setting, it is likely that quite a few children will have had little experience of sitting this way for meals before they get to school and puts the parents' attitude to the function of nursery school in perspective, a point teachers might bear in mind.

The number of children who were not put to bed and left to go to sleep on their own, in a conventional fashion, is surprising and seems to reflect the current ethos of tolerance in child-rearing practice. Several parents who perceived their child's sleeping habits as posing problems regretted that they had not taken a firmer stand earlier. They found it impossible to change the child's habit of having to go to sleep downstairs and then to be carried up to bed, or of having them stay with the child till he went to sleep. Impossible that is, in that a tough line meant shouting and crying from the child, and they were very conscious that this would be overheard and would disturb their neighbours, a pressing problem in terraced and semi-detached housing. Also, where there were other children in the family, either older or younger, they also would be disturbed. Some parents felt quite desperate about the situation, particularly when their own sleep was disrupted by the child coming into their bed during the night and again they were convinced that if they had foreseen how things were going to develop then they would never have permitted the habit to start.

Monitoring where the child went on his own varied widely with individual families and did not show the class difference we had anticipated, i.e. that working-class children would be permitted to wander further afield on their own. The lack of differential control over boys and girls at this age accords with the Newsons' findings with their study of children at four years of age (1968), where parents were not restricting the movements of one sex more than the other, in contrast to their later report on the children at seven years (1976). By then parents were taking greater care over accompanying their daughters, as opposed to their sons, on ventures outside the home. The authors attributed this development to parents' fears about the greater risk of molestation for little girls.

The close proximity of other families with different standards poses a variety of problems to urban parents, both street and estate dwellers. It is difficult to enforce a rule with a child when his neighbourhood friends are not bound by it. One family lived in a newly built cul-de-sac of half a dozen houses, one house still being unoccupied. Their son spent most of the time playing with the children from the two adjacent houses and they repeatedly all gathered in the back garden of the unoccupied house and attempted to pull down a newly erected fence to make 'a house'. The boy's mother retrieved her son three times and soundly told him off for going into the garden. The other parents ignored what their children were doing and finally the poor child stood at the corner of the plot, watching the other children play and silently shaking his head when they persistently called to him to join them.

While 38 per cent of the parents were observed to smack their children, this figure gives no guide to the proportion of families prepared to use smacking as a punishment. The majority of children gave little occasion for severe punishment and probably a much higher number of parents did smack their children very occasionally. The majority of children were cheerful and amenable and, as has been mentioned, all the parents saw themselves as proud of and interested in their children. It is this very deep reserve of good will and interest which has been tapped by various action research programmes, such as the Red House Project (Poulton and James, 1975) and could be utilized more by the teaching profession to forge the initial link between the home and the educational system.

## TOPICS FOR DISCUSSION

1. What *differences* in child-rearing practices did the authors find between working-class and middle-class parents? What *similarities* did they find?
2. 'The number of children who were not put to bed and left to go to sleep on their own, in a conventional fashion, is surprising and seems to reflect the current ethos of tolerance in child-rearing practice.' What other aspects of child-rearing practice would seem to support the authors' claim that there is an 'ethos of tolerance'?
3. 'The close proximity of other families with different standards poses a variety of problems to urban parents, both street and estate dwellers.' Discuss.

## SUGGESTIONS FOR FURTHER READING

1. Davie, C.E., Hutt, S.J., Vincent, E. and Mason, M. (1984) 'Language', in *The Young Child at Home*. Windsor, NFER-Nelson, chap. 8, pp. 129–52.

In studying the language environment of the young child at home the authors selected a small number of specific measurements which they considered were of theoretical importance. Because they felt that a measurement of the *total amount* of speech exchanged by the young child with both adults and other children was essential, Davie et al. recorded all speech between the subject and other people, identifying the speech recipient, and defined his general speech as:

*Communication*: any form of speech except moaning or aggressive speech to another individual.

They recorded separately:

*Auto-talk*: the subject talking to himself.

*Singing*: singing, humming and whistling.

*Telephone*: telephone talking.

The authors were interested to see how auto-talk related to the amount of general social communication, wondering, for example, whether high levels of communication to and from children would increase their 'chattiness' and therefore increase the likelihood of their talking to themselves, or, conversely, whether children tend to talk to themselves in the absence of social communication. According to Bernstein, language must be examined in different contexts and the predominant use, exposed in these contexts, can assign the subject to having access to a particular code (Bernstein specifies the following contexts: regularitive, instructional, imaginative or innovative, interpersonal); the authors, therefore, defined two categories – 'instructions' and 'abstracts' – in order to study patterns of language interaction of the young child in the home.

*'Instructions'* – giving of information, which may be used outside the child's own home, and which does not involve elaboration or expansion of a concept, such as specifically naming objects by drawing the child's attention to them, making statements of fact without justification, correcting the child's speech to the individual's own speech criteria.

*'Abstracts'* – statements or questions which involve abstractions to a class of individuals, objects or events, i.e. which includes a general principle.

The research team included an aspect of communication which they considered would be important in guiding and changing the child's behaviour, sustaining his or her interest in an outgoing activity or suggesting a new one. This they classified as an 'option':

*'Option'* – an invitation, a suggestion to the subject that he or she does something – includes non-verbal communication.

Finally, they distinguished the two categories of negative and positive speech:

*'Negative speech'* – direct verbal punishment and aggression and threats.
*'Positive speech'* – approval, praise, affection and promise of treats.

The research resulted in a number of important findings. Speech from the subject to adults did *not* vary with social class, age or sex, but showed differences according to family position. Only children spoke more to adults than either eldest or youngest children, and eldest children spoke more than youngest, i.e. youngest children were having least general conversation with adults. In particular, youngest children talked much less to their fathers than did either of the other two groups. Where speech to other children is concerned, the situation reverses: youngest subjects spoke far more to other children than either of the other two groups (p. 137).

Speech from other people to the subject showed a similar pattern to expressed speech, and again, although there was no difference between groups according to social class, sex or age, adult speech did tend to decline with age, and family position exerted an influence. Only children were talked to by adults far more than either of the other two groups, but eldest children did receive more adult speech than youngest. The authors found that although social class differences were apparent on some of the speech measures used in the research, they were not as widespread or as striking as those found by other researchers. Similarly, sex differences were not apparent – the girls were not interacting verbally more than the boys either generally with adults or specifically with their mothers. There were, however, some social class differences in the qualitative speech measures designed to assess speech that would increase the child's vocabulary, classificatory ability and concept formation. Middle-class adults were found to be more likely to provide their children with 'instructions' and their children were *significantly more likely* to ask for 'instructions'. Abstract explanations proved to be genuinely very rare events, probably because an abstract explanation is an extremely difficult thing to give to a young child, and parents of both social class groups tend to avoid attempting them. 'Options' and adult 'positive' and 'negative' speech showed consistent social class differences (pp. 148–9). The analysis of 'auto-talk' revealed that children who displayed frequent social talk did not also engage in high levels of auto-talk, which tended to occur when children had less opportunity for social speech from both adults and other children.

2. Tizard, B. and Hughes, M. (1984) 'Learning at home: play, games, stories and "lessons" ', in *Young Children Learning: Talking and Thinking at Home and at School*. London, Fontana, chap. 3, pp. 37–72.

Tizard and Hughes examine what children are learning from their mothers at home, and, specifically, the contexts in which this learning takes place. They dismiss the widely held view that many children – particularly in working-class areas – learn little or nothing at home, and spend most of their time watching television. Parents are frequently exhorted by professionals to play and talk more with their children in order to develop intellectual and linguistic skills. The authors set about to examine whether these opinions and advice are offered in the absence of any real knowledge of what 'typical' parents actually do at home in 'educating' their children.

The authors asked parents what they believed they were teaching their children at home, and found that *all* the parents they interviewed had definite ideas about what they were teaching their children. The answers parents gave were compared with detailed observations of what mothers actually talked to their children about, and in order to examine what the mothers were teaching, the authors scanned each of the mothers' turns of talk to see what kind of information was being conveyed. Thus, they looked at whether the information was about control (what the child should or should not do) or about other kinds of knowledge. Information not concerned with control was coded under one of 27 categories ranging from basic information about colour and size, through information about time relationships, family relationships, social interactions, to general knowledge and school-type subjects such as history, science and geography (pp. 38–9). The authors provide a fascinating account of how the children in the study received, on average, 150 turns an hour of information of all kinds, most of which was information that was *not* to do with control. Of particular importance is the examination of the contexts in which this vast amount of information was being transmitted and acquired; learning through play, for example, was seen as valuable by parents in helping the child understand the adult world by acting out roles. 'It's practice in life', 'She learns by copying adults', 'It brings us closer together' were typical parent responses to the question of whether they thought play was important and for what reasons (p. 41). The authors offer numerous examples of children learning through imaginative play, through games with rules, games for fun, through stories and 'lessons', demonstrating the very wide range of topics and learning contexts found in most of the homes of parents involved in the study.

3. Farquhar, D., Blatchford, P., Burke, J., Plewis, I. and Tizard, B. (1985) 'A comparison of the views of parents and reception class teachers'. *Education 3–13*, **13**, 2, 17–22.

If the chapter by Tizard and Hughes (no. 2 above) dispels some of the ideas that professionals hold as to what parents actually do in 'educating' their children, the study by Farquhar et al. highlights important discrepancies in parents' and teachers' views on what sorts of academic-related activities are felt to be appropriate *for parents* to engage in with their children at home. The differences in parents' and teachers' views are striking. Most teachers place clear restrictions on the range of 'academic-related' activities they think parents should attempt. They tend to favour *alternative* forms of parental involvement, for example reading *to* children at home rather than encouraging direct parental teaching of reading. Moreover, teachers have low expectations concerning the number of parents who will engage in activities involving general language development. Parents, on the other hand, whilst generally subscribing to the view that schools and teachers make the most significant contribution to children's educational progress, nevertheless *actively engage* in many academic-related activities with their children, *even before* they start school (p. 22). The authors report that 'of great interest is the fact that, *despite* a belief in the major influence of schools, many parents in the study not only stated that they intended to help their children at home once they started school, but also saw such help as part of their role as parents. If this is a reflection of the active role that a majority of parents take in their children's early education, then this is indicative of an important, and influential, educational resource' (p. 22).

## Reading 14
## 'HALLO, MISS SCATTERBRAIN. HALLO, MR STRONG': ASSESSING ATTITUDES AND BEHAVIOUR IN THE NURSERY
### *G. Thomas*

Research indicates that sexual inequalities are inherent in our education system (Whyte, 1983, p. 5). However, this research has largely been conducted in secondary schools, and it is perhaps because of the emphasis on academic achievement, subject choice and career options that primary teachers have displayed a reluctance to acknowledge their role in the shaping of sex-stereotyped behaviour. Undoubtedly much of the learning of sex roles occurs within the family and through the media, but the early years of schooling also have long-term effects. The outcome of learning experiences that occur during this period must contribute to the fact that girls 'do well academically but, in the long run, to less ambitious effect in their careers' (ILEA, 1982, p. 26).

It is during the primary years of schooling that girls begin the process of 'learning to lose' (Spender and Sarah, 1980) – not simply from the explicit curriculum but from the messages they receive from the 'hidden' curriculum, which includes school organization, books and resources, language, playground facilities, assemblies, extracurricular activities and above all the attitudes and expectations of the staff. Judith Whyte argues that education

Thomas, G. (1986) 'Hallo, Miss Scatterbrain. Hallo, Mr. Strong: assessing attitudes and behaviour in the nursery', in Browne, N. and France, P. (eds) *Untying the Apron Strings: Anti-sexist Provision for the Under-fives*. Milton Keynes, Open University Press, chap. 7, pp. 104–20.

in primary schools is unduly geared towards boys' interests, and maintains that they receive more teacher time and attention than do girls (1983, p. 11). Katherine Clarricoates' research revealed that teachers in the early years of schooling classify children according to their sex and expect sex-stereotyped behaviour from them (Clarricoates, 1980, pp. 26–41), a factor that tends to heighten rather than diminish the differences between the sexes.

This chapter describes an attempt I made during one academic year to investigate the extent to which these stereotyped attitudes towards sex roles were held by the children and staff in two nursery classes of an inner-city primary school. The following account matches the pattern of the study, which began with personal observations and went on to involve nursery staff in the monitoring of children's play preferences by means of tick-lists. The results of these lists were then discussed with the staff, and I also attempted to discover the teachers' feelings about sexism in general. One of the main questions raised in the discussions related to the amount of time staff allocated to girls and boys, and I then analysed my own practice with this in mind. Finally I discussed the issue with parents, in an attempt to determine whether or not staff were justified in their assertion that sexism in children is mainly a result of influences at home.

My reasons for attempting such a study relate to the fact that although in theory there may appear to be recognition of the need to eliminate sexism in primary schools, in practice it occurs only at an extremely superficial level, if at all. Fundamental attitudes remain unchanged; school staff refuse to acknowledge their own sexism or, if they do, fail to recognize it as a problem and thus maintain the status quo.

As a teacher attempting to change the sexist attitudes and actions that reveal themselves in my *own* behaviour and language, I hoped that any questions raised by my observations could be used as a basis for discussion with colleagues on the issue of sex-role stereotyping, and that we could work together towards the development of an anti-sexist school policy. The study, which in its entirety involved both nursery and infant classes, was not intended to be quantitative, and the resulting evidence was in fact insufficient to formulate generalizable statements about sex-role stereotyping. It nevertheless raised questions that have implications for the way we operate in the early years of schooling.

## FIRST IMPRESSIONS

On my initial visits to the nursery, conversations with staff revealed a belief that sex stereotyping occurred either at home or 'when they get higher up the school' and that for their part staff endeavoured to 'treat them all the same'.

As far as the activities provided were concerned, nursery staff considered they were used 'equally' by both sexes.[1]

However, from casual observations my perception of the situation did not correspond with that of the staff. It appeared to me that the girls generally occupied themselves in a quieter fashion and were 'better behaved' than the boys. Whilst the girls frequently played in the home corner, boys seemed to prefer activities using big bricks and constructional toys. The girls did not use the outside area as often as the boys, especially the climbing frame, and there was little evidence of cross-sex play, either in the classrooms or out of doors.

I began a closer observation of the situation by focusing on the home corner, where from experience I expected to find most evidence of stereotypical behaviour. During the first session, apart from a group of boys who rushed in and out again immediately, only one boy used this area together with five girls. The girls busied themselves pretending to be 'mummies cooking the dinner' and seemed prepared to allow the boy to participate in their role-play because of his quiet passivity. On another occasion four girls and a rather quiet boy took turns to manipulate a puppet behind a model television screen. During their play they were twice interrupted by several boys who attempted to break up the performance by overturning chairs, kicking, fighting with each other, snatching the puppet and throwing it to the floor. On the third visit I listened to the conversations of children as they dressed dolls in the home corner, and it was apparent that they had a very definite idea of what constitutes sex-appropriate clothing.

My observations in the home corner confirmed the impression I had gained on earlier visits, that girls *did* predominate in this area and engaged in domestic 'mothering' activities and in so doing they reinforced sex stereotypes. The majority of boys who visited the home corner came to disrupt activities. Their behaviour matched Whyte's (1983) description of boys 'making raids' on the Wendy house and threatening those playing there (p. 31).

## INVOLVING THE STAFF

Rather than simply discuss with the nursery staff the questions raised by my observations, it seemed more valuable at this stage to involve them in observing the behaviour of girls and boys. The children were allowed to move around both classrooms, playground and garden area, choosing from a range of activities. A simple method of monitoring was required to discover whether or not their play preferences revealed any patterns of behaviour that were sex related. Although not all the staff were convinced of

| Boy C | Boy B | Boy A | Girl C | Girl B | Girl A | | | |
|---|---|---|---|---|---|---|---|---|
| | | | | | | Sand | | |
| | | | | | | Water | | |
| | | | | | | Book corner | | |
| | | | | | | Home corner | | |
| | | | | | | Music corner | | |
| | | | | | | Painting | CREATIVE | INDOOR ACTIVITIES |
| | | | | | | Collage | | |
| | | | | | | Drawing | | |
| | | | | | | Other | | |
| | | | | | | Plasticine | PLIABLE | |
| | | | | | | Play-dough | | |
| | | | | | | Clay | | |
| | | | | | | Other | | |
| | | | | | | Lego | CONSTRUCTIONAL | |
| | | | | | | Sticklebricks | | |
| | | | | | | Building bricks | | |
| | | | | | | Large bricks | | |
| | | | | | | Other | | |
| | | | | | | Sewing | MANIPULATIVE | |
| | | | | | | Weaving | | |
| | | | | | | Other | | |
| | | | | | | Dressing-up | IMAGINATIVE | |
| | | | | | | Puppets | | |
| | | | | | | Maths games | MISCELLANEOUS | |
| | | | | | | Puzzles | | |
| | | | | | | | | |
| | | | | | | Bicycles | | OUTDOOR ACTIVITIES |
| | | | | | | Prams | | |
| | | | | | | Trolleys | | |
| | | | | | | Wheelbarrows | | |
| | | | | | | Scooters | | |
| | | | | | | Milk crates | | |
| | | | | | | Barrels | | |
| | | | | | | See-saw | | |
| | | | | | | Hoops | | |
| | | | | | | Balls | | |
| | | | | | | Climbing frames | | |

Figure 14.1   Tick-list.

the need to tackle sexism in the early years they were willing to be involved in these observations, and one of them suggested tick-lists.

Together we designed the lists to include all the available activities and involve all nursery staff (see Figure 14.1). It was originally intended that they should be checked at 30-minute intervals, but this proved impractical as staff, for various reasons, were unable to tick them at the prescribed times. It was agreed that a sheet bearing the children's names should be kept for each classroom and outside area and ticked at random intervals throughout the day, at the convenience of the staff, rather than at timed intervals. Obviously the results obtained were not statistically significant. However, as they were kept by a number of different people over a period of three weeks and revealed similar patterns of behaviour, they have some validity.

More important than the collection of scientific data was the fact that staff were involved in observing what was happening in the nursery and were therefore more likely to become aware of any sex-stereotyped behaviour. An increased awareness does not necessarily guarantee a change in attitudes and behaviour, but it is certainly a step towards it.

Figure 14.1 is a suggested plan for a tick-list, which in a modified form could provide staff with useful information about the behaviour of children in their charge. One such modification could be to concentrate on only one or two activities each week rather than the entire range simultaneously. Additionally the list could be modified to provide staff with an opportunity to record the way children used the various activities and whether or not their behaviour was consistent throughout, e.g. how girls behave in the playground area in comparison with the way they behave in the home corner. Where more than one member of staff is involved in making observations it is essential to spend time discussing and defining terms.

The main points revealed by the observations made by nursery staff at random intervals over a period of three weeks are described below. In addition I have included the opinions of the staff, which emerged during our subsequent discussion.

The teachers were not in total agreement with the findings, although they were not altogether surprised by them. When reminded of their original statement that all children used all activities equally they attributed this to the fact that in previous years there had been more boys than girls on roll and they felt this imbalance had to some extent masked the preferences displayed by the different sexes. Involvement in this type of classroom monitoring had made staff realize that all the children were capable of longer periods of concentration than they had previously believed possible; they were now more aware of the activities preferred by both sexes, although not all the areas monitored by the tick-lists revealed significant differences.

Our discussion of the findings was extremely valuable in that it raised a number of questions that have direct implications for education, which we later used to formulate some ideas for good practice.

## DISCOVERIES AND DISCUSSIONS

### Indoor activities

More girls than boys used the home corner, and girls used it more repeatedly than the boys.

The staff asserted that this was a hangover from the past when a great deal of unnecessary divisions by gender were made. Children had formerly to ask permission to use the home corner, and girls, because they were considered more likely to use it quietly, were allowed to use it more often than boys. Despite attempts of newer staff to change the ethos in the nursery, certain old attitudes still prevailed, especially amongst older and less flexible staff. However, I felt that positive efforts needed to be made to encourage girls to move out of the home corner, which appears to reinforce stereotyped behaviour. If girls practise only 'housework and childcare' then their opportunities to experience other activities will be limited. Boys need to be encouraged to use the home corner more often and in a less disruptive way and to realize that it is acceptable for them to be involved in 'caring' roles. If we ensure that this occurs then there is a greater possibility that boys will be able to express openly the range of emotions they feel.

More girls than boys used the pliable materials, which include clay, plasticine and play-dough.

The staff maintained that an activity like play-dough plus rollers and cutters was more likely to be used by the girls, whereas a 'messy' activity like clay or compost mixed with water was less likely. This could be related to the way in which female staff present such 'messy' activities to the girls, because often they find it difficult to conceal their own dislike of such play. So long as girls believe they shouldn't get dirty it precludes the possibility of engaging in a wide range of experiences.

More boys than girls used constructional toys, and boys used them more repeatedly than girls.

The boys' greater use of constructional toys was not regarded as typical, as the staff considered that their use varied enormously depending on the type of constructional play available. However, boys were more likely to construct cars, planes and guns, which they would incorporate into imaginative play. Probably the fact that girls are not exposed to constructional toys in their pre-nursery years to the same extent as boys tends to make them less confident and skilful in their use. If we believe that early experience of constructional play is a factor in determining a person's confidence in the use of scientific and technological ideas and equipment, then we need to ensure that all children's attempts are praised, *especially* the girls', who may lack experience.

More boys than girls were involved in imaginative activities.

It was felt that there were certain aspects of imaginative play that involved both sexes equally, such as play-people and puppets. However, staff should be aware of the fact that these toys are often used in very different ways, with girls 'putting baby to bed' and boys playing 'chase' games with toy cars and planes.

More girls than boys were involved in manipulative activities that require fine motor control, e.g. sewing, and fine interlocking pieces such as figure-craft.

Staff believed, contrary to the evidence of the tick-lists, that boys used these activities more than girls. Their disagreement suggests that checklists of this nature can be extremely useful in bringing the fact to one's attention that behaviours may not be exactly as one imagines. Such information should naturally inform future approaches.

## Outdoor activities

More boys than girls used the bicycles, and boys used them more often than girls.

Staff agreed that boys did dominate playground activities, especially the bicycles, which they 'saved' for each other. This was attributed to the particular type of boys present in the nursery at this time, who were always keen to play outside.

Prams were used more often by girls than by boys.

When boys were observed using prams, their use was described as 'wheel-barrows', whereas girls were seen to be 'caring'. Perhaps this description reflects the staff's stereotyped views.

Boys used the balls more than girls did.

There was agreement that the boys played with the balls more than the girls did, especially the footballs, which were rarely used for cross-sex play. Again, this was attributed to the nature of the particular group of boys. As boys seemed to dominate the outside space and activities, I felt we needed to discuss how we could encourage girls to use them more often, since they need the same opportunities as boys to be active and adventurous through physical exercise and spatial exploration.

Naturally, monitoring children's behaviour in this way required extra effort on the part of staff but as it resulted in a heightened awareness of stereotyped behaviour it seemed worth while. Such awareness should enable us to operate so that all children develop as 'highly individual people in their own right' (Byrne, 1978, p. 16).

## TALKING TO STAFF

It is understandable that many staff find an examination of their own attitudes and behaviour more 'threatening' than observations of children's behaviour. However, because this appears to be a crucial step in effecting any kind of change, I decided after using the tick-lists that loosely structured interviews would allow discussion of the issue of sex-role stereotyping and enable me to determine to some extent the attitudes held by the nursery staff.

The staff, who were all female, agreed that it was important that both sexes should be given equal opportunities in school. With one exception they believed that they had not been afforded the same opportunities in life as boys, because either brothers had been 'favoured' or facilities such as science laboratories and woodwork equipment had been lacking at single-sex schools. Only one member of staff expected different behaviour from the sexes, expecting girls to behave 'nicely' and boys to be 'rough but not bad'. The remainder considered that although they didn't necessarily expect different behaviour, parental and societal attitudes encouraged it.

Despite the fact that they all tried to treat children as individuals and not according to their sex, they admitted to not always being successful. Only one teacher seemed fully aware of how subtle this differential behaviour could be and attributed her awareness to recent attendance on in-service training courses concerned with the subject of sexism in the nursery environment.

Several of the staff were surprised by the information that girls achieved slightly better than boys in examinations up to O-level. They regarded poor career guidance as the reason why girls did not usually choose subjects to enhance their job prospects. Only one of them believed that expectations and attitudes held by staff involved in the early years of schooling could be influential in shaping these subject and career choices.

The nursery staff all believed that boys should be 'as gentle as girls and girls as tough as a boy can be' but considered that whilst society might be prepared to accept 'bossy' girls it was much harder for 'cissy' boys to be accepted. They were uncertain of the amount of time and attention they gave to each sex but felt it was unlikely that they gave more to boys. It was suggested that this was much more likely to be the case in the infant and junior departments where more direction of activities occurs.

From these discussions with the staff, further questions were raised, which were also used to develop ideas for good practice. One important question related to the way in which teacher time and attention are divided between the sexes and resulted in my own use of the GIST (Girls into Science and Technology) Classroom Observation Schedule.[2]

## CLASSROOM OBSERVATION SCHEDULE

Although I believe it to be extremely valuable to monitor the behaviour of children, if one seriously wishes to alter one's own attitudes and behaviour then it is essential to monitor and evaluate this in the classroom. I began to monitor my own practice by means of the GIST Classroom Observation Schedule, modified for nursery and infant classrooms. This schedule enables staff to discover how they share their time between the sexes by, for example, counting the number of times they ask questions of both sexes or how many times each sex comments spontaneously.

The observations were conducted in two lower infant classes but it seems appropriate to mention them here as the process of assessment can just as easily be carried out in a nursery. A colleague and I watched each other work and then agreed to arrange another of these reciprocal sessions on a future occasion. We considered that, although the results were insufficient to reach firm conclusions, they would provide a useful input at staff meeting and, we hoped, encourage colleagues to participate in this kind of critical evaluation of their own practice. Using this schedule reminded me that repeated assessment of one's practice is essential, and that the schedule, if operated reciprocally with a colleague, is an ideal instrument for building mutual trust.

## TALKING TO PARENTS

Parents have an enormous influence on the shaping of sex roles, which are already well established by the time children arrive at nursery school. If children do bring these sex-stereotyped attitudes it is easy for teachers to ignore the role of the school in reinforcing them. It is easier to blame parents than to recognize that one's own behaviour and the school organization are contributory factors. It would appear to be more beneficial to initiate a dialogue between parents and school, rather than apportion blame, so I decided to interview a number of the nursery children's parents in an attempt to discover if they considered that children of different sexes should be treated differently and encouraged to behave in a manner 'appropriate' for their sex.

Of the six parents I interviewed, four were women. Since it is usually mothers who collect their children from the nursery school it was more difficult to make contact with fathers. The interviews, which were loosely structured, were tape-recorded, as this enabled us to chat informally rather than me take notes and make parents feel they were being interrogated.

Both men believed that it was a better life for a man. Whilst the women all said that they were happy being women, all but one, who had been encouraged to continue her education, considered that they had not received the same opportunities as the males in their family when leaving school:

> When I wanted to do a hairdressing apprentice with no money, they wouldn't let me 'cos I was only going to get married, but he was encouraged to become an apprentice electrician, even though he didn't earn any money.

Everyone was in agreement that women and men should be given equal opportunities in life. However, when we discussed the career choices open to both sexes, it appeared they were unconvinced that 'equality' could be a reality. Although it was felt that

> as long as they're able then they should do whatever they want, even if they want to drive those big articulated lorries . . .

doubts were expressed about the possibility of this:

> the only drawback is that we have to have children. . . . But I think our build prevents us. I mean I can't imagine a woman humping a great big bin around.

According to the men there were differences that might prevent complete equality. One attributed it to physique and the other to intellect:

> she's too slow . . . I think it's because of her gender. She's . . . slow, so I said okay let's try for a man . . . then we realized that when we had that

man he was so quick in doing things. . . . I think maybe because she's a woman she's slow.

All the parents considered they tried to treat their daughters or sons in the same way and felt it was important for them to be encouraged to participate equally in household chores. However, when discussed at greater length it became clear that they did differentiate in their treatment of the sexes. Despite the fact that all except one male agreed that boys should be allowed to play with dolls, and girls to play with cars and planes, etc., only one woman had bought a doll specifically for her son. They all said that when faced with buying presents for children of friends and family they would buy only sex-appropriate toys. Action Man was greatly approved of as it had in some way made the notion of boys playing with dolls acceptable, but the aggressive nature of this doll appeared to have been overlooked. Only one parent insisted he would not allow his son to have a doll or any other toys he considered inappropriate for his sex: 'I always say, that's for a girl, because he knows anyway what is for boys and girls'.

When we discussed the subject of clothes it became apparent that attitudes about appropriate clothing for the sexes were still relatively traditional. The women appeared to favour feminine clothes for girls; while they considered it acceptable for girls to wear jeans, it was not totally right for boys to wear pink because 'It's that cissy thing again, isn't it?' or, as another parent said, 'It's just the way . . . the attitude of the world again'. Whilst one father was concerned to dress his children in practical clothes, the other insisted he would never allow his son to wear anything 'feminine'.

When we discussed the kind of emotional behaviour they considered appropriate for either sex, it was interesting that none of them chose to discuss this in relation to their daughters, but they considered it immediately in relation to boys. The women were in total agreement about the need for boys and men to be encouraged to 'show their feelings' and 'have the outlet to cry'. One of the men said he did not like to see people of either sex cry, but the other wished his son was less aggressive and more sensitive, like himself:

> I've always been more sensitive than many other males, especially in my family . . . I've always been quiet and enjoyed reading, whereas he seems to enjoy more boyish activities, fighting particularly.

Probably the greatest advances towards equality have been made in respect of housework, childcare and especially cooking, and the comments of male and female parents reflected this. However, given that changes have occurred, there was still the underlying assumption that these areas are nevertheless the province of women. Where husbands did participate in housework, cooking and childcare, none of them assumed responsibility for all the domestic chores. Even in one family where the husband was unemployed, although he was prepared to collect the children from school and do the cooking, he was not willing to be involved in housework. His wife considered it was her role to work full-time and do the housework – 'It's the law; we're made to fit in'.

When husbands did assume these roles, on occasions when their wives were working or sick, the women felt that they were fortunate or had 'a lucky one'. Whilst one man had undertaken the entire responsibility for the home and children because his wife worked while he studied, the other shared responsibility for the chores with his wife despite a certain reluctance: 'I know it's her job in a way . . . I said to myself it's her job, but we have to help each other'.

Overall there was a definite feeling that things had changed and women were given more equality of opportunity than in the past. What parents did not appear to be fully aware of, however, were the career choices that are in theory available to both sexes. They tended to consider the issue in terms of physique. They were unaware of the evidence suggesting that women are capable of great endurance; that there are greater differences in strength within the sexes than between them; and that women's gynaecological make-up does not necessarily restrict their involvement in physical exercise (ILEA, 1984). Only one parent clung to the notion that women were less intelligent than men.

In relation to the differential treatment of children the parents had somewhat ambivalent attitudes. While on one level they considered it important to treat both sexes in the same way and offer them similar experiences, on another level they were heavily influenced by societal attitudes and expectations. This was apparent in relation to the type of toys considered appropriate, the clothes worn and the emotional behaviour considered suitable for each sex. For although they believed that boys should be encouraged to be more 'caring' and sensitive, there was recognition that society does not regard these traits as admirable in a man.

Whilst advances have been made in relation to domestic responsibilities, and women today make more demands on their partners, these advances often obscure the fundamental attitudes that nevertheless exist about women's role in society. However, this does not alter the fact that we as teachers should avoid making assumptions about the behaviour and attitudes of parents. We must recognize that all parents want more equal opportunities for their children even if they are uncertain how they might be obtained. More important, just as many teachers are, they are attempting to make changes in their lives, however unsuccessful they may be, and in certain areas have already succeeded.

The immediate question to arise from this, which we as teachers must consider if we wish to work alongside parents in an attempt to counter the influences of society, is: how can a home–school dialogue best be promoted?

## TOWARDS AN ANTI-SEXIST POLICY

An investigation of this kind is useful in the formulation of a school anti-sexist policy. When questions are raised by such observations they can be used to promote discussion on the issue of sexism in school and to heighten teachers' awareness of the need to consider the issue seriously. There are other aspects of the school and its organization that will need investigation when developing a school policy, including language, books and resources, visual images, staffing and in-service training. A change in teachers' attitudes and behaviour or the development of such a policy will not necessarily overcome stereotyping, since schools are only part of the wider society. However, we must not use this as an excuse for apathy – 'countering sexism is part of the struggle to extend choices and opportunities for everyone' (Stones, 1983).

## NOTES

The title of this chapter is borrowed from *Little Miss Scatterbrain* by Roger Hargreaves (1981).
1. The term 'equally' was used in a very loose way, and staff did not make clear whether it meant that girls and boys engaged in an activity in the same way or for similar periods of time.
2. GIST Classroom Observation Schedule obtainable from Girls into Science and Technology, Manchester Polytechnic, 9a Didsbury Park, Manchester M20 0LH.

## TOPICS FOR DISCUSSION

1. 'Countering sexism is part of the struggle to extend choices and opportunities for everyone.' Discuss this statement with reference to Thomas' account of what she discovered about teachers' attitudes concerning sexism.
2. How important is it, do you think, that anti-sexist policies should be begun in the very early years of education?
3. What are the most important aspects of the school and its organization which need to be considered when developing an anti-sexist policy?

# SUGGESTIONS FOR FURTHER READING

1. France, P. (1986) 'The beginnings of sex stereotyping', in Browne, N. and France, P. (eds) *Untying the Apron Strings: Anti-Sexist Provision for the Under-Fives.* Milton Keynes, Open University Press, chap. 4, pp. 49–67.

Until comparatively recent times, sex-typing was considered by most psychologists, teachers and parents as an important and desirable goal of socialization. This assumption has provoked considerable criticism and for many educators, the explicit rejection of traditional sex-typing is a goal of socialization. This political and conceptual about-face justifies its viewpoint by arguing that sex-typed roles restrict personal fulfilment for *both* males and females by severely limiting the options that each can pursue. Pauline France illustrates this very point with illuminating insights into the ways in which sex role and behaviour difference are inculcated and established in the daily lives of very young children. The author asks the questions: 'Why do incidents (of sex-role typing) happen all too often in children's lives?, and what can anti-sexist parents and teachers do to broaden children's experiences and avoid channelling children into narrowly defined and unequal sex roles?' After a brief overview of the various influential theories that attempt to describe and explain sex differences, the author considers how a patriarchal society like Britain's is upheld and sustained. In the final part of the chapter she suggests strategies that may assist children to grow up with an approach to life that does not rely on sex and race stereotypes.

2. Davies, D. (1984) 'Sex role stereotyping in children's imaginative writing', in Cowie, H. (ed.) *The Development of Children's Imaginative Writing.* London, Croom Helm, chap. 4, pp. 73–87.

Although this reading is not specifically concerned with the pre-school age-group, it has been deliberately included to show how sex-role typing in the very early years shapes the attitudes, behaviours and values of children as they grow older. Maccoby and Jacklin (1974) found that 'Boys seem to have more intense socialization experiences than girls. They receive more pressure against engaging in sex-inappropriate behaviour, whereas the activities that girls are not supposed to engage in are much less clearly defined and less firmly enforced. Boys receive more punishment, but probably also more praise and encouragement . . . Whatever the explanation, the different amounts of socialization pressure that boys and girls receive surely have consequences for the development of their personalities' (p. 348). Similarly, Block (1978) found more consistent emphasis in the socialization of sons in the areas of achievement, competition, independence in the sense of personal responsibility, and in the control of emotion. Davies provides a very useful digest of recent research on sex-role stereotyping and discusses at length the subject of sex-role socialization of children by parents. She considers the evidence to show how teachers actively contribute to the process of sex-role stereotyping, describing a number of studies which suggest that teachers differentially encourage sex-appropriate behaviour and evaluate children's performances according to sex-stereotypical dimensions. Discussing sex-role stereotyping of children by the mass media, Davies writes, 'There is wide agreement as to the stereotypic characteristics and behaviour ascribed to males and females, and despite changes in many societal values over the last few decades these stereotypes have maintained an unchanging quality. Further, sex-role stereotypes have for most people been incorporated into the individual's self-concept' (p. 81). The author shows that throughout the media and in particular children's literature and television programmes 'males and females are presented in ways consistent with their sex-stereotyped image. Different messages are conveyed as to the appropriate behaviour for males and females, thus providing an important source in both learning and reinforcing existing stereotyped sex roles' (p. 86).

3. Whyte, J. (1983) *Beyond the Wendy House: Sex Role Stereotyping in Primary Schools.* Harlow, Longman for Schools Council.

The author's 'message' is that sexual equality is dependent on eliminating sex bias in the earliest years of education – and that to achieve this goal, the commitment and support of primary school teachers are of paramount importance. She describes a wide range of sex-stereotyped practices that are common experiences for many girls and boys during their primary education, emphasizing that such practices 'are insidious because they are unconscious and yet particularly persuasive in their long-term effects on girls' and boys' abilities, aspirations and achievements' (p. 5). Whyte reports that many nursery and reception teachers claim to be able to see differences between girls' and boys' behaviour, interests and attitudes as soon as they first come into school. She asks the question as to when and how this sex-typing occurs and considers whether it is inherent in the make-up of each sex or whether it is the result of social learning. Certainly it is the case that as children progress through the school system sex differences in 'learning styles' become increasingly apparent. 'The boy's learning style is active, participatory, demanding, lending itself to a confident, independent approach to learning. The girl's is more passive, less participatory, making fewer demands on the teacher's time and attention and leading to an underestimation of her own ability and lack of confidence, especially in science and mathematics' (p. 8).

Chapter Two of the book considers what children have learned before they come to school, summarizing some of the evidence about ways in which children adapt to the 'appropriate' sex-role behaviour expected of them by parents, teachers and society at large. Of particular relevance to Reading 14 is Whyte's account (in Chapter 4) of the 'hidden curriculum', which discusses how the experience of school can reinforce traditional sex-role stereotypes and exacerbate the polarization of the sexes. She highlights four aspects of school life which, she claims, constitute a 'hidden curriculum' from which children learn and adapt to different expectations and standards for boys and girls:

(a) the informal interactions between children in the classroom or outside it;
(b) common school experiences (practices and procedures) which divide or distinguish the sexes, often for no sound educational reason;
(c) teachers' expectations;
(d) patterns of teacher–pupil interaction in class.

# BIBLIOGRAPHY

Ainsworth, M.D.S., Bell, S.M. and Stayton, D.J. (1974) 'Infant–mother attachment and social development: socialization as a product of reciprocal responsiveness to signals', in Richards, M.P.M. (ed.) *The Integration of a Child into a Social World*. Cambridge, Cambridge University Press.

Atkinson, V.C. (1981) Selective group formation in pre-school children. Unpublished Ph.D. thesis, University of Edinburgh.

Barnes, S.B., Gutfreund, M., Satterly, D.J. and Wells, C.G. (1983) 'Characteristics of adult speech which predict children's language development'. *Journal of Child Language*, **10**, 65–84.

Barnett, L.A. and Storm, B. (1981) 'Play, pleasure and pain: the reduction of anxiety through play'. *Leisure Science*, **4**, 161–75.

Behan, B. (1963) *Hold Your Hour and Have Another*. London, Hutchinson.

Bernstein, B. (1971) 'Social class, language and socialization', in Bernstein, B. (ed.) *Class, Codes and Control, Vol. 1*. London, Routledge and Kegan Paul.

Blank, M. (1974) 'Pre-school and/or education', in Tizard, B. (ed.) *Early Childhood Education*. Slough, NFER.

Blatchford, P., Battle, S. and Mays, J. (1982) *The First Transition: Home to School*. London, Nelson.

Block, J.H. (1978) 'Another look at sex differentiation in the socialization behaviour of mothers and fathers', in Sherman, J.A. and Denmark, F.L. (eds) *The Psychology of Women: Future Directions in Research*. New York, Psychological Dimensions Inc.

Borke, H. (1978) 'Piaget's view of social interaction and the theoretical construct of empathy', in Siegel, L.S. and Brainerd, C.J. (eds) *Alternatives to Piaget*. London, Academic Press.

Bowerman, M. (1982) 'Reorganizational processes in language development', in Wanner and Gleitman (eds) (1982).

Bowlby, J. (1961) 'Process of mourning'. *International Journal of Psycho-Analysis*, **42**, 317–40.

Bowlby, J. (1969) *Attachment and Loss. Vol. 1, Attachment*. New York, Basic Books.

Bowlby, J. (1973) *Attachment and Loss. Vol. 2, Separation, Anxiety and Anger*. New York, Basic Books.

Bowlby, J. (1980) *Attachment and Loss. Vol. 3, Loss, Sadness and Depression*. New York, Basic Books.

Bradley, R.H. and Caldwell, B.M. (1978) 'Screening the environment'. *American Journal of Orthopsychiatry*, **48**, 114–29.

Breslow, L. (1981) 'Re-evaluation of the literature on the development of transitive inferences'. *Psychological Bulletin*, **89**, 325–51.

Brooks-Gunn, J. and Matthews, W.S. (1979) *He and She: How Children Develop Their Sex-role Identity*. New Jersey, Prentice-Hall Inc.

Brown, R. (1973) *A First Language: The Early Stages*. London, George Allen & Unwin.

Brown, R. and Bellugi, U. (1964) 'Three processes in the child's acquisition of syntax'. *Harvard Educational Review*, **34**, 133–51.

Browne, N. and France, P. (eds) (1986) *Untying the Apron Strings: Anti-sexist Provision for the Under-fives*. Milton Keynes, Open University Press.

Bruner, J.S. (1975) 'The ontogenesis of speech acts'. *Journal of Child Language*, **2**, 1–19.

Bruner, J. (1980) *Under Five in Britain*. London, Grant McIntyre.

Bruner, J.S. (1981) 'The pragmatics of acquisition', in Deutsch, W. (ed.) *The Child's Construction of Language*. London, Academic Press.

Bryant, P.E. (1982) 'The role of conflict and agreement between intellectual strategies in children's ideas about measurement'. *British Journal of Psychology*, **73**, 243–52.

Bryant, P.E. (1985) 'The distinction between knowing when to do a sum and knowing how to do it'. *Educational Psychology*, **5**, 3 & 4, 207–15.

Bryant, P.E. and Kopytynska, H. (1976) 'Spontaneous measurement by young children'. *Nature*, **260**, 773.

Bryant, P.E. and Trabasso, T. (1971) 'Transitive inferences and memory in young children'. *Nature*, **232**, 456–8.

Bryant, B., Harris, M. and Newton, D. (1980) *Children and Minders*. London, Grant McIntyre.

Byrne, E.M. (1978) *Women and Education*. London, Tavistock.

Campbell, R.N. and Bowe, T. (1977) 'Functional asymmetry in early language understanding', in Drachman, G. (ed.) *Salzburger Beitrage fur Linguistik, Vol. 3*. Tubingen, Gunter Narr.

Carey, S. (1978a) 'The child as word learner', in Halle, M., Bresnan, J. and Miller, G.A. (eds) *Linguistic Theory and Psychological Reality*. Cambridge, Mass., MIT Press.

Carey, S. (1978b) 'Less never means more', in Campbell, R.N. and Smith, P.T. (eds) *Recent Advances in the Psychology of Language. Vol. 1, Language Development and Mother–Child Interaction*. London, Plenum Press.

Central Advisory Council for Education (CACE) (1967) *Children and Their Primary Schools* (The Plowden Report). London, HMSO.

Central Statistical Services (1980) *Social Trends 10*. London, HMSO.

Chandler, M.J. (1972) 'Egocentrism in normal and pathological child development', in Monk, F., Hartup, W. and Dewit, I. (eds) *Determinants of Behavioural Development*. London, Academic Press.

Chandler, M.J. (1973) 'Egocentrism and antisocial behaviour: the assessment and training of social perspective-taking skills'. *Developmental Psychology*, **9**, 326–32.

Chomsky, N.A. (1959) Review of B.F. Skinner *Verbal Behaviour. Language*, **35**, 26–58.

Chomsky, N.A. (1964) Discussion of Miller and Ervin's paper, in U. Bellugi and R. Brown (eds) *The Acquisition of Language. Monographs of the Society for Research in Child Development*, **29**, 1, 35–42.

Chomsky, N.A. (1976) *Reflections on Language*. London, Fontana.

Christie, J.F. (1982) 'Sociodramatic play training'. *Young Children*, **37**, 25–32.

Clark, M.M. (1983) 'Early education: issues and evidence'. *Educational Review*, **35**, 2, 113–20.

Clark, M.M. and Cheyne, W.M. (eds) (1979) *Studies in Pre-School Education*. London, Hodder and Stoughton.

Clarke. A.D.B. (1968) 'Learning and human development – the 42nd Maudsley lecture'. *British Journal of Psychiatry*, **114**, 161–77.

Clarke, A.M. and Clarke, A.D.B. (1976) *Early Experience: Myth and Evidence*. New York, Free Press.

Clarricoates, K. (1980) 'The importance of being Ernest . . . Emma . . . Tom and Jane', in Deem, R. (ed.) *Schooling for Women's Work*. London, Routledge and Kegan Paul.

Cleave, S. (1982) 'Continuity from pre-school to infant school'. *Educational Review*, **24**, 3, 163–73.

Cleave, S., Jowett, S. and Bate, M. (1982) *And So to School: A Study of Continuity from Pre-School to Infant School*. Windsor, NFER–Nelson.

Commission for Racial Equality (1978) *Ethnic Minorities in the Inner Cities*. London, CRE.

Corrigan, R. (1982) 'The control of animate and inanimate components in pretend play and language'. *Child Development*, **53**, 1343–53.

Cross, T.G. (1978) 'Mother's speech and its association with rate of linguistic development in young children', in Waterson, N. and Snow, C.E. (eds) *The Development of Communication*. Chichester, Wiley.

Crowe, B. (1973) *The Playgroup Movement*. London, Allen & Unwin.

de Boysson Bardies, B. and O'Regan, K. (1973) 'What children do in spite of adults' hypotheses'. *Nature*, **246**, 531–4.

DES (1981) *Statistical Bulletin* (5/81). London, HMSO.

DES (1982) 'Pupils under five years in each LEA in England in January 1981'. *Statistical Bulletin*, February 1982.

DES/SSRC (1975) *Educational Priority: Vol. 4 The West Riding Project*. London, HMSO.

DHSS/DES (1976) *Low Cost Day Provision for the Under Fives*. Papers from a conference at Sunningdale, January 1976.

Doise, W. and Mugny, G. (1979) 'Individual and collective conflicts of centrations in cognitive development'. *European Journal of Social Psychology*, **9**, 105–8.

Donaldson, M. (1966) 'Discussion of McNeill (1966) "The Creation of Language" ', in Lyons, J. and Wales, R.J. (eds) *Psycholinguistics Papers*. Edinburgh, Edinburgh University Press.

Donaldson, M. (1978) *Children's Minds*. London, Fontana.

Duxbury, S. (1986) 'A comparative review of contemporary pre-school provision', in Browne, N. and France, P. (eds), chap. 3, pp. 32–48.

Edwards, A.D. (1976) *Language in Culture and Class*. London, Heinemann Educational.

Edwards, D. (1973) 'Sensory-motor intelligence and semantic relations in early child grammar'. *Cognition*, **2**, 395–434.

El'Konin, D. (1976) 'Symbolics and its function in the play of children'. *Soviet Education*, **8**, 2, 35.

Erikson, E.H. (1950) *Childhood and Society*. New York, Norton.

Erikson, E.H. (1959) *Identity and the Life Cycle*. New York, International Universities Press. (Reissued by Norton, 1980.)

Feitelson, D. (1977) 'Cross cultural studies of representational play', in Tizard, B. and Harvey, D. (eds) *Biology of Play*. London, Heinemann.

Ferri, E., Birchall, D., Gingell, V. and Gipps, C. (1981) *Combined Nursery Centres*. London, Macmillan.

Finch, J. (1984) ' "A first-class environment?" : working-class playgroups as pre-school experience'. *British Educational Research Journal*, **10**, 1, 3–17.

Freud, S. (1905) 'Three contributions to the theory of sex', in *The Basic Writings of Sigmund Freud* (trans. A.A. Brill). New York, Random House (Modern Library).

Freud, S. (1920) *A General Introduction to Psychoanalysis* (trans. J. Riviere). New York, Washington Square Press, 1965.

Freyburg, J.T. (1973) 'Increasing the imaginative play of urban disadvantaged kindergarten children through systematic training', in Singer, J.L. (ed.) (1973).

Garland, C. and White, S. (1980) *Children and Day Nurseries*. London, Grant McIntyre.

Garvey, C. (1977) *Play*. London, Fontana/Open Books.

Gelman, R. and Gallistel, C.R. (1978) *The Child's Understanding of Number*. Cambridge, Harvard University Press.

Golomb, C. and Cornelius, C.B. (1977) 'Symbolic play and its cognitive significance'. *Developmental Psychology*, **13**, 246–52.

Goodnow, J. (1977) *Children's Drawing*. London, Fontana/Open Books.

Grice, H.P. (1975) 'Logic and conversation', in Cole, P. and Morgan, J. (eds) *Syntax and Semantics. Vol. III, Speech Acts*. New York, Academic Press.

Grotberg, E. (1979) 'The parental role in education and child development', in Doxiades, S. (ed.) *The Child in the World of Tomorrow*. Oxford, Pergamon.

Halliday, M.A.K. (1975) *Learning How to Mean*. London, Edward Arnold.

Halliday, M.A.K. (1978) *Language as Social Semiotic*. London, Edward Arnold.

Hartshorn, E. and Brantley, J.C. (1973) 'Effects of dramatic play on classroom problem-solving ability'. *Journal of Educational Research*, **66**, 243–6.

Heber, F.R. (1978) 'Sociocultural mental retardation: a longitudinal study', in Forgays, D. (ed.) *Primary Prevention of Psychopathology, Vol. 2*. Hanover, NH, University Press of New England.

Herrmann, J. (1978) An observational study of two children perceived as aggressive problems in playgroup. Supplementary report to Peter Appleton's 1977–78 report on Project No. 15, financed by the East Anglian Regional Health Authority.

Hobson, D. (1978) 'Housewives: isolation as oppression', in Women's Studies Group, Centre for Contemporary Cultural Studies, *Women Take Issue*. London, Hutchinson.

Howell, A.A., Walker, R. and Fletcher, H. (1979) *Mathematics for Schools*. London, Addison-Wesley.

Hughes, M. (1981) 'Can pre-school children add and subtract?' *Educational Psychology*, **1**, 207–19.

Hughes, M. (1983) 'Teaching arithmetic to pre-school children'. *Educational Review*, **35**, 2, 163–73.

Hughes, M. (1986) 'Early education and the community (1)'. *Scottish Educational Review*, **18**, 1, 31–7.

Hughes, M. and Jones, M. (1986) 'Children's spontaneous written representations of simple arithmetical concepts' in G. Thomson and H. Donaldson (eds) *New Directions in Education Psychology*. Lewes, Falmer.

Hughes, M., Mayall, B., Moss, P., Perry, J., Petrie, J. and Pinkerton, G. (1980) *Nurseries Now: A Fair Deal for Parents and Children*. Penguin, Harmondsworth.

Hutt, S.J., Hutt, C., Tyler, S.T. and Foy, H. (1985) *A Natural History of the Preschool*. Windsor, NFER-Nelson.

Iannotti, R.J. (1978) 'Effect of role-taking experiences on role taking, empathy, altruism and aggression'. *Developmental Psychology*, **14**, 119–24.

ILEA (1982) *Equal Opportunities for Girls and Boys*. Report by the ILEA Inspectorate.

ILEA (1984) *Providing Equal Opportunities for Girls and Boys in Physical Education*. ILEA Study Group.

Jowett, S. and Sylva, K. (1986) 'Does kind of pre-school matter?' *Educational Research*, **28**, 1, 21–31.

Kagan, J. (1979) 'Family experience and the child's development'. *American Psychologist*, **34**, 886–91.

Kanter, R.M. (1976) 'The organisation child: experience management in a nursery school', in Dale, R., Esland, G. and McDonald, M. (eds) *Schooling and Capitalism: A Sociological Reader*. London, Routledge and Kegan Paul.

King, R. (1978) *All Things Bright and Beautiful*. Chichester, John Wiley.

Klackenberg, G. (1949) 'Thumbsucking: frequency and etiology'. *Pediatrics*, **4**, 418.

Leach, P. (1975) *Babyhood*. Harmondsworth, Penguin.

Lieberman, J.N. (1977) *Playfulness: Its Relationship to Imagination and Creativity*. New York, Academic Press.

Light, P. (1979) *The Development of Social Sensitivity*. Cambridge, Cambridge University Press.

Lindsay, G. (ed.) (1984) *Screening for Children with Special Needs*. London, Croom Helm.

Lloyd, I. (1983) 'The aims of early childhood education'. *Educational Review*, **35**, 2, 121–6.

Lovinger, S.L. (1974) 'Socio-dramatic play and language development in pre-school disadvantaged children'. *Psychology in the Schools*, **11**, 313–20.

Maccoby, E.E. (1980) 'Sex differences in aggression: a rejoinder and reprise'. *Child Development*, **51**, 964–80.

Maccoby, E.E. and Jacklin, C.N. (1974) *The Psychology of Sex Differences*. Stanford, Calif., Stanford University Press.

Manning, M. and Sluckin, A.M. (1979, 1980) A comparison of difficult and normal children in nursery schools. Unpublished reports to the Social Science Research Council (HR 6195).

Manning, M., Heron, J. and Marshall, T. (1978) 'Styles of hostility and social interactions at nursery, at school and at home: an extended study of children', in Hersov, L.A. and Berger, M. (eds) *Aggression and Anti-social Behaviour in Childhood and Adolescence.* Oxford, Pergamon.

Marsh, P., Rosser, E. and Harré, R. (1978) *The Rules of Disorder.* London, Routledge and Kegan Paul.

Matthews, W.S. (1977) 'Modes of transformation in the initiation of fantasy play'. *Developmental Psychology,* **13**, 212–16.

Matthews, W.S. (1978) 'Interruptions of fantasy play: a matter of "breaking frame" '. Paper presented to meeting of the Eastern Psychological Association, Washington, DC.

McCune-Nicolich, L. (1981) 'Toward symbolic functioning: structure of early pretend games and potential parallels with language'. *Child Development,* **52**, 785–97.

McGarrigle, J. and Donaldson, M. (1974) 'Conservation accidents'. *Cognition,* **3**, 341–50.

McGarrigle, J., Grieve, R. and Hughes, M. (1978) 'Interpreting inclusion: a contribution to the study of the child's cognitive and linguistic development'. *Journal of Experimental Child Psychology,* **26**, 528–50.

Mead, G.H. (1932) *Mind, Self and Society.* Chicago, Chicago University Press.

Midwinter, E. (1974) *Pre-School Priorities.* London, Ward Lock.

Miller, S. (1982) 'On the generalisability of conversation: a comparison of different types of transformation'. *British Journal of Psychology,* **73**, 221–30.

Milner, D. (1975) *Children and Race.* Harmondsworth, Penguin.

Milner, D. (1983) *Children and Race – Ten Years On.* London, Ward Lock Educational.

Montagner, H. (1978) *L'enfant et la communication.* Paris, Pernoud/Stock.

Moore, W. (1979) *Nuffield Maths I.* London, Longman.

Nelson, K. (1973) 'Structure and strategy in learning to talk'. *Monographs of the Society for Research in Child Development,* **38**, 1–2, Series No. 149.

Newson, J. (1978) 'Dialogue and development', in Lock, A. (ed.) *Action, Gesture and Symbol.* London, Academic Press.

Newson, E. and Newson, J. (1968) *Four Years Old in an Urban Community.* London, Allen and Unwin.

Newson, J. and Newson, E. (1976) *Seven Years Old in an Urban Community.* London, Allen and Unwin.

Ninio, A. and Bruner, J.S. (1978) 'The achievement and antecedents of labelling'. *Journal of Child Language,* **5**, 1–16.

Papert, S. (1980) *Mindstorms.* Brighton, Harvester Press.

Parten, M.B. (1932) 'Social participation among pre-school children'. *Journal of Abnormal and Social Psychology,* **27**, 243–69.

Perret-Clermont, A.N. (1980) *Social Interaction and Cognitive Development in Children.* London, Academic Press.

Piaget, J. (1951) *Play, Dreams and Imitation in Childhood.* London, Routledge and Kegan Paul.

Piaget, J. (1952) *The Child's Conception of Number.* London, Routledge and Kegan Paul.

Piaget, J. and Szeminska, A. (1952) *The Child's Conception of Number.* London, Routledge and Kegan Paul.

Pichault, C. (1984) *Day-care Facilities and Services for Children under the Age of Three in the European Community.* OPEC.

Pilling, D., Pringle, M.L., Kellmer, (1978) *Controversial Issues in Child Development.* London, Elek.

Poulton, G.A. and James, T. (1975) *Pre-school Learning in the Community: Strategies for Change.* London, Routledge and Kegan Paul.

Pre-school Playgroups Association (1972) *Playgroups in Education and the Social Services.* London, PPA.

Pre-school Playgroups Association (1980) *Playgroups in the Eighties: Opportunities for Parents and Children.* London, PPA.

Pulaski, M.A. (1973) 'Toys and imaginative play', in Singer, J.L. (ed.) (1973).

Ratner, N. and Bruner, J.S. (1978) 'Social exchange and the acquisition of language'. *Journal of Child Language*, 5, 391–402.

Richards, C. (ed.) (1982) *New Directions in Primary Education.* London, Falmer Press, p. 10.

Riegel, K.F. (1975) 'Adult life crises. A dialectic interpretation of development', in Datan, N. and Ginsberg, L.H. (eds) *Lifespan Developmental Psychology: Normal Life Crises.* New York, Academic Press.

Roper, R. and Hinde, R.A. (1978) 'Social behaviour in a play group: consistency and complexity'. *Child Development*, 49, 570–9.

Rosch, E. (1977) 'Classification of real-world objects: origins and representation in cognition', in Johnson-Laird, P.N. and Watson, P.C. (eds) *Thinking.* Cambridge, Cambridge University Press.

Rose, S. and Blank, M. (1974) 'The potency of context in children's cognition: an illustration through conservation'. *Child Development*, 45, 499–502.

Rubin, K.H. (1980) 'Fantasy play: its role in the development of social skills and social cognition', in Rubin, K.H. (ed.) *New Directions for Child Development: Children's Play.* San Francisco, Jossey-Bass.

Russell, J. (1981) 'Children's memory for the premises in a transitive measurement task assessed by elicited and spontaneous justifications'. *Journal of Experimental Child Psychology*, 31, 300–9.

Sachs, J. (1980) 'The role of adult–child play in language development', in Rubin, K.H. (ed.) *New Directions for Child Development: Children's Play.* San Francisco, Jossey-Bass.

Saltz, E. and Johnson, J. (1974) 'Training for thematic-fantasy play in culturally disadvantaged children: preliminary results'. *Journal of Educational Psychology*, 66, 623–30.

Samuel, J. and Bryant, P.E. (1984) 'Asking only one question in the conservation experiment'. *Journal of Child Psychology and Psychiatry*, 25, 315–18.

Schaffer, H.R. (1971) *The Growth of Sociability.* Harmondsworth, Penguin.

Schools Council (1978) *Early Mathematical Experiences.* London, Addison-Wesley.

Sestini, E. (1985) 'Pre-school education: recent developments in pre-school policies and provision in developing countries and the UK', in Lillis, M.K. (ed.) *School and Community in Less Developed Areas.* London, Croom Helm.

Singer, J.L. (1973) *The Child's World of Make-believe.* New York, Academic Press.

Skinner, B.F. (1957) *Verbal Behaviour.* New York, Appleton.

Slobin, D.I. (1981) 'The origin of grammatical encoding of events', in Deutsch, W. (ed.) *The Child's Construction of Language.* London, Academic Press.

Sluckin, A. (1981) *Growing Up in the Playground: The Social Development of Children.* London, Routledge and Kegan Paul.

Smilansky, S. (1968) *The Effects of Sociodramatic Play on Disadvantaged Pre-school Children.* New York, Wiley.

Smith, G. and James, T. (1975) 'The effects of pre-school education: some British and American evidence'. *Oxford Review of Education*, **1**, 223–40.

Smith, P.K. (1973) 'Temporal clusters and individual differences in the behaviour of preschool children', in Michael, R.P. and Crook, J.H. (eds) *Comparative Ecology and Behaviour of Primates*. London, Academic Press.

Smith, P.K. (1982) 'Does play matter? Functional and evolutionary aspects of animal and human play'. *The Behavioral and Brain Sciences*, **4**, 139–84.

Smith, P.K. and Connolly, K. (1977) 'Social and aggressive behaviour in pre-school children as a function of crowding'. *Social Sciences Information*, **16**, 601–20.

Smith, P.K. and Connolly, K. (1980) *The Ecology of Pre-school Education*. Cambridge, Cambridge University Press.

Smith, P.K. and Sydall, S. (1978) 'Play and non-play tutoring in preschool children: is it play or tutoring which matters?' *Child Development*, **48**, 315–29.

Snow, C.E. (1977) 'Mothers' speech research: from input to interaction', in Snow, C.E. and Ferguson, C.A. (eds) *Talking to Children: Language Input and Acquisition*. Cambridge, Cambridge University Press.

Spender, D. and Sarah, E. (eds) (1980) *Learning to Lose: Sexism and Education*. London, Women's Press.

Spock, B. (1955) *Baby and Child Care*. London, Bodley Head.

Sroufe, L.A. (1979) 'The coherence of individual development: early care, attachment, and subsequent developmental issues'. *American Psychologist*, **34**, 834–41.

Stannard, J. (1980) 'Communicating communication'. *Education 3–13*, **8**, 1.

Stern, D. (1977) *The First Relationship: Infant and Mother*. London, Open Books.

Stevens, A. (1981) 'What mothers learn at play'. *The Observer*, 10 May 1981.

Stones, R. (1983) *'Pour Out the Cocoa, Janet': Sexism in Children's Books*. Harlow, Longman for Schools Council.

Swann Report (1985) *Education for All*. Cmnd 9453. London, HMSO.

Sylva, K., Roy, C. and Painter, M. (1980) *Childwatching at Playgroup and Nursery School*. London, Grant McIntyre.

Tamburrini, J. (1982) 'Some educational implications of Piaget's theory', in Modgil, S. and Modgil, C. (eds) *Piaget: Controversy and Consensus*. London, Holt, Rinehart & Winston.

Taylor, P.H., Exon, G. and Holley, B. (1972) *A Study of Nursery Education*. Schools Council Working Paper 41. London, Evans/Methuen.

Taylor, W. (1980) 'Family, school and society', in Craft, M., Raynor, J. and Cohen, L. (eds) *Linking Home and School*, 3rd ed. London, Harper & Row.

Thayer, E. and Collyer, C. (1978) 'The development of transitive inference: a review of recent approaches'. *Psychological Bulletin*, **85**, 1327–43.

Thomas, V. (1973) 'Children's use of language in the nursery'. *Educational Research*, **15**, 3, 209–16.

Tizard, B. (1974) *Early Childhood Education*. Slough, NFER.

Tizard, B. (1979) 'Language at home and at school', in Cazden, C.B. (ed.) *Language and Early Childhood Education*. Washington, DC, National Association for Young Children.

Tizard, B., Philips, J. and Plewis, I. (1976) 'Staff behaviour in preschool centres'. *Journal of Child Psychology and Psychiatry*, **17**, 1.

Tizard, B., Carmichael, H., Hughes, M. and Pinkerton, G. (1980) 'Four year olds talking to mothers and teachers', in Hersov, L.A. and Berger, M. (eds) *Language and Language Disorders in Childhood*. Book supplement to the *Journal of Child Psychology and Psychiatry*, **2**. Oxford, Pergamon, pp. 49–76.

Tizard, B., Hughes, M., Pinkerton, G. and Carmichael, H. (1982) 'Adults' cognitive demands at home and at nursery school'. *Journal of Child Psychology and Psychiatry*, **23**, 105–16.

Tizard, B., Hughes, M., Carmichael, H. and Pinkerton, G. (1983) 'Children's questions and adults' answers'. *Journal of Child Psychology and Psychiatry*, **24**, 269–81.

Tizard, J. (1975) 'The objectives and organisation of educational and day care services for young children'. *Oxford Review of Education*, **1**, 211–22.

Tizard, J., Moss, P. and Perry, J. (1976) *All Our Children*. London, Temple Smith/New Society.

Traisman, A.A. and Traisman, H.S. (1958) 'Thumb and finger-sucking: a study of 2,650 infants and children'. *Journal of Paediatrics*, **52**, 566–79.

Trevarthen, C. (1979) 'Communication and cooperation in early infancy: a description of primary intersubjectivity', in Bullowa, M. (ed.) *Before Speech: The Beginnings of Human Communication*. Cambridge, Cambridge University Press.

Turner, I.F. (1977) Preschool playgroups: Research and evaluation project. Department of Psychology, Queen's University, Belfast.

Van der Eyken, W. (1977) *The Preschool Years*. Harmondsworth, Penguin.

Ungerer, J.A. and Sigman, M. (1981) 'Symbolic play and language comprehension in autistic children'. *Journal of the American Academy of Child Psychiatry*, **20**, 318–37.

Vygotsky, L.S. (1967) 'Play and its role in the mental development of the child'. *Soviet Psychology*, **12**, 62–76.

Vygotsky, L.S. (1977) *Thinking and Speech*. Selected passages of *Myshlenie i Rech*, translated by A. Sutton. Centre for Child Study, University of Birmingham.

Wales, R.J. (1974) 'Children's sentences make sense of the world', in Bresson, F. (ed.) *Les problèmes actuels en psycholinguistique*. Paris, PUF.

Wanner, E. and Gleitman, L.R. (eds) (1982) *Language Acquisition: The State of the Art* (Introduction). Cambridge, Cambridge University Press.

Watt, J. (1977) *Co-operation in Pre-school Education*. London, SSRC.

Weir, R. (1962) *Language in the Crib*. The Hague, Mouton.

Wells, C.G. (1985) *Language Development in the Pre-school Years*. Cambridge, Cambridge University Press.

Whyte, J. (1983) *Beyond the Wendy House: Sex Role Stereotyping in Primary Schools*. Harlow, Longman for Schools Council.

Wolf, D. and Grollman, S.H. (1982) 'Ways of playing: individual differences in imaginative style', in Pepler, D.J. and Rubin, K.H. (eds) *The Play of Children: Current Theory and Research*. Basel, S. Karger.

Wolkind, S.N. and Everett, B. (1974) 'A cluster analysis of the behavioural items in the pre-school child'. *Psychological Medicine*, **4**, 422–7.

Wood, D.J., Wood, H.A., Griffiths, A.J., Howarth, S.P. and Howarth, C.I. (1982) 'The structure of conversations with 6- to 10-year-old deaf children'. *Journal of Child Psychology and Psychiatry*, **23**, 295–308.

Woodhead, M. (1976) *Intervening in Disadvantage*. Slough, NFER.

Woodhead, M. (1985) 'Pre-school education has long-term effects: but can they be generalized?' *Oxford Review of Education*, **11**, 2, 133–54.

Yawkey, T.D. (1979) 'The effects of social relationships, curricula and sex differences on reading and imaginativeness in young children'. *Alberta Journal of Educational Research*, **25**, 159–68.

Zeskind, P.S. (1981) 'Preventing intellectual and interactional sequelae of fetal malnutrition: a longitudinal, transactional, and synergistic approach to development'. *Child Development*, **52**, 213–18.

# INDEX